The History of World Literature
Parts 1–4
Grant L. Voth, Ph.D.

PUBLISHED BY:

THE TEACHING COMPANY
4151 Lafayette Center Drive, Suite 100
Chantilly, Virginia 20151-1232
1-800-TEACH-12
Fax—703-378-3819
www.teach12.com

Copyright © The Teaching Company, 2007

Printed in the United States of America

This book is in copyright. All rights reserved.

Without limiting the rights under copyright reserved above, no part of this publication may be reproduced, stored in or introduced into a retrieval system, or transmitted, in any form, or by any means (electronic, mechanical, photocopying, recording, or otherwise), without the prior written permission of The Teaching Company.

Permissions Acknowledgments begin on page 306 and constitute a continuation of the copyright page.

Grant L. Voth, Ph.D.

Professor Emeritus, Monterey Peninsula College

Grant L. Voth earned his B.A. degree in Philosophy and Greek from Concordia Senior College, Ft. Wayne, Indiana, in 1965. He received his M.A. in English Education from St. Thomas College, St. Paul, Minnesota, in 1967 and his Ph.D. in English from Purdue University in 1971.

Professor Voth taught at Northern Illinois University in DeKalb, Illinois; Virginia Tech in Blacksburg, Virginia; and Monterey Peninsula College in California, from which he retired in 2003 and where he is Professor Emeritus in English and Interdisciplinary Studies. For several years he was a consultant for the National Endowment for the Humanities, reading proposals for interdisciplinary studies programs and advising colleges that wished to initiate such programs; he was also an N.E.H. Fellow at the University of California-Berkeley. He served as Director of an American Institute of Foreign Studies program for a consortium of California colleges in London in 1988, and he has led travel-study tours to England, Ireland, France, Greece, Turkey, and Egypt. He has been taking students to the Oregon Shakespeare Festival and the Santa Cruz Shakespeare Festival for 30 years, and he is currently a Discovery Series Lecturer for the internationally acclaimed Carmel Bach Festival in Carmel, California.

Professor Voth is the author of more than 30 articles and books on subjects ranging from Shakespeare to Edward Gibbon to modern American fiction, including the official study guides for many of the plays in the BBC The Shakespeare Plays project in the late 70s and early 80s. He was the recipient of the first Allen Griffin Award for Excellence in Teaching, and in 1996 was the Students' Association Teacher of the Year. He created a series of mediated courses in literature and interdisciplinary studies for the Bay Area Television Consortium and the Northern California Learning Consortium, one of which won a Special Merit Award from the Western Educational Society for Telecommunication. This is his first course for The Teaching Company.

Table of Contents
The History of World Literature

Professor Biography i
Course Scope 1

Part I: Lectures 1–12

Lecture One	Stories and Storytellers	4
Lecture Two	The *Epic of Gilgamesh*	7
Lecture Three	The Hebrew Bible	12
Lecture Four	Homer's *Iliad*	16
Lecture Five	Homer's *Odyssey*	20
Lecture Six	Chinese Classical Literature	24
Lecture Seven	Greek Tragedy	29
Lecture Eight	Virgil's *Aeneid*	33
Lecture Nine	Bhagavad Gita	38
Lecture Ten	The New Testament	43
Lecture Eleven	*Beowulf*	48
Lecture Twelve	Indian Stories	52

Timeline for Lectures 1–12 57
Glossary for Lectures 1–12 59
Biographical Notes for Lectures 1–12 62
Bibliography for Lectures 1–12 70

Part II: Lectures 13–24

Lecture Thirteen	T'ang Poetry	74
Lecture Fourteen	Early Japanese Poetry	78
Lecture Fifteen	*The Tale of Genji*	83
Lecture Sixteen	*Inferno*, from Dante's *Divine Comedy*	87
Lecture Seventeen	Chaucer's *The Canterbury Tales*	92
Lecture Eighteen	*1001 Nights*	96
Lecture Nineteen	Wu Ch'eng-en's *Monkey*	101
Lecture Twenty	The *Heptameron*	106
Lecture Twenty-One	Shakespeare	111

Lecture Twenty-Two	Cervantes's *Don Quixote*	115
Lecture Twenty-Three	Molière's Plays	120
Lecture Twenty-Four	Voltaire's *Candide*	125

Timeline for Lectures 13–24 129
Glossary for Lectures 13–24 131
Biographical Notes for Lectures 13–24 136
Bibliography for Lectures 13–24 141

Part III: Lectures 25–36

Lecture Twenty-Five	Cao Xueqin's *The Story of the Stone*	146
Lecture Twenty-Six	Goethe's *Faust*	151
Lecture Twenty-Seven	Emily Brontë's *Wuthering Heights*	156
Lecture Twenty-Eight	Pushkin's *Eugene Onegin*	161
Lecture Twenty-Nine	Flaubert's *Madame Bovary*	166
Lecture Thirty	Dostoevsky's *Notes from Underground*	171
Lecture Thirty-One	Twain's *Huckleberry Finn*	177
Lecture Thirty-Two	Dickinson's Poetry	183
Lecture Thirty-Three	Ibsen and Chekhov—Realist Drama	188
Lecture Thirty-Four	Rabindranath Tagore's Stories and Poems	193
Lecture Thirty-Five	Higuchi Ichiyō's "Child's Play"	198
Lecture Thirty-Six	Proust's *Remembrance of Things Past*	203

Timeline for Lectures 25–36 207
Glossary for Lectures 25–36 209
Biographical Notes for Lectures 25–36 214
Bibliography for Lectures 25–36 220

Part IV: Lectures 37-48

Lecture Thirty-Seven	Joyce's *Dubliners*	225
Lecture Thirty-Eight	Kafka's "The Metamorphosis"	230
Lecture Thirty-Nine	Pirandello's *Six Characters*	236
Lecture Forty	Brecht's *The Good Woman of Setzuan*	242
Lecture Forty-One	Anna Akhmatova's *Requiem*	247
Lecture Forty-Two	Kawabata Yasunari's *Snow Country*	252
Lecture Forty-Three	Faulkner—Two Stories and a Novel	258

Lecture Forty-Four	Naguib Mahfouz's *The Cairo Trilogy*	264
Lecture Forty-Five	Achebe's *Things Fall Apart*	270
Lecture Forty-Six	Beckett's Plays	276
Lecture Forty-Seven	Borges's *Labyrinths*	281
Lecture Forty-Eight	Rushdie's *Haroun and the Sea of Stories*	286
Timeline for Lectures 37–48		291
Glossary for Lectures 37–48		293
Biographical Notes for Lectures 37–48		296
Bibliography for Lectures 37–48		301
Permissions Acknowledgments		306

The History of World Literature

Scope:

In 48 half-hour lectures, *The History of World Literature* explores cross-cultural themes, techniques, and modes of representation over nearly 5,000 years of history. The focus of the individual lectures is on themes as they are repeated, echoed, and modified through time, but the unifying thread for the course as a whole is the evolution of storytelling, beginning with the relatively straight-forward relationship of teller to tale in the earliest works in the course and ending with the much more complicated relationships in the works of contemporary writers. Along the way we also notice the many different functions narratives have fulfilled vis-à-vis the cultures and times in which they were produced.

The first lecture suggests some of the many different kinds of stories that the course treats—explaining the inclusion of a few lyric poems and plays among the narratives—and some of the most important ways stories have functioned for people: defining cultures and nations, offering ways to remember the past, explaining the reasons for and nature of our presence in the universe, and helping us to survive in a world in which we think of ourselves as alien. We also define such terms as "literature" and "history" as they are used in the course.

Lectures Two through Eleven focus on epic poems and epic heroes who are larger-than-life and who define a people or a culture or a nation, from the Middle Eastern *Epic of Gilgamesh* to the Germanic *Beowulf*. The three religious texts treated in these lectures—the Hebrew Bible, the Bhagavad Gita, and the New Testament—form a subset of epic literature, focusing on the relationship between God and human beings while subordinating other aspects of epic narrative. In all of these works, the writers speak in more or less official capacities as spokespersons for their cultures, and the stories they tell are important in helping people define their nature and values. The early literature of China is the exception in the first unit of the course; while their writers help to define their cultures, they do so outside the parameters of the epic, in lyric poetry and writings whose focus is on the everyday and the commonplace rather than the extraordinary and the heroic.

Lectures Twelve through Thirty-Five, the major portion of the course, cover the periods in Western history from the Middle Ages through the Renaissance, the Enlightenment, the Romantic Movement, and the Industrial Revolution up to about the time of the First World War. They also deal with these corresponding periods in the Middle East, India, China, and Japan. The focus of these lectures is on narrative techniques and strategies—on the ways writers learn to write their stories in more complicated ways. In these lectures, Dante is our last epic writer, speaking for an entire culture (in his case, medieval Christendom). Most of the other writers speak for segments of their cultures, sometimes in opposition to the dominant voices in those cultures (in new genres like the novel) that use new narrative strategies designed to place some distance between the writer and the narrator on the one hand, and the narrator and the tale he or she tells on the other. Frames—that is, envelope narratives containing other narratives—become increasingly important in this development, as seen in the work of Indian storytellers, Murasaki, Chaucer, the *1001 Nights*, Marguerite of Navarre, Cervantes, *The Story of the Stone*, and Goethe. In Lecture Twenty-Nine we arrive at the Realist mode in fiction, whose purpose was to abstract the narrator out of the story altogether and give what purports to be an unmediated picture of reality. Since the Realist Movement in the West corresponded with the height of the colonial period, realism had a huge impact on the literature of the rest of the world, and we trace that impact in succeeding lectures. From this point on in the course, all literary movements are international. Before we get to realism we deal with Emily Brontë's *Wuthering Heights,* an extraordinarily experimental novel in its own time that embeds all of the storytellers inside the story; in so doing, the novel anticipates techniques that we think of as modern or even contemporary.

In Lecture Thirty-Six we deal with Marcel Proust, who in rejecting the Realist mode in fiction redefined the novel and narrative technique for the modern world, so that the final 13 lectures in the course deal with the amazing innovations in stories and storytelling that carry us to the present. Modernists such as Joyce, Kafka, Faulkner, and Kawabata in fiction and Pirandello and Brecht in drama move the action of literature from the external to the internal world and question many of the fundamental assumptions about the self, the meaning of existence, and the human place in the universe with techniques that are dazzlingly new and sometimes difficult for readers. By the time of the Postmodernists (Beckett, Borges, and Rushdie in this course) the foregrounded question of literature is in fact the relationship between literature and life. As Rushdie puts it in the last lecture of the course, "What's the use of stories that aren't even true?" Rushdie himself provides one answer in *Haroun and the Sea of Stories*, but alternative answers are given by Beckett, Borges, and several other

Postmodernist writers whose works will be referenced in the last three lectures.

Thus the course is really about both literature and history. The individual literary works treated are as alive today as they were when they were written, and they still call us to think about questions humans have been asking since the first cave-man or -woman told the first story. But the course is also about the relationships among those works; the ways that writers across history have learned from each other, responded to and reacted against each other; the ways in which stories and storytelling have changed through time; and finally the ways the many different streams of stories have blended into Rushdie's "Sea of Stories"—which is itself, as we discover in the course, both a very old and a very new conceptual metaphor.

Lecture One
Stories and Storytellers

Scope: In this lecture we identify the common threads of our course—stories and storytelling—and trace the ways stories have been used across history. In Part One we focus on *epics*: stories about representatives of cultures written by official spokesmen of those cultures. Parts Two and Three deal with narrative strategies; as storytellers learn to put distance between themselves and their stories, allow space for disagreement with their dominant cultures, and invite readers to make their own interpretations. In Lecture Twenty-Nine we arrive at *realism*, in which the storyteller tries to evaporate himself or herself out of the story to allow it to speak for itself. Beginning with Proust in Lecture Thirty-Six and continuing through Part Four, we trace the experiments in storytelling prompted by the loss of faith in external values and the extreme subjectivity of the modern world. We conclude this lecture by defining "literature" and "history" as they will be used in this course and with a warning about the addictive properties of good stories.

Outline

I. Stories have been important through all of history, but they have served different functions, including entertaining people, helping them remember the past, and providing a personal and cultural identity.
   A. The first part of this course will explore primarily epic stories that deal with larger-than-life characters who help to define a people, a culture, or a nation.
      1. Examples of these epics include the *Iliad*, the *Odyssey*, the *Epic of Gilgamesh*, the *Aeneid*, and *Beowulf*.
      2. The three religious texts—the Old and New Testament and the Bhagavad Gita—will focus on the relationship between God and humanity while marginalizing other aspects of epic tales.
      3. Chinese literature will be the exception to the rule in the first unit, since it focuses on more ordinary aspects of life than on extraordinary ones.

4. Three collections of Indian short stories, including Somadeva's *Ocean of the Rivers of Story*, provide a transition to the concerns of the next 24 lectures.
- **B.** The second and third parts of this course will treat stories in the West, the Middle East, and the Far East from the Middle Ages to World War I, illustrating the way stories become artful through time.
   1. These lectures will focus on narrative strategies and techniques, as writers spoke less as official spokespersons for their cultures and more for certain segments of them—and sometimes in opposition to those cultures.
   2. Writers also used framing devices and other narrative techniques to create distance between a tale's writer and narrator and between the narrator and the tale, allowing space for a variety of interpretations.
   3. With the emergence of the Realist Movement, storytelling either tried to evaporate the narrator out of the work altogether or tried to embed the narrator inside the story.
   4. Realism had a profound impact on the literature of non-Western cultures and is still the most popular mode for fiction across the world.
- **C.** The fourth part of this course will deal with a century of experimentation in stories and storytelling.
   1. Prompted by the erosion of foundations of belief and a radical subjectivity, writers created new techniques—such as broken chronology, interior monologue, and stream of consciousness—to try to capture in their stories a sense of life as it is experienced, not as it is reported.
   2. The Postmodernist Movement used the relationship between art and life as its subject and theme.
   3. We will use literary examples from various countries to illustrate the international impact of Modernist and Postmodernist literature.
   4. We will also see how literary techniques from one era get played out in another.

II. What do we mean by "literature" and "history"?
- **A.** By *literature* we mean primarily poems, plays, short stories, and novels, with occasional excursions into what we might call "philosophy" or "religion."

> **B.** By *history* we mean an effort to see the storytellers of the world as an international community across time and space, in which individual members learn from each other, are influenced by each other, and rewrite each others' stories.
>   1. We will try to read individual works as living pieces, which still have much to say to us.
>   2. We will also see each work as a separate current that eventually flows together with others to make up an ocean of stories.

III. Reading books can be addictive, become all-consuming, and disrupt our ordinary routines—costs which most of us gladly incur for the pleasures of a good story.

Supplementary Reading:

Erich Auerbach, *Mimesis: The Representation of Reality in Western Literature*.

Questions to Consider:

1. Can you think of any American books that attempt to define American culture and national identity and try to describe what it means to be "American"? If so, which ones, and what do they say about us?

2. When you read a story written long ago, are you usually more interested in what the story tells us about the people for whom it was written, or in the ways the story still addresses our contemporary concerns? Do you think that the two ways of reading are compatible with each other?

Lecture Two
The *Epic of Gilgamesh*

Scope: We begin our study of world literature with the Mesopotamian *Epic of Gilgamesh*. The lecture begins with a brief look at the life of the poem across two millennia in the Middle East. We then consider the two parts of the epic: the heroic first part, in which Gilgamesh and his friend Enkidu journey to far lands, kill monsters, and return home as conquerors, assured of their lasting fame; and the second part, in which Gilgamesh undertakes a solitary spiritual journey in quest of a remedy for his own mortality. Next we consider Enkidu's story as a parable of culture and Gilgamesh's as a recognition of the positive and negative aspects of mortality. We conclude by suggesting some of the many ways in which the poem is a template for much of the literature that follows, including a great deal that we will treat in this course.

Outline

I. One of the oldest literary works in the world is the Middle Eastern Epic of Gilgamesh.
   A. The modern text is based on a 7th-century B.C.E. copy found in the library of the Assyrian King Assurbanipal.
   B. The poem itself dates to about 2800 B.C.E., when Gilgamesh was king of the Sumerian city of Uruk.
      1. The poems written about him were passed down from the Sumerians to the Akkadians, Babylonians, and Assyrians as these people succeeded to power in the Middle East.
      2. The poems were woven into a single narrative in the 2nd millennium B.C.E. by a Babylonian scribe known as Sin-liqe-uninni.
      3. Professor Vandiver tells the story of the poem's rediscovery in the 19th century in The Teaching Company course *Great Authors of the Western Literary Tradition, 2nd Edition*.

II. The poem is divided into two parts: a heroic story about the exploits of a legendary king, and a narrative about a spiritual quest by a man who has just recognized his own mortality.

A. Gilgamesh is heroic in that, like Achilles and Aeneas, he is partly divine and hence larger than life in all respects. His adventures are told in an epic, which is a narrative poem about a heroic figure who defines his culture.

B. Gilgamesh begins the story as a ruler who wears out his people, who pray to the gods for relief.
  1. The gods create Enkidu as an alter-ego for Gilgamesh: half animal, half human in complement to Gilgamesh's half-human, half-divine nature.
  2. Enkidu is civilized by a prostitute who has sex with him, introduces him to shepherds—who teach him to eat human food, wear clothing, and groom himself—and then takes him to meet Gilgamesh.
  3. The two wrestle and become fast friends, the first instance in literature of the kind of male friendship that we will later encounter between Achilles and Patroclus or David and Jonathan.
  4. The pair cements the friendship and seeks lasting fame by going to the cedar forests and killing their guardian, Humbaba, in an anticlimactic action that angers the god Enlil. Because there was no wood or stone in Sumeria, this may have been meant as a necessary quest by a builder-king.
  5. This is the world's first "Saint George and the Dragon" story if we can see Humbaba as a threat to Gilgamesh's community.

C. The death of Enkidu provides a transition to the second part of the poem.
  1. Gilgamesh spurns an offer of marriage from Ishtar, the goddess of love.
  2. In retaliation, Ishtar sends the Bull of Heaven against Uruk, but Gilgamesh and Enkidu kill it.
  3. The gods decide that the pair of heroes has crossed into forbidden territory and that one of them—Enkidu—must die.
  4. Gilgamesh stays by Enkidu until and after he dies; then, frightened by death, he lays aside his regalia and goes out searching for a more literal immortality than a name that will live after him.

D. The second part of the poem is about the quest for a remedy against death.

1. Gilgamesh travels to the end of the world, crosses over the Ocean of Death, and arrives at the island of Uta-napishti; he and his wife are the only humans ever granted immortality by the gods.
2. Uta-napishti tells Gilgamesh the Mesopotamian version of the story of the Great Flood, in which he built a boat that saved animals and people. As a reward for this act, he was given eternal life; the act will never be repeated for any other human being.
3. Gilgamesh is given a plant that renews one's youth, but a snake eats it as Gilgamesh is returning to Uruk.
4. The connections between this flood story and the one in the Old Testament have stimulated much scholarship, which can be reviewed in Heidel's *The Gilgamesh Epic and Old Testament Parallels*.
5. The poem presents a pattern identified in such books as Joseph Campbell's *The Hero with a Thousand Faces*, in which a hero of unusual birth undergoes heroic trials, seeks a treasure, and then returns to ordinary reality a changed person.
6. Gilgamesh returns home empty-handed but becomes reconciled to the human lot: his own immortality will be the walls of Uruk.
7. The Sumerians' depiction of life after death—the first in literature—is grim; there is no happy afterlife to console human beings.
8. The poem insists that Gilgamesh is a hero not just because of what he did but because of what he learned.

III. The poem is rich and complex enough to be interpreted in various ways.
   A. Enkidu's story is a Mesopotamian parable of culture in which the *protagonist* moves from wilderness to pastoral to city life—from prehistory to history.
      1. The story is also a fall from primeval innocence and union with nature into self-consciousness and the severing of the bond with nature.
      2. Enkidu as a civilized man kills animals that were once his friends and slays the guardian of the forests so that they can be plundered.
   B. Gilgamesh's story is about coming to terms with mortality.

      1. As part of his maturation process, Gilgamesh comes to see everything in a new way and better understands who he is and what he can accomplish.
      2. The deepest wisdom comes to Gilgamesh from Uta-napishti: It is about understanding one's role and responsibility in life and then performing it—in Gilgamesh's case, to go home and resume his duties as king.
      3. The poem also encourages one to find time for some civilized pleasures throughout life.

IV. The Epic of Gilgamesh is a good work to start off this course.
   A. It provides a kind of template for so much of the literature that follows.
   B. In addition to the themes and techniques already noted, this work also deals with many themes for the first time in literature: the relationship between gods and humans, the immortalizing power of art, the nature of a paradisial garden, the hunter or shepherd as a mediating figure between nature and civilization, dreams as portents of the future or as messages from another world, the ferryman across the waters of death, and the fantastic journey to strange places, including the Land of the Dead.

Essential Reading:

The *Epic of Gilgamesh.*

Supplementary Reading:

Andrew George, trans. *The Epic of Gilgamesh: The Babylonian Epic Poem and Other Texts in Akkadian and Sumerian*, the "Introduction."

Alexander Heidel, *The Gilgamesh Epic and Old Testament Parallels.*

Thomas Van Nortwick, *Somewhere I Have Never Travelled.*

Questions to Consider:

1. A variety of characters tell Gilgamesh on his solitary journey that his quest is fruitless, yet he continues. What is it that finally convinces him? Is the spiritual and emotional state in which we find Gilgamesh at the poem's end a victory or a defeat? How so?

2. Other themes have suggested themselves to readers of this epic: that of male-male friendship, the relationship between civilization and the feminine, and the attitudes of these Middle Eastern cultures to nature. What do you make of these—and other themes you might discover as you read the poem for yourself?

Lecture Three
The Hebrew Bible

Scope: This lecture focuses on the Hebrew Bible. After an account of the immigration of the Hebrews into Canaan, their own story as told in the *Tanakh* (the Old Testament for Christians), and ways in which they were influenced by surrounding cultures, we deal with the unique elements in Hebrew literature: monotheism and the Jews' covenant with their God, *Yahweh*. We treat the ways in which the Tanakh is neither pure literature nor history nor theology, but a blending of all three which foregrounds the relationship between God and his people. We go on to show the paradoxical ways this blending expresses itself in narrative, and we illustrate that paradox with a reading of passages from 1 Samuel, containing two versions of part of the David story in which human and divine agency are set side by side in ways that explain the Hebrew experience within history but which remain mysterious and defy reconciliation with each other.

Outline

I. The Hebrew Bible is one of the most important books in history, both for literature and for culture.
   A. For centuries, all writers within the Judeo-Christian culture wrote either consciously or unconsciously within its framework.
   B. It is a sacred text for Jews and Christians and an important one for Muslims.
   C. It is the *Old* Testament only for Christians, so we will call it by one of its Hebrew names, Tanakh, made up of the first letters of the Hebrew words for "law," "prophets," and "writings." The Torah, the first five books of the Tanakh, was assembled around the 10th century B.C.E.

II. The Tanakh tells the story of the Hebrews' immigration into Canaan around 2000 B.C.E.
   A. Abram, Sarai, and Lot leave Mesopotamia and travel to Canaan and institute the age of the great patriarchs: Abraham, Isaac, and Jacob.

    B. When a famine in Canaan sends some Jews to Egypt, they are enslaved and subsequently rescued by their God and the *prophet* Moses in the exodus.
    C. Some scholars see the story of the Jews from creation to the possession of the Promised Land as a kind of national epic, even though there is much more history to come in the Tanakh.

III. Hebrew thought and literature show striking similarities to that of Mesopotamia and Egypt and also some even more striking original features.

    A. The Hebrew flood story is indebted to the flood story in *Gilgamesh*; the story of Moses in a pitch-lined basket in the river reflects that of Sargon, an Akkadian ruler; Sheol bears a likeness to the afterlife depicted in *Gilgamesh*; and Psalm 104 is remarkably similar to Pharaoh Akhenaten's "Hymn to the Sun."
    B. The Hebrews, however, were or became monotheists.
        1. They believed either that there was only one God or that at least they as a people had only one.
        2. This contrasts with the many gods of the Mesopotamians and Egyptians.
    C. The Hebrews also believed that their God, Yahweh, had made a *covenant* with his people: a contract where God and people could meet and bind themselves to each other.
        1. Yahweh thus submits himself and his people to a rule of law and promises that he will behave in certain ways if they do.
        2. This idea was stunningly different from the *polytheistic* cultures of the ancient world, in which gods and goddesses could and did frequently behave in whimsical and unpredictable ways.
        3. The earliest covenant was between Abram and Yahweh in Genesis 12; the covenant was renewed with Isaac and Jacob and reaffirmed when Yahweh delivered his people from Egypt.
        4. The Ten Commandments more explicitly spelled out the obligations and rewards of this covenant.
    D. The combination of monotheism and the idea of a covenant makes the Tanakh part history, part literature, and part theology.
        1. It is history in that it is the story of people achieving an identity and a land of their own.

      2. It is literature in that it uses such devices as characterization, symbols, invented speeches, and interior monologue.
      3. It is theology in that it shows that when a nation keeps the law, things go well; when a nation breaks the law, it is punished.
      4. The Tanakh thus becomes what Robert Alter calls "historicized fiction" or "fictionalized history."
      5. The relationship between gods and men is part of the context in epic poems like *Gilgamesh*; here, the relationship occupies center stage.

IV. The combination of genres results in some paradoxes.
    A. The Creation story illustrates these paradoxes: God making history and human beings making history, the universe as God's harmonious creation and as a muddle, human beings as part of God's plan and human beings as free agents capable of making plans that may not coincide with God's.
    B. In *The Art of Biblical Narrative,* Robert Alter suggests that one of the ways the paradox is expressed in biblical literature is by telling the same story twice in different ways that are irreconcilable. He demonstrates this by considering two versions of the David story, set side by side in 1 Samuel 16 and 17.
      1. In 1 Samuel 16, David is a passive agent selected by Yaweh to be his chosen one. David then becomes Saul's armor-bearer and kills Goliath.
      2. In 1 Samuel 17, David, who does not know what to do with armor, uses his cunning, verbal skills, and courage to kill Goliath.
      3. The details of these two chapters cannot be reconciled.
      4. According to Alter, the stories show two different conceptions of David and two different theologies; one shows that David is God's instrument, the other that David is making history himself.
    C. Perhaps the Hebrews' greatest contribution to world literature is this paradox, which becomes a formative story for all of subsequent Western literature.
      1. Every writer until the 19th century will know these stories, which will form part of the background of values, beliefs, and assumptions of literature from Dante to Shakespeare.
      2. The code of ethics these stories produced was bequeathed in large measure to Christianity and, to a lesser extent, Islam.

Essential Reading:
The book of Genesis.
1 Samuel 16–17.

Supplementary Reading:
Robert Alter, *The Art of Biblical Narrative*.

Bernard M. W. Knox and Jerome Wright Clinton, "Introduction" to "The Bible: The Old Testament" in *The Norton Anthology of World Literature*.

Questions to Consider:
1. There are two different accounts of creation in the first two chapters of Genesis. Using Alter's idea of the paradox at the heart of Hebrew thought, how would you account for these two different versions? What does each one assert, and in what ways are they irreconcilable?
2. Read the rest of the story of David in 1 and 2 Samuel and the beginning of 1 Kings. In what ways is David himself a paradoxical character, apart from theological considerations? What kind of figure is he? What do you make of him, both as a man and as a king?

Lecture Four
Homer's *Iliad*

Scope: This lecture deals with the *Iliad*, beginning with an account of the origins of the Trojan War as recounted by Homer. We then treat the elements of an epic poem, whose conventions were established for the Western world by Homer's two poems, including heroic characters, the participation of gods and goddesses, the grand style (including epic similes), beginning the poem *in medias res*, and the *invocation*. After a description of a "shame culture," the way it functions in Book 1, and a brief recounting of the events of the rest of the poem, we present two ways in which this work influenced all subsequent Western literature: its individualistic notion of heroism and the hero, using both Achilles and Hector as examples, and its treatment of the enemy as equal in dignity and worth to the protagonists, giving to literature an impersonal order which has enhanced its authority ever since.

Outline

I. According to Harold Bloom, the Hebrew Bible and Homer's epics "compete for the consciousness of Western nations" as the most important literary works in history.
   A. According to the Greeks themselves, the Trojan War was a 10-year siege of the city by a consolidated force of mainland and island kings and their armies.
      1. The traditional date for the fall of Troy is 1184 B.C.E., about the same time the Hebrews were moving into Canaan.
      2. It occurred during the Mycenaean Age (c. 1500–1150 B.C.E.), named after Mycenae: the largest, wealthiest city on the mainland, ruled by Agamemnon.
      3. It was fought because Paris (or Alexandros), son of King Priam of Troy, abducted Helen, the wife of King Menelaus of Sparta.
      4. King Agamemnon, Menelaus's brother, led an armada of a thousand black ships to Troy to avenge the insult and to retrieve Helen.
      5. Homer's *Iliad* does not tell the entire story; rather, it deals only with about 52 days during the 10th year of the siege.

B. Stories about the Trojan War survived orally for about 400 years until Homer—whoever he was—somewhere around 700 B.C.E. wove some of them into an epic poem. The distance shows up in the poem sometimes in such details as Homer's unawareness of how chariots were used in battle.
II. An epic—a long narrative poem dealing with large and important characters and events—was defined for the Western world by Homer's two poems.
  A. Homer's techniques became the conventions of succeeding epic poems in imitation of the *Iliad* and the *Odyssey*.
   1. Characters are larger and stronger than men and women are in contemporary life and are able to achieve great feats of physical strength and courage.
   2. Gods and goddesses are more directly involved in human life as well, making life's meanings more transparent than they are now. The gods and goddesses are characters in the poems and will later be called the "supernatural machinery" of the epic.
   3. The epic's style is lofty and avoids vulgarities and colloquialisms.
   4. Even its rhetorical devices are on the grand scale, like its *epic similes*, comparisons introduced by "like" or "as" which continue on for many lines (e.g., the comparison in Book 8 between fires on the plain before Troy and stars in the sky).
   5. The poem begins with an invocation to the Muse, who sings *through* the poet, helping him tell a story he was not there to see for himself.
   6. The epic begins *in medias res*, "in the middle of things" (i.e., in the middle of the story), and fills in the necessary background in flashbacks.
  B. Homer's subject—warfare—was likewise crucial, so that most future epics will be about heroes on the battlefield and the honor they win there.
III. The poem begins with a dispute between Agamemnon, the great king, and Achilles, the greatest fighter, over a slave girl, leading to the "anger of Achilles," the announced theme of the poem.
  A. The Greeks lived in what is sometimes called a "shame culture," an other-directed culture in which one's worth is based on how one's peers value him.

        1. A warrior's worth is based on the prizes awarded him by the army.
        2. When Agamemnon strips Achilles of one of his prizes—the slave girl—Achilles loses face.
        3. Agamemnon would lose face by backing down to Achilles before the whole army, which he commands, and so they reach an impasse.
        4. Achilles withdraws from the fight and stays in his tent until his best friend, Patroclus, wearing Achilles' armor, is killed in battle by Hector, the greatest Trojan fighter.
        5. Then Achilles, who has been angry with Agamemnon, directs his anger at the Trojans and Hector until he meets Hector in battle, kills him, and then dishonors the body, refusing to allow it burial.
    B. The anger of Achilles ends when Priam, Hector's aged father and the King of Troy, travels alone to Achilles' tent to beg the return of his son's body.
        1. Achilles and Priam weep together, and Achilles returns Hector's body.
        2. When the anger of Achilles ends, so does the poem; its final event is the funeral of Hector in Troy.
IV. Among the *Iliad's* myriad legacies, two are especially important for the history of literature.
    A. The first enduring legacy is that heroism is defined in the poem as fighting hand-to-hand in battle—like the gunfights on Main Street in later Westerns.
        1. Considerations for family and community come after that for one's own reputation.
        2. Hector, who is a very good man, nevertheless chooses his own dignity and integrity over that of his community and his wife and child.
        3. As Moses Hadas reminds us, heroism for the ancient Greeks was an individualistic quest, and the hero's ultimate loyalty is always to himself, not to his family, nation, or even his gods.
    B. The second enduring legacy is Homer's treatment of the enemy—the Trojans—as equal in dignity and humanity to the army of Agamemnon and Achilles.
        1. Both armies speak the same language, worship the same gods, and live by the same codes.

2. The Trojans can be seen as more sympathetic, since we see them with their families, while the Achaeans are an army on the prowl.
3. Northrop Frye says that the demonstration in the poem that the fall of an enemy is as tragic as that of a friend or leader gives a disinterested quality to this literature which is part of its authority, moving it beyond entertainment, propaganda, or devotion toward "the vision of nature as an impersonal order."

Essential Reading:

Homer, the *Iliad*.

Supplementary Reading:

Harold Bloom, ed. *Homer (Bloom's Modern Critical Views)*.

Jasper Griffin, *Homer (Past Masters)*.

Moses Hadas, *Humanism: The Greek Ideal and Its Survival*.

Questions to Consider:

1. As you read the quarrel between Agamemnon and Achilles in Book 1 of the *Iliad*, with which of them do you find yourself sympathizing? Who is in the right? Who the wrong? On what basis can we decide in this kind of conflict?
2. Consider a modern hero in a modern novel or movie and try to decide what motivates him or her. Is he or she serving personal and individualistic interests in becoming a hero, or is he or she subordinating personal interests to larger issues and causes? The example of Marshall Kane in *High Noon*, discussed in this lecture, can guide your consideration of this complicated issue.

Lecture Five
Homer's *Odyssey*

Scope: This lecture discusses the *Odyssey*, which shares most of the characteristics of an epic with the *Iliad*. Among its thematic concerns, it shares with the *Iliad* the hero's need to win personal fame and make a name for himself; Odysseus's confrontation with the Cyclops is analyzed to demonstrate this theme. The lecture then treats the many times Odysseus is tempted to give up and to settle for a long but anonymous life (culminating with Calypso's offer of immortality) and shows that in important ways Achilles and Odysseus make the same heroic choice. This poem, however, is set in peace time, and we conclude by discussing some of the ways in which this is reflected: in the emphasis on domestic events, the nonheroic opponents Odysseus confronts on his journey home, the variety of skills he needs in this different ambience, and the importance of powerful and interesting women in the poem.

Outline

I. Modern scholarship suggests that the *Odyssey* was written about a generation after the *Iliad* but by a different poet who knew the *Iliad* very well and patterned this poem on the earlier one.
   A. It is written in 24 books, is about larger-than-life characters and events, is written in the grand style which uses epic similes, features the same supernatural machinery as the *Iliad*, and begins *in medias res*.
   B. It features a hero who more than anything else wants to make a name for himself and achieve enduring fame.
      1. This is the primary motivation for the warriors at Troy.
      2. Sometimes it involves sacrificing the good of one's community or family.

II. The episode with the Cyclops illustrates this motif of honor in the poem.
   A. Odysseus does not have to confront the Cyclops, but he does. Despite the loss of six of his best men, Odysseus adds to his reputation and glory.

- **B.** Once he has escaped, Odysseus makes sure that the Cyclops knows who it was who bested and blinded him, even at the risk of getting himself or more of his crew killed by the one-eyed giant.
- **C.** As in the *Iliad*, in this poem one has to expose oneself to risk in order to become somebody, a hero with a name that reaches to the ends of the world.

III. The motif is underscored by the kinds of temptations Odysseus resists on his way home, all of which encourage him to lay down his arms and live a long, happy, and anonymous life.
- **A.** The Lotus-Eaters, Circe, the Sirens, and the Phaiakians all make this offer to Odysseus.
- **B.** Most notably, Calypso offers him immortality but at the cost of reputation, fame, and being remembered. Odysseus turns down all of them.
    1. Achilles in the *Iliad* had the same choice: stay home and live a long but undistinguished life, or go to Troy and die young but be remembered forever. He goes to Troy; Odysseus makes the same choice.
    2. By the time of the *Odyssey,* Achilles has rethought his decision, as he tells Odysseus, who visits him in Hades.
    3. Odysseus, however, still persists, risking his life in order to win the kind of honor that outlives and thus defeats death.
    4. Odysseus constantly chooses the difficult and dangerous way to keep on adding to his name—to be a mortal hero rather than an anonymous immortal.

IV. The *Odyssey* is different in many ways from the *Iliad* as well.
- **A.** The poem is set in peacetime and has an entirely different ambience from the great war poem on which it is modeled.
- **B.** A third of this poem deals with hospitality and feasts and sacrifices. Odysseus in a way is fighting to get back home to this kind of life.
- **C.** Odysseus's antagonists are giants, monsters, witches, and nymphs, who observe none of the rules of heroic fighting and therefore have to be opposed with wit and guile rather than the straightforward fair fighting of the *Iliad*.

- **D.** Odysseus's triumphant return home is no heroic victory, since—appallingly outnumbered—he is forced to kill in cold blood 108 suitors for his wife Penelope.
    1. Hence his *heroic epithet*, which translates as "wily" or "many-faceted," as opposed to the heroic epithets of the heroes of the Trojan War (e.g., Achilles being described as "swift-footed").
    2. Hence Odysseus's ability to tell stories and lie when in a tight spot, as opposed to the hatred of the heroes of the Trojan War for a man "who says one thing but hides another in his heart."
- **E.** The differences between the heroic world of the *Iliad* and the peacetime world of the *Odyssey* are illustrated in Odysseus's meeting with Aias in Hades.
    1. Aias, a hero from the heroic world of the Trojan War, turns his back on Odysseus and walks away, refusing to acknowledge someone who has survived by compromising the heroic code.
    2. The distance from the heroic world is also reflected in Odysseus's frequent disguises and the sometimes deflating epic similes applied to him by the poet.
- **F.** Women characters play a far more important part in this poem than they do in the *Iliad*; they are not depicted as slave women.
    1. Helen, Circe, Calypso, and Penelope are formidable women who easily control men and whose power is challenged only by Odysseus (who sometimes needs divine help to do so).
    2. Helen in Sparta, visited by Telemachus, is marvelously in charge of her household; Circe changes men into swine; and Calypso captures Odysseus and keeps him with her until forced to release him by Zeus.
    3. Penelope's beauty, wit, and intelligence have turned 108 suitors into metaphorical swine; in the poem's penultimate scene, she tricks the great trickster Odysseus into losing his temper, making her the only character in the poem ever able to do so.
    4. We hope that Odysseus and Penelope will spend the rest of their lives as equals—a hope that this peacetime poem makes possible in a way the *Iliad* cannot.
- **V.** The impact of the *Odyssey* and the *Iliad* on the subsequent history of literature is incalculable.
    - **A.** Both Achilles and Odysseus bequeathed an idea of personal heroism that never disappears.

    B. We will encounter Achilles again in Greek tragedy and the works of Shakespeare, Goethe, Faulkner, and Achebe.
    C. We will meet Odysseus again in the Chinese novel *Monkey* and many of the tales from Chaucer and the *1001 Nights*.

Essential Reading:

Homer, *Odyssey*.

Supplementary Reading:

M. I. Finley, *The World of Odysseus*.

Jasper Griffin, *Homer (Past Masters)*.

Questions to Consider:

1. Odysseus's name translates roughly as "trouble." If his goal throughout the poem is to win a name, or to deserve the name he has already won at Troy, what is the significance of his given name? Does he earn or deserve it by the poem's end and, if so, in how many ways?
2. The most fantastic adventures in the poem are narrated by Odysseus himself at the Phaiakian banquet when he finally reveals his identity. It has been suggested that he is making up these adventures—or at least elaborating and heightening them—in order to impress the highly domesticated Phaiakians, to convince them to take him home, and to get them to load him up with gifts. What do you think about that thesis? Is it plausible? Is there any corroborating evidence, supplied by the poet, to confirm any of Odysseus's tales?

Lecture Six
Chinese Classical Literature

Scope: This lecture features three works from China's Classical Age: a lyric poem and two prose works that fall somewhere between philosophy and literature—all of which demonstrate how different Chinese literature is in its earliest stages from that of Mesopotamia, Israel, and Greece. After looking briefly at a lyric poem from *The Book of Songs*, whose voice is that of an ordinary person in ordinary life, we take a closer look at Confucius's *Analects* and Chuang Chou's *Chuang Tzu*. Confucius's book is designed to train young men for government service and argues for manners, benevolence, and a sympathetic putting of oneself in another's place to recreate the self, the family, and the state. Chuang Chou's is an early Taoist work which advocates political, intellectual, and emotional freedom as the basis for "going with the flow"; several of his stories are analyzed to demonstrate the values of learning to do this.

Outline

I. While other early civilizations created epic stories, Chinese literature begins with lyric poetry in which we hear the voices of ordinary people going about everyday events. This can be illustrated with a poem from the *Shih Ching (Classic of Poetry)*, or *The Book of Songs*.

   A. The collection comes from the Chou Dynasty, and it was compiled between the 10th and 7th centuries B.C.E. It consists of 305 poems, 160 of which are folk songs.
   1. Tradition assigned its editing to Confucius.
   2. It is probably, however, an independent work of the Chou court, later adopted for teaching purposes by Confucian scholars.

   B. The collection would later become one of the five Confucian classics, used as the basis for Chinese education for millennia. For over 2000 years every educated person in China would have known these poems.

   C. Poem 26, "Boat of Cypress," is typical of certain qualities of the entire collection.

1. It is the voice of an anonymous someone whose concerns are of the mundane, not the epic, sort.
2. Like many Chinese poems, it starts with a picture that both suggests a situation and sets a mood.
3. Most critics have decided that the voice is that of a young woman being coerced into something she does not want to do.
4. The poem then gives a series of negative images for a heart that will not be forced, and it ends with a wish to fly away.
5. The subject and tone of the poem are in amazing contrast to those of the works we have looked at from other cultures.

II. The same contrast can be seen in the *Analects* of Confucius.
   A. Confucius (551–479 B.C.E.), like Socrates and Jesus, was a teacher who did not write a book. The *Analects* are sayings of his which are frequently responses to questions or parts of larger discussions, and they appear in random order. It is one of the most influential works in Chinese history.
      1. His teachings are this-worldly, focused on human relationships which he sees as hierarchical, based on the fundamental one between parent and child. They stress moral propriety and social responsibility.
      2. The right is expressed for Confucius in ceremony, ritual, and social forms which A. C. Graham says we might think of as "good manners" that should always be observed unless there is a compelling reason not to.
      3. The right is something like benevolence, and it can be axiomatically stated in what has been called the *Confucian Golden Rule*: "Do not impose on others what you yourself do not desire." The key to benevolence is "likening to oneself" (i.e., putting oneself in the place of the other).
      4. The ultimate goal of Confucius's teachings is to prepare young men for government service, and his teachings contain visions of what a government would be like if every ruler were to observe the right. Like other belief systems, these ideas run the risk of leading to hypocrisy and authoritarianism.
   B. Confucius was looking for a balanced individual in a balanced state, which he believed can be achieved.
   C. Confucius arrived at a place where instinct and duty are identical; thus, he never has to choose between them again.

    D. The combination of virtue, manners, custom and ritual can harmonize all human relations and can harmonize the individual soul so that instinct and duty are identical. The vision has had profound influence on Chinese thought throughout history.

III. While Chuang Chou (c. 369–286 B.C.E.) created a philosophy in opposition to that of Confucius (he is considered one of the founders of Taoism), his focus is likewise on the everyday and the here-and-now.

    A. Unlike Confucius, who trained young men for government posts, Chuang Chou did not found a school or seek out disciples. Instead, he advocated keeping the mind free of politics, authority, and conventional ways of thinking.

    B. The idea of his teaching is to get one into harmony with the order of things: "going with the flow."
        1. In order to do this we must free ourselves from all the sectarian and limited ideas, training, and advice we receive from parents, teachers, and priests.
        2. The two fundamental principles of Chuang Chou are that language is not an accurate reflector of reality and that everything we know is based on categories which are defined by language and shaped by our own perspective.
        3. Since *Chuang Tzu* is made up of words, Chou turns his skepticism on his own book, frequently working in paradox and parable.
        4. Almost everything he says is illustrated with a story, which makes *Chuang Tzu* as much a work of literature as of philosophy.

    C. Given the unreliability of language and the relativity of perspective, how does Chuang Chou suggest we live?
        1. He tells a story about hunting a magpie in a park.
        2. He asserts that everything in the world is unified and cooperates with everything else.
        3. Humans miss "the Way" by sticking to codes laid down by sages; the true "Way" is the entire universe.
        4. The heroes of his stories are mostly craftspeople who are not analytical but who can size up an entire situation and respond to it using both eye and hand in a way that usually cannot be put into words.

> 5. The point is to size up a situation based on experience, without imposing definitions and categories, and then cooperate with the way things are.
>
> **D.** "The Way" also teaches us to rise above the distinction between life and death, since all is process and all is one.
> 1. He tells a story of how he played music and sang at his wife's funeral, which shocked people for whom burial rites are of supreme importance.
> 2. He gives instructions for the disposal of his body after death, suggesting a view of death that had no precedent in literature before this time.

IV. Chinese literature of the classical period stands in high contrast to the literature of other early civilizations.

  A. In general terms, the literature of most early cultures is heroic and leans toward the tragic. Heroes try to bend the universe to their will, fight against it, and frequently fail.

  B. Early Chinese literature, on the other hand, is not heroic and leans toward a broad sense of the comic. It allows forces larger than ourselves to carry us along and suggests that we try to align ourselves with these forces.

Essential Reading:

Confucius, D.C. Lau, trans., the *Analects*.

Chuang Chou, *Chuang Tzu: Basic Writings*.

Stephen Owen, ed. and trans., *An Anthology of Chinese Literature: Beginnings to 1911*.

Supplementary Reading:

A. C. Graham, *Disputers of the Tao*, Chapters 1 and 3.

Burton Watson, *Early Chinese Literature*.

Questions to Consider:

1. Is Confucius's claim that a ruler can be truly great by doing nothing a possible state of affairs or an impossibly lofty vision? Does Confucius seem to believe that it is literally possible? What would Machiavelli say about it?

2. Imagine yourself spending one full day trying to get into harmony with things as described by Chuang Chou. What would you have to do to be able to spend such a day? What would the day be like? What would be its rewards?

Lecture Seven
Greek Tragedy

Scope: This lecture pursues the idea that the three great Athenian tragic dramatists—Aeschylus, Sophocles, and Euripides—reflect the developing intellectual life of the city in their plays, particularly regarding the nature of the gods and their relationship with humanity. Aeschylus's *Oresteia* concerns a series of difficult choices which are resolved in the Athenian institution of trial-by-jury and a belief that Zeus leads humanity through suffering into wisdom. For Sophocles, in *Antigone,* the gods are part of the furniture of the universe, but they have their own concerns and cannot be counted on to create or validate human morality. Euripides's *Medea* suggests that the Greek gods are merely the forces of nature; the most uncontrollable of human passions anthropomorphized into deities. Medea, whose overwhelming desire for revenge in the play includes killing her own children, demonstrates this idea by becoming a deity at play's end.

Outline

I. The origins of Greek theater are treated in other Teaching Company courses such as *Greek Tragedy*, *Masterpieces of Ancient Greek Literature*, and *Age of Pericles*.

   A. By the 5th century B.C.E. there is a fully developed theater in Athens featuring the two kinds of plays that would remain standard in Western drama until the time of Ibsen: *comedy* and *tragedy*.

   B. We will deal in this lecture only with tragedy. Tragedy is a serious drama in verse that deals with the lives of characters of significance and usually carries a protagonist from happiness to unhappiness.

   C. Socrates said that the unexamined life was not worth living; tragedy was one of the ways the Greeks examined their lives, especially in terms of their understanding of the relationship between humans and the gods.

II. Aeschylus (c. 524–456 B.C.E.) is the most religious and patriotic of the three great tragedians, and also the greatest poet.

A. His *trilogy*, *Oresteia,* is based on the myth of the House of Atreus and goes back to events just after the Trojan War. It reinterprets old stories in order to illuminate contemporary life.
   1. The trilogy is organized around a series of difficult choices.
   2. In *Agamemnon*, the first play, we are reminded of Agamemnon's dilemma of 10 years earlier: being forced to choose between his family and his army, either one of which carries both human and divine sanctions and either of which will doom him.
   3. In *The Libation Bearers,* the second play, Agamemnon's son Orestes is forced to choose between avenging his father by killing his mother or leaving his father's murder unavenged—again, a choice with terrible sanctions either way.
   4. In *Eumenides*, the third play, Orestes is acquitted for killing his mother after a trial before a jury of Orestes's peers, arbitrated by Athena.
   5. In *Eumenides*, the difficult choice is resolved by the institution of trial-by-jury, in which the law of vendetta is replaced by a court of law and a system of communal justice.
   6. Aeschylus sees this as evidence of the way Zeus leads humans through suffering into truth—making him the most religious and patriotic of the three playwrights.

III. Sophocles (c. 496–406 B.C.E.) played an important part in Athenian public life, but in his plays he expressed more skepticism than Aeschylus regarding the participation of the gods in human life and their concern for humans or human morality.
  A. He never doubts the existence of the gods, but he finds no support from them for human morality or conduct, which humans always have to create for themselves.
   1. In *Antigone* the protagonist is forced to make another difficult choice: loyalty to the state or loyalty to her family. Again, there are sanctions on both sides of the choice.
   2. She chooses her family by burying a brother whom King Creon had commanded should lie unburied. She is caught, imprisoned, and anticipates starving slowly to death by committing suicide.
   3. The gods are remarkably silent until too late, and the king suffers punishment as a result of his own actions, not divine

interference. The gods do not endorse or validate human morality.

B. Moses Hadas suggests that for Sophocles the spheres of the gods and humans are separate, and that humans must create their own moral codes without expecting divine assistance.

IV. Euripides (c. 480–406 B.C.E.) was the most private of the three playwrights, the most modern, and the most skeptical of the existence of the gods as they were conceived in ancient Greece.

A. He was influenced by the *Sophists*, who argued that man—not the gods, nature, or universe—is the "measure of all things," and thereby introduced a radical subjectivity into Greek thought. Characters like the Chorus in *Hippolytus* and Talthybius in *Hecuba* echo this Sophist position.

B. *Medea* is a play made out of this kind of skepticism. A tailpiece to the story of Jason and the Argonauts, it is drawn from Greek myth and set a generation before the Trojan War.

  1. The play attacks traditional Greek attitudes about foreigners and women, echoed in the relationship between Medea and Jason.

  2. The play makes Medea into a "masculine" tragic hero who is given the same kind of treatment that Achilles or Hector received in earlier Greek literature.

  3. The play suggests that the gods are simply personifications of the most powerful forces in nature and the most powerful human passions.

  4. In this play Medea becomes a deity and is whisked away in a reverse *deus ex machina* (usually a device used to bring a god onto the Greek stage to solve some otherwise insoluble problem but here used to carry Medea *off* the stage).

  5. Medea is deified for killing her own children, the king of Corinth, and his daughter, Jason's betrothed—a stunning idea in Athens in its time.

C. Where Aeschylus sees the gods participating in human life and working toward a greater good, and Sophocles sees them as simply part of the furniture of the universe whose involvement in human life is minimal, Euripides sees them as *anthropomorphic* projections of our own uncontrollable lusts.

1. In this way, tragedy in Athens' Golden Age was part of the examined life—raising questions and debating current issues in the intellectual life of the city.
2. These are all intellectual positions that will recur in the Western world beginning with the Renaissance.

Essential Reading:

Aeschylus, *The Oresteia (Agamemnon, The Libation Bearers, Eumenides)*, Robert Fagles, trans.

Euripides, *Mêdeia. Euripides: The Complete Plays*, Carl R. Mueller, trans.

Sophocles, *Antigone*.

Supplementary Reading:

Moses Hadas, *Introduction to Classical Drama*.

Questions to Consider:

1. How much of the Greek theology that we get in these plays depends on Greek religion being polytheistic, vis-à-vis Hebrew monotheism? That is, in a theology that posits many gods, is an attitude like Euripides's inevitable, just as a monotheistic religion inclines a people towards belief in a God who cares about people? Conversely, are the differences between Greek and Hebrew thought about God or the gods attributable to other factors?

2. In reading Euripides's *Medea*, where do you locate your sympathies: with Medea, Jason, or some combination? How much of what you feel is attributable to modern sensibilities about gender relations? How do you think the original Greek audience would have felt about these issues? Is Medea, either for you or (do you think) for the original audience, an admirable character, a reprehensible character, or both?

Lecture Eight
Virgil's *Aeneid*

Scope: This lecture explores Virgil's *Aeneid* and illustrates the Greek idea of heroism transformed into the Roman one. Where Greek heroes are individualistic, Roman heroes—of which Aeneas is the prototype—are responsible and dutiful, subordinating their individualism to larger and more abstract causes. Book 2, the story of the fall of Troy, and Book 4, featuring the love affair between Aeneas and Dido, are summarized and used to show Aeneas's transformation from a Greek hero to a Roman hero. Virgil's attitude toward this new type of hero is complex: while he understands and celebrates the greatness of Rome's achievement and the contribution its heroes made to that achievement, he cannot help but wonder about its high cost, both to the individual and to the people who are destroyed in Rome's advance. The ambiguous ending of the poem is considered as a demonstration of Virgil's subtle and humane analysis of Roman history.

Outline

I. As Sumeria became the foundation of all subsequent cultures in the Middle East, so did Greece for Rome.

    A. Rome adopted and adapted much of Greek culture when it conquered Greece: its philosophy, literature, historiography, and even parts of its religion.

    B. When Virgil (70–19 B.C.E.) set out to write a national Roman epic poem, he modeled his very closely on Homer's, even to the extent of linking Roman history with Greek history by tracing the founder of Rome back to Aeneas, a Trojan warrior in the *Iliad*.

    C. In typical Roman fashion, however, Virgil adapted his Greek models to his own needs.

        1. Where Greek heroes are individualistic, the prototypical Roman hero, Aeneas, will subordinate his individuality to a body of laws, his family, and his state.

        2. Where the Greek heroes have epithets like "swift-footed" (Achilles) or "many-faceted" (Odysseus), Aeneas's will be *pius*, which means "responsible" or "dutiful."

3. *Pietas* really implies four levels of responsibility: to the gods, to the state, to the family, and to fellow human beings.
4. Aeneas begins the poem as a Greek hero who fought at Troy, but he becomes a Roman hero throughout the course of the poem, learning to subordinate his private to his public self.

II. The poem begins, like Homer's, *in medias res*, in the ninth year since the fall of Troy, during which Aeneas has been at sea, looking to found a new Troy.
  A. Juno (the Greek Hera) still hates the Trojans and stirs up a storm that lands Aeneas's ships dispersedly at Carthage in North Africa.
    1. Carthage is Juno's city; she wants Aeneas and Queen Dido to fall in love so that Aeneas's glorious destiny will be fulfilled in Carthage.
    2. She enlists the aid of Venus (Aphrodite), Aeneas's mother, and Dido falls in love with Aeneas and invites him and his refugee Trojans to a huge banquet, where he tells the story of their wanderings in flashback, as Odysseus did for the Phaiakians in the *Odyssey*.
    3. We get to hear what the fall of Troy was like for the losing side, which makes this one of the great books of the *Aeneid*.
  B. Aeneas's story describes the first stages in the transformation of a Greek hero into a Roman one.
    1. Aeneas tries to die with his city, as a good Greek hero would, but is prevented by signs from Venus and Jupiter, who require him to leave to found a new Troy in the west.
    2. The picture of Aeneas leaving Troy—carrying his aged father, leading his son and wife, carrying the household gods and then taking responsibility for the many Trojans outside the city—is a perfect illustration of all of the aspects of *pietas*.
    3. In Book 3, Aeneas describes nine years of wandering, during which he visited many of the same spots that Odysseus did in the *Odyssey*.

III. Book 4 is Dido's story.
  A. Maneuvered by Venus and Juno into consummating their love, Aeneas and Dido spend the winter together in Carthage, and for one of the few times in the poem, Aeneas seems happy.
  B. In the spring, however, Jupiter commands that Aeneas move on to fulfill his destiny, which he does reluctantly.

- **C.** Dido builds a funeral pyre and kills herself upon it, asking for eternal enmity between Carthage and Rome as she dies.
- **D.** Throughout Book 4, Virgil forces us to see events through Dido's eyes, generating a great deal of sympathy for her and distancing us from the poem's nominal hero.
  1. In Book 6, Aeneas sees Dido's shade when he visits Hades, and she treats him as Aias did Odysseus in the *Odyssey*.
  2. In many ways Dido is a Greek-type heroine who fulfills her *nature*, while Aeneas is a Roman-type hero who fulfills his *duty*.
  3. Book 4 also raises some haunting questions about Roman destiny: Why does it cost the destruction of so many innocent and admirable people? What has Dido done to deserve such a fate?

IV. In Books 6 and 8, Aeneas is given visions of the future greatness of Rome, whose gifts to the world will increase military might and rule, and provide security, peace, and prosperity. The visions are designed to justify to Aeneas the personal sacrifices he has made and will make in Rome's establishment.

V. The last six books of the *Aeneid* are modeled on the *Iliad*, as the first six were on the *Odyssey*.
- **A.** Aeneas must fight another Trojan War over Lavinia, whom he must win away from Turnus so that he can marry her and found a race blended from Trojan and Latin blood.
  1. In the battle, Turnus is another Greek-style hero fighting for personal reasons, while Aeneas is by now *pius* Aeneas, fighting for duty, destiny, and Rome.
  2. As in the *Iliad*, where Hector's killing of Patroclus precipitates the climactic fight between Hector and Achilles, the killing of Pallas precipitates the climactic fight between Aeneas and Turnus.
  3. Turnus is defeated, concedes victory to Aeneas, and begs for mercy; after hesitating, Aeneas kills him.
- **B.** Readers and critics have argued for 2000 years about the meaning of the killing of Turnus.
  1. Is it yet another illustration of *pietas*, with Aeneas doing what he must do in spite of his own impulses?

        2. Is it the last impulsive thing Aeneas ever does: striking back at a destiny which has cost him his individuality just before he disappears into history?
    C. The second half of the poem keeps the question of the cost of Roman achievement before us through the deaths of beautiful young men in what seems an unnecessary war, the pervading sadness of its tone, and the making of Dido and Turnus into the poem's most attractive characters.
        1. The unprecedented era of peace and prosperity across the Roman world will be achieved by force (all the future Roman heroes Aeneas sees in Hades are soldiers).
        2. Aeneas must give up art, beauty, and personal happiness to become an agent of destiny.
        3. It is in addressing both sides of the issue of establishing peace and rule of law that Virgil shows his greatness as a poet and makes the *Aeneid* the most subtle analysis of Roman history that we have.
VI. Rome created a new kind of hero for our course: the one who fights for a cause.
    A. We will run across both kinds in future stories.
    B. The Christian tradition in the Western world especially found this Roman conception of heroism attractive and useful.

Essential Reading:

Virgil, the *Aeneid*.

Supplementary Reading:

William S. Anderson, *The Art of the Aeneid*.

Adam Parry, "The Two Voices of Virgil's *Aeneid*." *Virgil: A Collection of Critical Essays*.

Viktor Pöschl, *The Art of Virgil: Image and Symbol in the Aeneid*.

Questions to Consider:

1. Try to find as many parallels as you can among the *Aeneid* and the *Iliad* and *Odyssey*, and then think about the ways Virgil subtly adapts everything he borrows to put it to new use in his poem.
2. How do you read the poem's ending? Is it a final Roman triumph for Aeneas, or a final Greek-type defeat? Are there other ways to think about what the last lines of the poem mean or suggest?

Lecture Nine
Bhagavad Gita

Scope: This lecture deals with the Indian Bhagavad Gita ("Song of the Lord"). It begins by characterizing the *Mahabharata*, the epic poem that contains the Gita, in relation to the Homeric epics. It then considers the Gita's big question: How can Arjuna fight in a battle against his kinsmen without accumulating a devastating amount of *karma*? The rest of the Gita is a dialogue between Krishna (the incarnated Vishnu) and Arjuna, in which Krishna introduces new ideas into traditional Hinduism—ideas which allow any person from any caste to establish a direct and personal relationship with Krishna and to facilitate the progression of the soul towards freedom from rebirth (*mokṣa*) and union with the One (*Brahman*). Krishna validates his teaching by revealing himself to Arjuna in his glory as a god. We conclude by asking how the Gita relates to ideas in other literature we have considered in the course.

Outline

I. The *Mahabharata*, the larger epic poem in which the Bhagavad Gita is contained, may be the longest poem in the world—about seven times longer than the *Iliad* and *Odyssey* combined.

   A. The *Mahabharata* grew by accretion from about the 4th century B.C.E. to about the 4th century C.E.

   B. Its roots are with the Indo-Aryans, who came into the Indus River Valley around 1500 B.C.E. These peoples were part of the Indo-European language group, which implies that the *Mahabharata's* amazing similarities to Homer's epics may be a result of common origins rather than direct influence.
      1. Both poems share an epic war that brings an entire age to a close.
      2. They also share supernatural machinery, characters who are part divine, an initial situation involving loss of a possession that reflects personal honor, and a cosmic war fought over a woman, Draupati.

   C. There are also differences between the two poems.

1. The *Mahabharata*—especially the Bhagavad Gita, added to the epic around the 1st century C.E.—has always had a more scriptural status than the Greek epics.
2. The *Mahabharata* also marks an important evolution in Hindu thought that revolutionizes traditional Hindu theology.

II. The setting for the Bhagavad Gita is the moment before the great cosmic battle is about to begin.
   A. Arjuna, one of the warriors, notices that the enemy's ranks are made up of relatives, teachers, and friends—all of the antagonists are in fact children of Bharata (as the Hebrews are all children of Jacob/Israel).
   B. Arjuna has the same kind of difficult choice as that of protagonists in Greek epic and tragedy: he has a duty to fight but fears that he will accumulate a devastating amount of *karma* by killing kinsmen and friends.
      1. *Karma* is a law of moral nature that holds that actions produce effects which are enacted over a period of births, deaths, and rebirths.
      2. Since the goal of Hinduism is the release from the cycle of death and rebirth, *karma* makes that goal ever more remote.
   C. Arjuna lays down his bow and declares that he will not fight.
   D. His chariot driver is Krishna, an incarnation of the god Vishnu, who responds to Arjuna. The rest of the poem is a dialogue between the two, centering on the question of how Arjuna can participate in this battle without condemning himself to an eternity of rebirths.

III. Krishna's teaching is a redefinition of the relationship between God and humans in Hindu thought.
   A. Krishna assures Arjuna that a soul is immortal, so death is an illusion; no one can ever really be killed.
   B. He argues that to live is to act, and that action is necessary to keeping the self, society, and the cosmos healthy. Vishnu incarnates himself and acts in history just for this reason.
   C. Krishna says that one can act in the world without accumulating *karma* if one acts from duty rather than from the hope of personal gain—what Krishna calls "the fruits of action."

1. This can be done by undertaking every action as a personal sacrifice made directly to God.
2. Then, paradoxically, action can lead to liberation, but only if it is done with discipline (*yoga*).

D. This is a new teaching, since it allows anyone from any caste to establish a direct relationship with God.
   1. In traditional Hinduism, only a few Brahmins (members of the top caste) could liberate themselves by not acting and by perfecting knowledge and discipline; lower castes were mired in consequential action and continuously piled up *karma*.
   2. Now, anyone from any caste can establish a direct relationship with God by dedicating action to God and thereby perfecting his or her own life.
   3. This new teaching will set up the rich body of future religious poetry in Hinduism, most of which will be dedicated to Krishna.

E. To define what one's duty is, Krishna explains the caste system in Hinduism to Arjuna.
   1. Humans are divided into four classes: Brahmins (intellectuals and priests); warriors, rulers, and statesmen; businessmen; and workers and servants.
   2. Each class is divided into four stages of life (student, householder, retirement, and renunciation) and each has its appropriate goal (wealth, pleasure, social duty, and release or liberation).
   3. What one does to find one's duty is to find one's place on these superimposed grids.
   4. Arjuna is in the warrior class; Krishna reminds him that this is no ordinary war but one whose purpose is to set the cosmos right again for a while.

F. Krishna clinches his teaching by revealing himself to Arjuna in all his glory, and the poem gives us Arjuna's response to the vision.
   1. As in Hebrew and Greek stories, Arjuna cannot long endure the sight of unmediated divinity.
   2. After Arjuna begs Vishnu to return to being Krishna, he picks up his bow and prepares to fight.

IV. Modern Indian commentators have given the Gita a metaphoric, psychological reading, in which Arjuna learns to kill the enemies of his

true Self—his illegitimate desires and passions—in order to achieve union with his real, Supreme Self.
- **A.** Once he does this, he realizes three things:
  1. The universe is one, and we cannot escape its continuity.
  2. Arjuna's own interests and those of the universe coincide: what is done for the Supreme Self is done for the universe and vice versa.
  3. These awarenesses lead to a union in love with his Supreme Self (Vishnu) and to the ability to accept the entire universe with joy and to join in its universal aims.
- **B.** This reading matches up with Confucius' saying that at a certain stage in life instinct and duty are identical, or with Plato's assertion that the life of the just man is many times happier than the life of the unjust man.

V. The Bhagavad Gita touches on many important issues.
- **A.** It tempts us into a hypothetical round-table discussion of important issues among famous literary characters.
- **B.** It has influenced and touched many people in history.
  1. It influenced Goethe, Carlyle, Emerson, and Thoreau.
  2. Mahatma Gandhi used it as an everyday guide to action.

Essential Reading:
Bhagavad Gita.

Supplementary Reading:
Eliot Deutsch, *The Bhagavad Gita*, the "Introduction."

V. S. Sukthankar, *On the Meaning of Mahabharata.*

Questions to Consider:
1. What do you think of Krishna's argument in the Gita as a justification for war? Are there other conceptual frameworks—for example, that of a "just" or "unjust" war—that need to be invoked? Would these justifications for fighting be the same as Arjuna's? If you were on the other side in this war, how would Krishna's counsel strike you? Is the idea that if one is a soldier, one's duty is to fight sufficient justification? Why or why not?

2. Pick three or four of the writers treated in this course so far and set them at one of Steve Allen's round tables to discuss a question raised by one of the works treated so far: the withdrawal of Achilles or Arjuna from fighting; the treatment of women by Hector, Jason, Creon, and Aeneas; the idea that one's primary loyalty is to God rather than to any earthly good; or some other idea that the course has suggested to you so far.

Lecture Ten
The New Testament

Scope: This lecture considers the New Testament, which focuses on Jesus. We begin by seeing Jesus in the letters of Paul, for whom Christ's death and resurrection were the text's essential items and could be explained to Gentiles (non-Jews) in terms of the mystery religions which had sprung up all over the Mediterranean world. We then look at the Gospels of Matthew, Mark, Luke, and John and consider that their differences might be the result of different emphases and target audiences. Next we examine Jesus's preference for teaching in parables and look at one of their recurring themes: God's concern for the lost, the errant, and the lowly—a striking contrast to the way the gods valued humans in Greek and Roman literature. This concern for the meek and the poor in spirit has implications for future literature, as we demonstrate with Erich Auerbach's analysis of the story of Peter's denial of Jesus in Matthew's Gospel.

Outline

I. For Christians, this book is the *new* covenant, transcending or fulfilling the *old* one made with the Hebrews.
   A. For Christians, Jesus died a blameless death for the sins of the world, thus undoing the primal sin of Adam and Eve and reconciling God and humans.
   B. His resurrection validates his sacrifice and establishes a pattern in which humans can participate, as all people are now God's chosen people.

II. This was the message of Paul, the first great Christian missionary, who wrote the oldest books in the New Testament, dating from 50 C.E.
   A. Paul was writing to Gentiles (non-Jews) who would not have known Old Testament prophecies about an expected Messiah.
   B. Paul explained Jesus's death and resurrection in terms of mystery religions which had sprung up all around the Mediterranean world as personal alternatives to the official and public state religion of Rome.

©2007 The Teaching Company.

1. According to Robert Payne, Rome's religion was a duty; it offered little by way of moral code and no promise of personal immortality.
2. *Mystery religions* were dedicated to various gods (Isis, Dionysus, Mithra) and involved initiation, ritual, and the promise of immortality through participation in the death and resurrection of the deity.
3. For Paul, Jesus was the fulfillment of all other mystery religions: a god who was not from mythology, who did not die annually but did so once and for all time in history, and whose death and resurrection via belief and participation in his sacred meal—the Eucharist—promised immortality.

III. The Gospels were written perhaps as late as the 2nd century in the case of John, and they add information about Jesus's life and teachings to Paul's account of Jesus's death and resurrection.
   A. The Gospel according to Mark is the oldest and shortest gospel.
   B. Matthew and Luke seem to have drawn on Mark but had other sources, since they include material not in Mark. Luke includes material in neither Mark nor Matthew, so he may have had access to a third collection of sources.
   C. The Gospel according to John is very different from the other three.
      1. It includes much material that is not in the synoptic Gospels.
      2. It is deeply indebted to Greek philosophy for its explanation of Jesus's life and death.
      3. It is more a meditation on Jesus than a history or biography.
   D. For this lecture we will set John aside to focus on the other three Gospels.

IV. The Gospels of only Matthew, Mark, and Luke are called the synoptic Gospels, since their accounts, while differing in details, can be reconciled with each other, and can probably be accounted for by their different aims and intended audiences.
   A. The Gospel according to Mark is probably designed to get as much information about Jesus into writing before those who remembered him died.
      1. Its central question concerns Jesus's identity as the awaited Jewish Messiah.

      2. In the first verse, Mark says that Jesus is the *Christ*, and *Christos* is the Greek word for "Messiah."
      3. When the Jewish high priest asks Jesus if he is the Christ, Jesus says simply, "I am."
   B. The Gospel according to Matthew is written for fellow Jews, and its intent is to show that Jesus fulfilled all the Old Testament prophecies about the Messiah.
      1. Matthew's story is dense with allusions to the Old Testament prophets (reminding us of the way Virgil uses Homer in his *Aeneid*).
      2. Matthew includes some narrative details to show fulfillment of Old Testament stories—like Mary and Joseph taking the baby Jesus to Egypt, which sets up interesting parallels between Jesus and Moses, the deliverer of Israel from Egypt.
   C. Thus, target audiences may have a great deal to do with the differences between the synoptic Gospels.

V. The synoptic Gospels all agree that Jesus preferred to teach in *parables*, which answer questions indirectly with a narrative rather than a discursive answer.
   A. Parables—as we have seen in those of Chuang Chou—are more resonant than discursive answers, handing more of the responsibility of understanding them to the hearer/reader.
   B. Mark's comment that Jesus told parables in public and then explained their meaning to his disciples in private has given rise to a long tradition that posits a secret society which has always known the *real* meaning of his teachings.
   C. Most of Jesus's parables seem not to need secret interpretation. Many of them—like the Prodigal Son, the man who loses one sheep out of 100, or the woman who loses one piece of silver out of 10—show God's concern for the lost, the lowly, and the outcast.
   D. In our course, this is strikingly new, since in most of the theologies we have looked at, God or the gods favor the strong, the beautiful, and the successful—those who are most like them.
   E. There are exceptions to this idea.
      1. In the Hebrew Bible, Yahweh takes such unlikely people as Moses and David and turns them into heroes.

      2. In the Bhagavad Gita, Krishna says that he will love anyone, from any caste, who will sacrifice the actions of his life to Vishnu.
- **VI.** The idea that God has a special care for the lost, the straggler, the ordinary—underscored in the Sermon on the Mount in the Gospel according to Matthew—announces a new age with powerful implications for the future of literature.
    - **A.** In *Mimesis,* Erich Auerbach argues that there had never been a serious treatment of common people in literature before the New Testament. If they appeared at all before, they were treated comically.
    - **B.** There is nothing in classical literature like the story of Peter's denial of Jesus as told in Matthew.
        1. The scene, in classical terms, is too serious for comedy, too contemporary for tragedy, and too politically insignificant for history.
        2. The story engenders a new style in which what was once material for the comic reaches out to the sublime and the eternal.
    - **C.** After the New Testament, it became possible in literature to treat fishermen, prostitutes, tax collectors, the sick, the paralyzed, the lame, the lost, and the erring seriously.
    - **D.** In literary terms, this may be the greatest revolution brought about by the New Testament.

Essential Reading:

The New Testament: The Gospels according to Matthew, Mark, and Luke.

Supplementary Reading:

Erich Auerbach, *Mimesis: The Representation of Reality in Western Literature,* Chapter 2.

Humphrey Carpenter, *Jesus (Past Masters).*

Questions to Consider:

1. How practical are the admonitions in Jesus's Sermon on the Mount in the Gospel according to Matthew? Should their practicality even be a consideration? Compare their rubrics with those of the ideal ruler in Confucius: in either or both cases, are we talking about a possible situation or an ideal which cannot be reached but which should be aimed at?

2. What are the advantages and disadvantages of teaching in parables rather than in discursive statements and answers? Try to make up a parable that contains the most essential things you would like to teach your children or grandchildren, then ask a friend to interpret the parable. How does your friend's interpretation help you to understand the nature of parables?

Lecture Eleven
Beowulf

Scope: This lecture deals with the Germanic heroic poem, *Beowulf*. After a summary review of its story, we suggest some similarities with earlier heroic literature in this course. Then, as a way of opening up the poem for readers, we suggest three different readings of *Beowulf:* a nostalgic tribute to a heroic and pagan past age and culture; the poem as an extended meditation on the destructive nature of the perpetual internecine fighting that characterized Germanic cultures; and the poem as deeply influenced by Christian values and concerned with community and the ways community is fostered and destroyed. We conclude with the reminder that all of good literature is capable of multiple interpretations—part of its appeal and its ability is to stimulate response and thought.

Outline

I. *Beowulf* seems to have come from southern Sweden to England with the Angles, Saxons, and Jutes, who started arriving in the 5th century C.E.
   A. It seems to have survived orally for several centuries before being written down somewhere between the 8th and 10th centuries C.E.
   B. It survives in a single manuscript which was damaged in a fire.

II. The plot of the poem has three climaxes with each featuring a great fight between Beowulf and a monster; but the poem includes a great deal of other material as well.
   A. A great portion of the poem is given over to feasts and celebrations.
   B. *Beowulf* digresses off into about 10 other stories from Germanic history and legend—stories which are only allusively referred to, so we need footnotes to help us sort them out.
   C. *Beowulf* shares features with other epic poems we have discussed.
      1. Like Gilgamesh, Achilles, Odysseus, and Arjuna, Beowulf is a hero, larger and stronger than other men but nevertheless mortal.

- **2.** Like Gilgamesh and Odysseus, Beowulf must deal with monsters of more-than-human size and strength.
- **3.** Like virtually all the heroes we have considered, Beowulf is eager to win fame and be remembered in song and story after his death.
- **4.** Like the other *epic heroes* in this course, he helps us understand the values of Germanic culture and especially the virtues of a great chieftain.

III. Like all good literature, this poem is capable of being read and understood in different ways. We will focus on three interpretations to illustrate the flavor of the debate and explore some of the poem's possibilities.
- **A.** One of the most famous readings of the poem is by J. R. R. Tolkien, author of *The Lord of the Rings* trilogy.
    - **1.** Tolkien argues that *Beowulf* is essentially a pre-Christian poem with a few inadvertent Christian details, unavoidable because the poem was written by a Christian looking back at a pre-Christian past with admiration and some nostalgia.
    - **2.** The poem's definition of a "good king" is solidly Germanic, emphasizing fighting, winning treasure, and being remembered after one's death.
    - **3.** Beowulf's principal enemies—trolls and dragons—are creatures from Germanic mythology associated with cold, darkness, and the wilderness; they are enemies of human values and achievements, and they reflect the hostile environments from which Germanic people came.
    - **4.** Beowulf's death during his battle with the dragon is no surprise; for these Germanic peoples, all stories end in death and destruction, as does their mythology about the world itself. What makes Beowulf a hero is that he takes the dragon with him when he dies.
    - **5.** Beowulf's death means the destruction of his people—another reminder of the gloomy Germanic world view that is underscored by a favorite device of the poet: understatement.
- **B.** Another reading sees the poem as a meditation on the futility of tribal warfare and the Germanic love of fighting.
    - **1.** Most of the digressions—and all of them that can be accurately identified—are about inter-tribal feuds, most of which end badly.

- 2. Beowulf's own people know what lies ahead for them now that their protector is gone.
- 3. Paradoxically, violence can only be controlled with violence, which merely perpetuates the vicious cycle.
- 4. In this reading, the monsters are not symbols of a hostile universe but of a social sickness that pervades the whole culture. They can be killed, but the violence goes on.

C. A reading by John D. Niles sees the poem permeated with the Christian values that Tolkien found only on its margins.
- 1. This reading sees the poem's concern as that of community, which accounts for the emphasis on feasts, ceremonial speeches, and gift exchanges—the values for which Beowulf fights.
- 2. The poem opens with an account of how a thriving community is founded, and it ends with an account of how one is destroyed: Beowulf's tribe will fall because his people did not support him in his fight with the dragon.
- 3. The digressions are about the ways anger, pride, self-will, or the breaking of oaths can destroy a society. The monsters are symbols for these dangers; they live outside the community and are without language, ceremony, or gift exchange.
- 4. Beowulf comes to the Danish court to help Hrothgar because of a reciprocal network of obligations; in the first two monster fights, the emphasis is on the celebration of bonds after the fights, not the fights themselves.
- 5. Wiglaf, who stands beside Beowulf in his last battle with the dragon, demonstrates that heroism binds communities together and is preserved through loyalty. Three speeches at the end of the poem confirm these values.
- 6. For Niles, the poem is not about heroism *per se*, but about how leaders need to act if society is to be held together. All gifts are merely loans from God; it is how gifts are used that matters, and the digressions reiterate this point.

D. *Beowulf*, like all good literature, demonstrates its richness by the number of different readings it can support.
- 1. It can be a poem about humankind's losing battle with the universe.
- 2. It can be a meditation on the futility of a culture that defines itself in terms of war.

3. It can be an analysis of the uses and misuses of heroism within the human community.

IV. *Beowulf* represents the end of our study of epic heroes and serves as a transition point for future works.
   A. We have seen epic heroes who are individualistic, who fight for causes outside themselves, who dedicate their actions to God or the gods, who fight against other heroes, and who fight against monsters.
   B. Although many heroes in later literature borrow traits from the ones we have studied, we will modify our definitions to discuss the heroism of future characters.
   C. We will also encounter stories of ordinary people doing ordinary things.
   D. Over time, we will see that storytelling becomes more artful, sophisticated, and complicated.

Essential Reading:

Beowulf.

Supplementary Reading:

John C. McGalliard and Lee Patterson, *The Norton Anthology of World Literature*, "Introduction" to *Beowulf.*

John D. Niles, *Beowulf: The Poem and Its Tradition.*

J. R. R. Tolkien, "*Beowulf:* The Monsters and the Critics."

Questions to Consider:

1. How obvious are the Christian details in *Beowulf*? Are they an integral part of the poem, or are they tacked on to an essentially pagan poem? How important are the Christian allusions to an understanding of the poem?
2. What similarities do you notice between the Germanic peoples and the Mycenaeans during the time of Agamemnon as you read *Beowulf*? Are the comparable values of a warrior or leader in some measure dependent on this kind of social structure?

Lecture Twelve
Indian Stories

Scope: In this lecture we turn from mostly epic literature to one of the themes of our next two units: narrative strategies. This theme is illustrated in three seminal collections of stories from India: the *Jātaka* (*Story of a Birth*), the *Pañcatantra* (the *Five Books* or the *Five Strategies*), and the *Kathāsaritsāgara* (*Ocean of the Rivers of Story*), each of which is complexly framed within larger stories so that individual tales are nested or emboxed. Each of the three collections is briefly characterized: the *Jātaka* tells of the many earlier lives of the Buddha, the *Five Books* gives practical advice to rulers, and *Ocean of the Rivers of Story* gathers together an amazingly diverse group of tales organized roughly around making money and being successful. The sophisticated framing techniques of each are discussed, as well as the amazing and long-lasting legacies of these books, ranging from the *1001 Nights,* Boccaccio, and Chaucer to Aesop's Fables, the animal fables of La Fontaine, Shakespeare, the Brothers Grimm, Hans Christian Andersen, and even Uncle Remus. The lecture concludes with an anticipation of some of the many ways in which these brilliant Indian techniques will be used in future literature across the world.

Outline

I. We move now from essentially epic literature to a subject that will be of primary concern in our next two units: narrative strategies. We begin with three collections of Indian stories whose influence is unparalleled by any comparable body of work in the world.

II. India's reliance on the oral tradition for entertainment and instruction has made its storytelling an incredibly rich tradition, as folklorists to this day remind us.

    A. The simple abundance of stories from that country, however, does not explain the amazing sophistication of the collections' organization.

    B. All three of the collections under consideration use the device of *framing*, which sets stories inside other stories so that each is nested or emboxed in a larger story.

III. The *Jātaka*, formally collected around the 4th century B.C.E., frames its hundreds of stories within the 550 prior incarnations of the Buddha.
- **A.** As in Hinduism, *karma* is carried over from one lifetime to the next; each life is made up of actions and remembered knowledge from previous lives. Each individual story in the *Jātaka* is set inside this framework.
  1. In each story, the Buddha recalls a prior life in order to make a point about Buddhist doctrine or ethics.
  2. In each story, the main point is underscored with an epigram, and the Buddha makes clear what role he played in the story.
- **B.** The stories were written not in Sanskrit but in Pali, a dialect intended for popular consumption, and they make use of many older folktales, none of which—prior to their reworking—had any connection with Buddhism.
  1. Some of the stories seem only tangential to Buddhist truths, and some—like the story about a hare who thinks that the sky is falling—carry within them suggestions of their older meanings and values.
  2. These lively stories have simply been adapted to Buddhism, teaching Buddhist values—such as not to destroy life, not to take what is not given, to keep from alcohol, to love selflessly, and to be useful—while keeping at least some of their original focus.
  3. The story of the self-sacrificing hare, for example, teaches the Buddhist value of selfless acts of charity while at the same time explaining how the shape of a hare gets onto the moon.
- **C.** These stories were translated by the Greeks, Persians, Jews, and Arabs, and they traveled across the world. Aesop's animal fables, for example, are likely primarily Indian in origin.
  1. Because the stories are largely optimistic and have happy endings, they also have been a rich source of fairytales for children.
  2. An estimated 50 percent of the tales eventually collected by the Brothers Grimm are Indian in origin; there is even an early version of Uncle Remus's "Brer Rabbit and the Tar Baby."
- **D.** The stories contain touches of realism which can charm adult readers: for example, the Monkey King's failure to factor into his

calculations the length of vine he has tied around his waist and thus his failure to make it all the way to the next tree.

IV. The *Pañcatantra* has as its main frame a sage attempting to teach a king's three dull-witted sons the fine points of governing.
- **A.** This book, written in Sanskrit, was also translated almost immediately into many languages and brought to Europe by the Arabs in the 8th century C.E., where its stories and framing devices inspired such works as the *1001 Nights,* the *Decameron,* and *The Canterbury Tales.*
  1. Each of the work's five books has its own frame, and both in the frame and within the stories characters tell each other stories which illustrate points of governance.
  2. The work is always multi-leveled; many different plots go on simultaneously without ever losing track of the main plot.
  3. The work's framing plot also is plotted, so that stories within stories play a part in the plots in which they are enclosed.
- **B.** Especially notable in this collection are the animal stories, in which various animals teach useful lessons.
  1. A wise old crow teaches how to defeat a stronger enemy.
  2. A pigeon king shows the most important quality of one who deserves to rule.
- **C.** There are stories about humans as well.
  1. A foolish man with a pot full of rice illustrates the dangers of fantasizing a magnificent future before one has the means to achieve it.
  2. A farmer's son shows the extreme dangers of greed and impatience.
- **D.** The stories offer a vision of life that is complex and multi-layered, with complicated appraisals of social and political life.
- **E.** Some of the same stories appear in different Indian collections; Roy C. Amore and Larry D. Shinn's *Lustful Maidens and Ascetic Kings* helps us to see the different ways in which Buddhists and Hindus make use of them.

V. The largest and most famous of the three collections is Somadeva's *Kathāsaritsāgara,* an 11th-century C.E. Sanskrit adaptation of an earlier 7th-century work in dialect, *The Great Romance.*
- **A.** This collection has a multi-layered frame.

1. In one frame, the 7th-century author writes the stories as a penance imposed on him by a goddess who turned him into a troll.
2. His stories rejected by a king (because they were written in "troll's tongue"), the author burns all but one volume—this one.
3. The penance is demanded because, in another frame, two heavenly creatures overhear and repeat stories the god Śiva tells his consort Pārvatī while she sits in his lap. Both creatures are banished to earth and not allowed to return until they have disseminated all the stories.
4. Stories within stories keep proliferating until we lose the thread of the main narrative.
5. A more immediate frame is provided by the adventures of a prince, within whose story characters tell each other stories, much as Śiva told his to Pārvatī.
6. Individual collections of tales are sometimes themselves framed, as is the famous collection of 25 riddle stories told by a vampire or ghoul to a king (one of these riddle stories turns up centuries later in Hans Christian Andersen's "The Princess and the Pea").

B. The theme of most of these stories is success, and most of its protagonists are merchants and bankers.
1. The prince whose story provides the most immediate frame is named "Gift of the God of Riches," suggesting something of the ambience for the tales.
2. A few rogues and thieves get into the stories as well due to the blurred distinction between a sharp-dealing merchant and a thief. Harisarmon, whose story eventually will metamorphose into part of "Rumpelstiltskin," is one of these characters.

C. Indian collections of stories from this period tend not to feature women as central characters, but this book has some notable women characters who match in wit, resourcefulness, and courage to their male counterparts.
1. The tale of "The Red Lotus of Chastity" is a good example.
2. It also provided, via many intermediaries, one of the plots for Shakespeare's *Cymbeline*.

D. The framing technique is important because it emphasizes the seriousness of stories in Indian life. Even the gods tell stories, and hearing them can help us overcome our own demons and discover new selves which can begin to move us toward liberation.

VI. The stories in these collections are good reading in themselves. They provided later writers with framing techniques that will be put to brilliant uses in the books treated in future lectures.

Essential Reading:
The *Jātaka*.

Somadeva, *Kathāsaritsāgara*.

Viṣṇuśarman, *Pañcatantra*.

Supplementary Reading:
Roy C. Amore and Larry D. Shinn, *Lustful Maidens and Ascetic Kings: Buddhist and Hindu Stories of Life*.

Edward C. Dimock Jr., et al. eds. *The Literatures of India: An Introduction*.

J. A. B. Van Buitenen, trans. *Tales of Ancient India*.

Questions to Consider:
1. What values or storytelling skills do you find in these hundreds of stories that allow them to move out of the specifically Indian contexts in which they were created and into so many different languages and cultures, where they have been equally cherished and admired? Are there some kinds of nearly universal values or assumptions in the stories that allow this?

2. Why are we not offended or put off by the amount of casual and quite brutal violence in these stories? Is there something about the tone that keeps us comfortably detached from the sometimes awful things that happen to characters? Is it the context of the collection itself or is it something else that allows us to be at ease with this kind of violence in ways that we would not be in stories of a different kind?

Timeline
(Lectures 1–12)

B.C.E.

c. 2800	Gilgamesh is King of Uruk.
2600–2100	Age of the Great Pyramids in Egypt.
c. 2000–1400	Hebrew migration to Canaan; age of the Hebrew Patriarchs—Abraham, Isaac, Jacob; the Egyptian Captivity.
c. 1700–1600	The *Epic of Gilgamesh* is formed (Standard Version 7th century B.C.E.).
1500	Aryan tribes speaking Sanskrit settle in the Indus Valley.
c. 1200	Exodus of the Hebrews from Egypt.
1184	Traditional date for the fall of Troy.
1027–256 C.E.	The Chou Dynasty in China, the early part of which was China's Classical Age.
c. 10th century	Hebrew Torah is assembled.
c. 1000–600	The *Classic of Poetry* is collected.
753	Traditional date for the founding of Rome.
c. 700	Homeric epics written down.
563	Birth of Gautama Buddha.
5th century	Confucius's *Analects*.
490	The Battle of Marathon: Athens defeats the Persians.
458	Aechylus's *The Oresteia*.
441	Sophocles's *Antigone*.
431	Euripides's *Medea*.

c. 400–c. 400 C.E.	Creation of the *Mahabharata*.
4th century	Writings of Chuang Chou; earliest version of the *Jātaka*.
334–323	Conquests of Alexander the Great.
27	Rome becomes an empire under Caesar Augustus.
c. 19	Virgil's *Aeneid*.
c. 5	Birth of Jesus.
c. 1st century	Bhagavad Gita added to the *Mahabharata*.

C.E.

50s	The letters of Paul in the New Testament.
c. 60–c.100	The Gospels in the New Testament.
2nd–3rd century	Visṇuśarman's *Pañcatantra*.
335–470	The Gupta Period in Northern India.
476	The fall of Rome in the West.
c. 500	Angles, Saxons, and Jutes begin migrating to England.
800	Charlemagne is crowned Holy Roman Emperor.
c. 9th century	*Beowulf* is written down.
11th century	Somadeva's *Kathāsaritsāgara*.

Glossary
(Lectures 1–12)

anthropomorphism: The attribution of human shape or characteristics to nonhuman entities like objects or gods.

comedy: A dramatic form which generally deals with ordinary people in contemporary life and ends happily.

deus ex machina: Literally, "god out of the machine." A device used in Greek drama whereby a god or goddess was flown down onto the stage by special machinery to solve an otherwise insoluble problem.

epic hero: The central character of an epic, usually of impressive strength, occupying an important position in history or legend and hence of value in defining the qualities of a people, culture, or nation.

epic poem: A lengthy narrative poem in the high style presenting characters of significant stature in a series of adventures which help to define a nation or culture. From Homer onward it also possesses mandatory conventional elements which are itemized in Lecture Four.

epic simile: An extended comparison, often running to many lines, in which the secondary object is occasionally developed in sufficient detail to displace the primary object it is illuminating.

frame: A narrative structure which contains within it other stories, making the stories themselves "stories-within-a-story." The device allows characters within the frame to tell the narratives. The use of this device—in ingeniously complex forms—seems to have originated with Indian storytellers (see Lecture Twelve).

furens: The heroic epithet for Turnus, Aeneas' antagonist in the *Aeneid*. It means "raging" or "furious."

heroic epithet: An adjective or adjective phrase used so frequently in conjunction with a name that it becomes almost a part of that name: e.g., "swift-footed Achilles" or "dutiful Aeneas."

in medias res: Literally, "in the middle of things." A literary technique which starts a story in the middle and then fills in the background via flashbacks. It has been a convention of the epic since Homer.

invocation: A request to a Muse or deity for aid in writing. Since Homer, it has been a convention of the epic to begin with an invocation.

karma: Literally, "deed" or "act." In Hinduism and Buddhism, the totality of one's actions in any single lifetime, the consequences of which have to be lived out and worked off in successive rebirths and lifetimes.

logos: Literally, "word." In Greek philosophy it came to mean reason, which controls the universe through the manifestation of speech. John calls Jesus the *Logos* in the first sentence of his Gospel.

lyric poetry: The poetry of a single voice, expressing perception and emotion subjectively.

mokṣa: In Hinduism and Buddhism, the liberation from the cycle of death and rebirth (see *karma*).

monotheism: The belief that there is only one God.

mystery religions: Cults which required initiation before taking part in rituals designed to allow individuals to achieve immortality by participating in the death and resurrection of a god or goddess (e.g., Dionysus or Isis).

parable: A story answering a question or illustrating a moral or a truth. It can vary from a point-by-point parallel with the situation illustrated to a looser parallelism, allowing more room for interpretation.

Pax Romana: Literally, "Roman peace." For the Romans it meant an era of world peace ushered in by the end of the civil wars and the establishment of empire by Caesar Augustus in 27 B.C.E.

penates: The household gods of the ancient Romans.

pius: Literally, "dutiful" or "responsible." Aeneas's heroic epithet in the *Aeneid* (see also *furens*).

polytheism: The belief that there are many gods.

prophet: In Judaism and Islam, a person who speaks for God under divine guidance (e.g., Moses or Muhammad).

protagonist: The chief or central character in a play or story.

scop: An Anglo-Saxon poet or bard.

Sophists: A group of teachers in ancient Greece who taught rhetoric and philosophically argued for subjectivity in values and morals.

Tanakh: An acronym for the Hebrew Bible, made up of the first letters of the Hebrew words for "law," "prophets," and "writings."

tragedy: A drama which treats serious events in the lives of significant characters, usually set in the past, using an elevated style, and generally leading its protagonist from happiness to unhappiness.

trilogy: The three tragedies written for the annual competition by a Greek dramatist, usually related by tone, theme, or story. Aeschylus's *Oresteia* is the only Greek trilogy which has survived.

Yahweh: One of the Hebrew names for God.

yoga: A set of disciplined practices designed to focus complete attention on God so as to achieve identity. Krishna redefines *yoga* in the Bhagavad Gita.

Biographical Notes
(Lectures 1–12)

Historical Figures

Aeschylus (c. 524–456 B.C.E.): The first of Athens's great tragedians. Much of his life is lost in obscurity or legend, but his epitaph (which he seems to have written himself) suggests that he fought at the Battle of Marathon in 490. He wrote more than 90 plays, of which seven survive, including the only surviving complete trilogy, *The Oresteia* (*Agamemnon, The Libation Bearers,* and *Eumenides*).

Chuang Chou (c. 369–286 B.C.E.): Little is known about his life, and only the first seven chapters of *Chuang Tzu* are securely attributed to him (the rest of the book was probably written by later Taoists). He founded no school and seems not to have sought disciples, but his amazingly imaginative and witty book is one of the basic texts of Taoism.

Confucius (551–479 B.C.E.): A teacher and scholar whose only work, *Analects* (or *Sayings*) was written by disciples many years after his death. He was credited with editing the six "classics" of Chinese literature, but modern editors are skeptical about this claim. He attained the position of chief magistrate during his lifetime, but he is remembered, like Socrates, as a teacher rather than a public official.

David (r. c. 1005–c. 965 B.C.E.): The second king (succeeding Saul) of a united Israel and the father of Solomon, whose succession brought an end to the united Israel.

Euripides (480–406 B.C.E.): The third and youngest of the three Athenian tragedians; 18 of his plays survive, including *Medea.* Unlike Aeschylus and Sophocles, he seems not to have participated much in public life in Athens; rather, he was the kind of intellectual who lived a life of introspection and study. He was the least popular of the three great Athenian tragedians during his lifetime, winning first prize in the annual competition only four times. He ended his life in Macedon, to which he had exiled himself, and his last plays were written there.

Geats: A Germanic people living in southern Sweden. According to *Beowulf*, Beowulf was one of their kings.

Gilgamesh (r. c. 2800 B.C.E.): A king of Uruk who, after his death, became the subject of legends and eventually the hero of the epic poem named after him.

Homer (c. 8th century B.C.E.): Traditionally the author of the *Iliad* and the *Odyssey*. Nothing whatever is known about him, and many scholars believe that the two works were written by different poets.

Jesus (c. 5 B.C.E.–c. 30 C.E.): The protagonist of the New Testament, the Messiah according to his disciples, the ultimate figure of a mystery religion for Paul, and the divine *Logos* for the Gospel of John.

Paul (d. c. 65 C.E.): A Jew from Tarsus, he became the first important Christian missionary to the Gentiles. He was the author of the Pauline epistles in the New Testament.

Peter (d. c. 64 C.E.): One of Jesus's 12 apostles. The story of his betrayal in the New Testament is a new kind of story in the history of world literature.

Sargon the Great (r. c. 2350 B.C.E.): An Akkadian king and empire builder in the Middle East; the story of his origins strikingly anticipates that of Moses in the Hebrew Bible.

Sin-liqe-uninni (c. 13th–11th centuries B.C.E.): The traditional author, compiler, or redactor of the Old Babylonian version of the *Epic of Gilgamesh*.

Somadeva (11th century C.E.): The author of the illustrious *Kathāsaritsāgara*. We know virtually nothing about him except that he was a Brahmin. He wrote the book, he says in its preface, for the Queen of Kashmir.

Sophocles (496–406 B.C.E.): The second and most successful (in his own lifetime) Athenian tragedian, based on the number of first prizes he won in the annual competition. He wrote about 125 plays, of which seven survive, including *Antigone* and *Oedipus the King*. He also served in several public offices in Athens during his lifetime; like Aeschylus and unlike Euripides, he seems to have been fully integrated into the culture of his time, even though his extant tragedies suggest some independence of thought.

Tacitus (b. c. 56 C.E., d. after 117 C.E.): Little is known for certain about his life aside from the fact that he was a successful lawyer and government official, including service as Proconsul of Asia. He is known to us as a historian whose major works are *Histories*, which records Roman history from 69 to 90 C.E., and *Annals*, which deals with the earlier period from 14 to 68 C.E. He also wrote *Germania,* an account of Germanic peoples in the 1st century which is the best contemporary source we have on the culture of *Beowulf.*

Virgil (70–19 B.C.E.): The greatest Roman poet, author of *Eclogues, Georgics* (poems about the pastoral and agricultural life), and, by imperial commission, the Roman national epic the *Aeneid.*

Viṣṇuśarman (2nd–3rd century C.E.): By attribution, the author of the *Pañcatantra.* By tradition, he was an elderly sage summoned by a king to teach statecraft to his three slow-witted sons, and the result was one of the most famous and appealing works ever written.

Mythical, Legendary, and Fictional Characters

Achilles: The greatest of the Greek warriors at Troy. His quarrel with Agamemnon over a slave girl, his subsequent anger, and its consequences for his army are the subjects of the *Iliad.*

Aeneas: The son of Anchises (a mortal) and Aphrodite/Venus, he is a Trojan warrior in the *Iliad* who becomes the hero of Virgil's *Aeneid* and the ultimate founder of Rome.

Agamemnon: King of Mycenae, leader of the expedition to Troy, brother of Menelaus. He sacrificed his daughter Iphigenia to Artemis to secure the winds needed to sail his ships to Troy; his quarrel with Achilles precipitates the action of the *Iliad.* He was killed by his wife, Clytemnestra, upon his return from Troy in Aeschylus's *Agamemnon.*

Aias: The second most-powerful warrior in the Greek army after Achilles. He commits suicide when he is not awarded Achilles' armor after Achilles' death. Odysseus has a poignant encounter with him in Hades in the *Odyssey.*

Anchises: The father of Aeneas.

Andromache: The wife of Hector, the greatest of the Trojan warriors. She warns Hector in the *Iliad* that their son will be killed and she sent into slavery when he is killed.

Antigone: A daughter of King Oedipus, she is the protagonist of Sophocles's tragedy named after her.

Apollo: A son of Zeus, his special provinces include reason, government, and music. He favors the Trojans in the *Iliad*, and he becomes Orestes's special patron and helps Athena establish the institution of trial by jury in *The Oresteia*.

Arjuna: The great Indian warrior whose hesitation before battle and subsequent debate with Krishna is the subject of the Bhagavad Gita.

Ascanius: Aeneas's son, he accompanies his father in his wanderings on the way to found a new Troy in the West.

Athena: The daughter of Zeus and one of the most important Greek goddesses, whose special provinces are wisdom and warfare. She favors the Greeks in their war at Troy and is Odysseus's special patron in the *Odyssey*. She helps Apollo establish the institution of trial by jury in Athens in Aeschylus's *Eumenides*.

Beowulf: King of the Geats and monster-slayer; the protagonist of *Beowulf*.

Bharata: The ancestor of all the Indians whose great battle is the climax of the *Mahabharata*, whose title contains his name.

Briseis: The slave girl over whom Achilles and Agamemnon quarrel, which starts the *Iliad*.

Calypso: A divine nymph who falls in love with Odysseus when he is washed up on her island and keeps him with her for seven years. He is on her island when the poem begins.

Circe: A beautiful witch encountered by Odysseus on his travels. She lures men to her house and then turns them into swine.

Clytemnestra: Sister of Helen of Troy and wife of Agamemnon. Her murder of her husband and then her murder by her son are the focus of Aeschylus's *Oresteia*.

Creon: Brother-in-law of Oedipus and King of Thebes in Sophocles's *Antigone*. He is Antigone's uncle, and it is his decree that she cannot bury her brother that sets in motion the plot of the play.

Cyclops: The son of Poseidon, a one-eyed giant whom Odysseus encounters and blinds on his way back to Ithaca. His name is Polyphêmos.

Dido: The Queen of Carthage in Virgil's *Aeneid*, she falls in love with Aeneas. When he leaves, she commits suicide, setting up eternal enmity between Carthage and Rome.

Enkidu: The companion the gods create for Gilgamesh in his poem. Enkidu's death precipitates Gilgamesh's awareness of his own mortality and sends him on his quest to find a remedy for death.

Enlil: The god in *Gilgamesh* who decides that Gilgamesh and Enkidu have gone too far in killing Humbaba and that one of them must die.

Furies: The *Eumenides* by their Greek name, they are goddesses whose responsibility is vengeance, especially when the victim is a blood relative. They thus vow to punish Orestes for killing his mother in Aeschylus's *Oresteia*.

Grendel: The first monster killed by Beowulf at Hrothgar's mead hall. The second is Grendel's mother and the third is a dragon.

Hector: The greatest of the Trojan warriors. His death at Achilles' hands is the climactic battle of the *Iliad*, and Achilles' anger ends when Hector's father and King of Troy, Priam, comes to Achilles' tent to reclaim the body.

Helen: Sister of Clytemnestra and wife of Menelaus. Her abduction by Paris sets in motion the events of the Trojan War. She is back at home with Menelaus in the *Odyssey*, where she is visited by Odysseus's son, Telemachus.

Hrothgar: King of the Danes, whose mead-hall is under siege from Grendel and whom Beowulf travels to rescue to start the main action of the poem.

Humbaba: The guardian of the cedar forest killed by Gilgamesh and Enkidu and whose destruction is part of the reason the gods demand that one of the heroes must die.

Iphigenia: Daughter of Agamemnon and Clytemnestra. Her sacrifice by her father at the start of the Trojan War provides the background to Aeschylus's *Agamemnon* and in part prompts Clytemnestra's murder of her husband.

Ishtar: Goddess of love and war in the *Epic of Gilgamesh*. Gilgamesh's refusal of her proposal of marriage causes her to send the Bull of Heaven against Uruk in retaliation.

Jason: The hero of the adventure of the Argonauts and the Golden Fleece. It is his decision to marry the daughter of the King of Corinth that prompts Medea's revenge in Euripides's *Medea*.

Juno: Hera is her Greek name, and she is the sister/consort of Jupiter/Zeus. She is the goddess who still hates the Trojans years after the war and hence harries Aeneas throughout the *Aeneid*.

Krishna: The incarnation of the god Vishnu in the Bhagavad Gita, who serves as Arjuna's chariot driver.

Lavinia: The Latin princess who is part of the cause of the war between Aeneas and Turnus in the *Aeneid*. She is the equivalent in this war of Helen in the first Trojan War.

Medea: Daughter of the King of Colchis and consort of Jason. She dabbles in magic and is hence a dangerous antagonist when Jason shames her in Euripides's *Medea*.

Menelaus: Brother of Agamemnon and husband of Helen.

Odysseus: The King of Ithaca. A warrior and strategist at Troy (the Trojan Horse was his idea), his many adventures on the long trip home are the subject of the *Odyssey*.

Oedipus: King of Thebes who unintentionally murders his father and marries his mother in Sophocles's *Oedipus the King*. He is also—by Jocasta, his mother—the father of Antigone.

Orestes: Son of Clytemnestra and Agamemnon. His murder of his mother to avenge his father's death is the focus of Aeschylus's *The Libation Bearers* and *Eumenides*.

Pallas: The young protégé of Aeneas whose killing by Turnus sets up the climactic fight between Aeneas and Turnus. He is the Patroclus of the *Aeneid*.

Paris: Also called Alexandros, he is the son of King Priam of Troy. His abduction of Helen from Menelaus triggers the Greek expedition of revenge that becomes the Trojan War.

Pārvatī: An important goddess in the Hindu pantheon. She is the wife/consort of Śiva.

Patroclus: The dearest friend of Achilles, his killing by Hector brings Achilles back into the Trojan War and precipitates the climactic events of the *Iliad*.

Penelope: Wife of Odysseus, she holds 108 suitors for her hand at arm's length while she waits and hopes for Odysseus's return. Their reunion—and the way she gets the better of him—constitute the climax of the *Odyssey*.

Phaiakians: A very sheltered and perhaps over-civilized people who live on an island protected by Poseidon. It is to them that Odysseus tells the story of his years of wandering, and they provide him transportation home to Ithaca, for which Poseidon punishes them.

Priam: King of Troy and father of Hector and Paris.

Scylla and Charybdis: Two monsters—one which eats men and the other which sucks ships to the sea's bottom, respectively—between which Odysseus has to sail on his way home in the *Odyssey*.

Shiduri: A goddess who keeps a tavern at world's end. Gilgamesh encounters her on his way to find Uta-napishti.

Sirens: Dangerous nymphs who sing irresistible songs that lure ships to their destruction on rocks. Odysseus is the only one ever to hear the song and live to tell about it.

Śiva: One of the principal gods in Hinduism, or one of the three most important aspects of God.

Teiresias: The blind prophet who appears in Sophocles's *Oedipus the King* and *Antigone* and in Hades, where Odysseus goes to see him in the *Odyssey*.

Telemachus: Odysseus's son. He sets out looking for his father at the beginning of the *Odyssey* and eventually helps him kill the 108 suitors.

Thetis: A sea nymph and Achilles' mother. She enlists Zeus's help in defeating the Achaeans while Achilles remains in his tent.

Turnus: The Latin prince who turns out to be Aeneas's antagonist in the war that ends the *Aeneid*. He takes on many of the qualities of Achilles in the war scenes, in contrast to the more controlled and altruistic behavior of Aeneas.

Ur-shanabi: The ferry man for Uta-napishti. Gilgamesh takes him to Uruk to show him the magnificent walls.

Uta-napishti: The Noah of the *Epic of Gilgamesh* who survives the Great Flood and is awarded eternal life for his part in saving creation.

Venus: Her Greek name is Aphrodite. She is the goddess of love and, in the *Iliad*, a Trojan sympathizer. In the *Aeneid* she is the mother of Aeneas, who helps him escape from burning Troy.

Bibliography
(Lectures 1–12)

Essential Reading:

Note: Every work treated in this part of the course is available in multiple editions and translations, many of them excellent. I have listed here the ones from which my text citations were taken. In general, the best strategy is to find a translation that gives you sufficient introductory material to help orient you to the text and sufficient editorial help to understand what you are reading. If you find those things, you have found the recommended translation for you.

Aeschylus. *The Oresteia.* Robert Fagles, trans. New York: Viking Penguin, 1975.

An Anthology of Chinese Literature: Beginnings to 1911. Stephen Owen, ed. and trans. New York: W. W. Norton, 1996.

Beowulf. Seamus Heaney, trans. New York: Farrar, Straus, Giroux, 2000.

The Bhagavad-Gita. Barbara Stoler Miller, trans. New York: Bantam, 1986.

Chuang Chou. *Chuang Tzu: Basic Writings.* Burton Watson, trans. New York: Columbia University Press, 1964.

Confucius. *The Analects.* D.C. Lau, trans. New York: Penguin, 1979.

Euripides. *Mêdeia. Euripides: The Complete Plays.* Volume I. Carl R. Mueller, trans. Hanover, New Hampshire: Smith and Kraus, 2005.

Homer: The Iliad. Robert Fagles, trans. New York: Viking Penguin, 1990.

Homer: The Odyssey. Robert Fitzgerald, trans. Garden City, New York: Doubleday, 1961.

Jātaka. E. B. Cowell, ed. 6 vols. Cambridge, U.K.: Cambridge University Press, 1895–1907. This is the complete and still standard edition, which has been frequently reprinted. There are many other translations of selected stories.

The New Oxford Annotated Bible. New Revised Standard Version with Apocrypha. 3rd ed. Michael D. Coogan, ed. New York: Oxford University Press, 2001.

Somadeva. *Kathāsaritsāgara.* C. H. Tawney and N. M. Penzer, trans. 1st ed. Calcutta: Baptist Mission Press, 1880. Privately printed for subscribers in London in 10 volumes in the late 19th century, this translation has been reprinted in full and in selections many times. For a selection of stories from Somadeva, see entry under van Buitenen in "Supplementary Reading" below.

Sophocles. *Antigone. Three Theban Plays.* Robert Fagles, trans. New York: Viking Penguin, 1975.

Virgil. *The Aeneid.* Allen Mandelbaum, trans. New York: Bantam, 1972.

Viṣṇuśarman. *Pañcatantra.* Arthur W. Ryder, trans. Chicago: University of Chicago Press, 1956.

Supplementary Reading:

Alter, Robert. *The Art of Biblical Narrative.* New York: Basic Books, 1981. A provocative and stimulating series of lessons in reading the Hebrew Bible as literature while preserving its original textual spirit and ambience.

Amore, Roy C. and Larry D. Shinn. *Lustful Maidens and Ascetic Kings: Buddhist and Hindu Stories of Life.* New York: Oxford University Press, 1981. As the title suggests, the book selects stories from various sources and then organizes them by topic, contrasting Hindu stories with Buddhist ones. The introduction and head notes help to demonstrate the similarities and differences in the uses of storytelling in the two cultures.

Anderson, William S. *The Art of the Aeneid.* Englewood Cliffs, New Jersey: Prentice-Hall, 1969. A good general introduction to the poem, featuring some of the ways Virgil transforms an oral genre into a written, "artistic" one.

Auerbach, Erich. *Mimesis: The Representation of Reality in Western Literature.* Willard R. Trask, trans. 1946; rpt. Princeton: Princeton University Press, 1953. A brilliant and interesting book tracing the ways in which literature has tried to capture reality, from the ancients to the modern period. In a way, this is a more sophisticated version of the storytelling theme that runs through this entire course.

Bloom, Harold, ed. *Homer (Bloom's Modern Critical Views).* New York: Chelsea House, 1986. Like all of the volumes in this series, this one features a number of modern readings of the Homeric epics along with an interesting introduction by the editor.

Carpenter, Humphrey. *Jesus (Past Masters).* New York: Oxford University Press, 1980. This is a coherent and well-documented account of the life and teachings of Jesus, based on the Gospels. Some of the arguments in Lecture Ten were based on material from this book.

Deutsch, Eliot. *The Bhagavad Gita.* San Francisco: Holt, Rinehart, Winston, 1968. The introductory essay is a great orientation to the poem, explaining key Hindu words and providing a comprehensive intellectual context for what happens in the Gita.

Dimock, Edward C., Jr., et al., eds. *The Literatures of India: An Introduction.* Chicago: University of Chicago Press, 1974. This contains essays by various hands on various aspects of the literature of India. It contains a very good essay on *Ocean of the Rivers of Story* by J. A. B. van Buitenen.

The Epic of Gilgamesh: The Babylonian Epic Poem and Other Texts in Akkadian and Sumerian. Andrew George, trans. New York: Penguin, 1999. George's introduction is well worth reading.

Finley, M. I. *The World of Odysseus.* 1954; rpt. New York: Penguin, 1979. This book contains a wealth of background information regarding families, economics, social structures, and values for Homer's two epic poems.

Graham, A. C. *Disputers of the Tao.* La Salle, Illinois: Open Court, 1989. A comprehensive and challenging survey of the Classical Age in Chinese thought.

Griffin, Jasper. *Homer (Past Masters).* New York: Hill and Wang, 1980. A readable and insightful introduction to Homer's two epic poems.

Hadas, Moses. *Humanism: The Greek Ideal and Its Survival.* London: George Allen & Unwin, 1961. A series of essays on Greek culture and literature. One chapter is devoted to "The Heroic Code," part of the subject of Lecture Four.

_____. *Introduction to Classical Drama.* New York: Bantam, 1966. An extremely accessible and lucid introduction to the basic themes and techniques of classical drama, from Aeschylus to Seneca.

Heidel, Alexander. *The Gilgamesh Epic and Old Testament Parallels.* Chicago: University of Chicago Press, 1949. A book on the importance of the Mesopotamian poem for biblical studies.

Knox, Bernard M. W. and Jerome Wright Clinton. "Introduction" to "The Bible: The Old Testament" in *The Norton Anthology of World Literature.* 2nd ed., Volume A. Sarah Lawall et al., eds. New York: W. W. Norton, 2002. This is an anthology widely used in world literature courses. Its introductory material and bibliographies are all excellent, including those on the Hebrew Bible.

McGalliard, John C. and Lee Patterson, "Introduction" to *Beowulf* in *The Norton Anthology of World Literature.* 2nd ed. Volume B. Sarah Lawall et al., eds. New York: W. W. Norton, 2002. See "Knox" entry above.

Niles, John D. *Beowulf: The Poem and Its Tradition.* Cambridge: Harvard University Press, 1983. Contains a wealth of useful information about the poem in its context, and it does an interesting and persuasive "Christian" reading of what is usually thought of as a pagan poem.

Parry, Adam. "The Two Voices of Virgil's *Aeneid.*" *Virgil: A Collection of Critical Essays.* Steele Commager, ed. Englewood Cliffs, New Jersey: Prentice-Hall, 1966. A fine essay demonstrating the brilliant ambivalence of the poet about his materials.

Pöschl, Viktor. *The Art of Virgil: Image and Symbol in the Aeneid.* Ann Arbor: University of Michigan Press, 1962. A close reading of many passages in the poem, illustrating Virgil's stunning control of his material.

Sukthankar, V. S. *On the Meaning of Mahabharata.* Bombay: The Asiatic Society of Bombay, 1957. Sukthankar provides a psychological reading of the Gita which does not conflict with the theological one but gives readers an entirely different way to approach and think about the poem.

Tolkien, J. R. R. "*Beowulf:* The Monsters and the Critics." 1936. Rpt. *Beowulf. A Norton Critical Edition.* Joseph F. Tuso, ed. New York: W.W. Norton, 1975, pp. 105–113. A seminal essay reprinted many times in many places on the poem which rescued it from critical neglect and is almost as good a read as Tolkien's famous trilogy.

Van Buitenen, J. A. B. trans. *Tales of Ancient India.* Chicago: University of Chicago Press, 1959. This is a translation of selected tales from Somadeva and a second, earlier adaptation of the original *The Great Romance.* It also contains a very useful introduction to the material.

Van Nortwick, Thomas. *Somewhere I Have Never Travelled: The Second Self and the Hero's Journey in Ancient Epic.* New York: Oxford University Press, 1992. A study of the alter ego as it occurs in ancient epics, along with the reminder that in all of them, the second self needs to die in order to help the protagonist grow up: spiritual death always precedes spiritual rebirth.

Watson, Burton. *Early Chinese Literature.* New York: Columbia University Press, 1962. A survey of Chinese literature to about 100 A.D., full of perceptive insights about individual works and literary movements.

Lecture Thirteen
T'ang Poetry

Scope: This lecture treats three poets of the T'ang period (618–907 C.E.) in China: Wang Wei, Li Po, and Tu Fu. After a reminder of how and why poetry was so essential in so many aspects of life in China in the period, we describe the traditional ways the Chinese have thought about and interpreted poetry, the characteristics of the five-character couplet, and some of the problematic issues in translating classical Chinese verse. Then we illustrate these points with readings of one poem by Wang Wei, two by Li Po (plus an Ezra Pound poem based on one by Li Po), and one by Tu Fu. We conclude with reminders of the intensely visual nature of Chinese poetry and its focus—especially vis-à-vis other cultures we have looked at in this course—on ordinary events and people instead of the epic, the heroic, and the grand.

Outline

I. China achieved one of its Golden Ages during the T'ang period, so that in about 850 C.E. the four greatest centers of learning and art in the world were Constantinople, Alexandria, Baghdad, and Ch'ang-an, the capital city of China.

II. From 690 C.E. on, poetry was part of the Chinese civil service examination, so that throughout the T'ang period—and well beyond it—every government official would have been able to quote from *The Book of Songs* (which we looked at in Lecture 6) and to write respectable poetry for special occasions and events. The official anthology of T'ang poetry contains 50,000 poems by 2,300 poets, a selection of the vast number of poems from which the editors had to choose.

III. The Chinese theory of the way poetry *means* is a bit different from that of the Western world.
   A. A poem in Chinese theory is generated by something "intensely on the mind," which seeks expression in language.
   B. The reader of a Chinese poem must work backwards to the specific situation that created the emotion that generated the poem, and then to the poet and to his or her entire world, making a Chinese

poem "true" in an almost literal way that is different from the metaphorical truth we assume in a Western poem.

- **C.** A Chinese poem was understood as an authentic presentation of a historical experience.
- **D.** Formally, a Chinese poem from the T'ang period works in five- or seven-character couplets which rhyme on even-numbered lines.
    1. Couplets can be combined into longer or shorter verse forms.
    2. The Chinese wrote in characters rather than letters, so a couplet is two five-character lines.
- **E.** In a poem by Li Po, "heavens-clear-one goose-far" in the first line parallels "lake-vast-lone-sail-slow" in the second to suggest "The sky is clear, a single goose afar; / The lake, vast—a lone sail moves slowly."
    1. The point of the poem is in the parallels: each line describes a white speck on a vast body of blue, in which the distant bird seems to move as slowly as the nearer sail on the water.
    2. If the reader tries to reconstruct the mental pressure that generated the poem, he or she can recreate the poet watching a sail carrying a traveler away, with the feeling of sadness that such a moment always implies.
- **F.** A first-person perspective is almost always assumed by a Chinese poem, but the reader is required to do a certain amount of work to recreate the moment that inspired it.
- **G.** Typically, the Chinese poet keeps the reader focused on what he or she is seeing, which allows for a certain amount of interpretive freedom. Eliot Weinberger's *Nineteen Ways of Looking at Wang Wei* gives 19 quite different readings of the same four-line poem.

IV. Much T'ang poetry seems to have been written about recluses and is about living in the country, far from the court.
- **A.** This was the result of a 722 edict severely limiting the size of the entourages kept by royal princes, which sent many officials back to their homes.
- **B.** The emphasis on nature and the country makes much of this poetry sound like that of Wordsworth and Coleridge.

V. Wang Wei was a painter and devout Buddhist who late in life took the vows of a Buddhist layman.

- **A.** "Written Crossing the Yellow River to Ch'ing-Ho" focuses on what the poet sees rather than on the poet himself.
    1. The poem is about a traveler's experience: concentrating so hard on one's destination that one forgets about the place of departure and realizes with a shock and a touch of homesickness that it has now disappeared.
    2. In many of Wang Wei's poems, feelings are not expressed but implied by what the poet sees and what he shows to us.

VI. Li Po was the rogue of the three great T'ang poets and led a colorful life.
- **A.** His poems are frequently about love, wine, and friendship.
- **B.** Some of his most famous poems are about being happy by oneself.
    1. In "Drinking Alone Beneath the Moon," Li Po (unlike Wang Wei) forces us to focus on the poet instead of the scene.
    2. "Sitting Alone in Ching-t'ing Mountain" uses the parallelism, which is one of the structural principles of Chinese poetry, to focus on Li Po himself.

VII. Chinese poetry strongly influenced modern poetry in its emphasis on images and pictures rather than explanation.
- **A.** Ezra Pound used Chinese poetry as part of the inspiration for the Imagist Movement, which stressed that poetry should work through pictures or images rather than discursive argument.
- **B.** Pound used this theory to edit T. S. Eliot's "The Waste Land," which helped launch Modernist poetry.
- **C.** Pound also opened the doors to the beauty of Chinese poetry, helping to make the 20th century a great age of translation. His *Poems of Cathay* includes a translation of Li Po's "The River Merchant's Wife."

VIII. Tu Fu was less popular than Wang Wei and Li Po during his lifetime but is now sometimes called the Shakespeare of Chinese poetry.
- **A.** He was a Confucian who believed in social concerns and the importance of the family.
- **B.** His poems combine the descriptive aspects of Wang Wei and the subjectivity of Li Po. This combination is illustrated in "Spending the Night in a Tower by the River."
    1. The poem uses parallels as one of its structural principles.

2. Everything in the poem is poised to go one way or another, which worries the poet, who cannot yet know which way things will move.
   3. Chinese poetry is dependent on pictures that we can use to reconstruct the feeling of the poem.
   4. The poem does its work through images, which lead the reader back to the solitary man in a study in a tower on the river bank in a troubled time.
   C. Chinese readers thought that if they were good readers, they would come to know the poet as a kind of friend.

IX. As with the Chinese literature treated in Lecture Six, Chinese poetry is about ordinary people doing ordinary things, not about monsters or heroes or the gods. T'ang poetry celebrates the ordinary lives of ordinary people and makes high art out of the everyday.

Essential Reading:
Poems of Wang Wei, Li Po, and Tu Fu.

Supplementary Reading:
Wu-chi Liu. *An Introduction to Chinese Literature.*
Stephen Owen, *Traditional Chinese Poetry and Poetics.*
Eliot Weinberger, *Nineteen Ways of Looking at Wang Wei.*

Questions to Consider:
1. What difference does it make in the way we read whether we believe a poem is literally or metaphorically true?
2. After reading a sufficient number of poems by the three poets discussed in this lecture, try your hand at constructing character portraits of the three, using the classical Chinese approach to reading poetry. In what ways are they very different kinds of people? Which of the three would you most like to know in person?

Lecture Fourteen
Early Japanese Poetry

Scope: In this lecture we look at two collections of Japanese poetry: the *Man'yōshū* of the 8th century and the *Kokinshū* of the 10th century. We note some of the many ways Japanese poetry is indebted to its Chinese models, but we also describe some uniquely Japanese features that are part of what has been called the *Japanese aesthetic*; we note especially the Japanese love of suggestion, irregularity, simplicity, and perishability. After a brief description of Japanese poetics and verse forms, which illustrates the Japanese aesthetic, we use a series of poems by Kakinomoto Hitomaro from the *Man'yōshū* and several by a woman poet, Ono no Komachi, from the *Kokinshū* as examples of how Japanese poetry works. We conclude by discussing some of the features of Japanese poetry that are difficult to capture in translation, and some techniques we need to learn in order to read and appreciate that poetry.

Outline

I. After the agricultural revolution came to Japan in the 3rd century B.C.E., Japan reinvented itself in terms of Chinese models, borrowing—among other things—Confucianism, Taoism, China's writing system, and (by the 7th and 8th centuries C.E.) Buddhism.

II. The *Man'yōshū* of the 8th century is an equivalent of the Chinese *Book of Songs* (which we treated in Lecture Six).

    A. Its breadth is roughly equivalent to that of its Chinese predecessor, including folk songs, farming songs, and a wide variety of poetic voices.

    B. It includes a large number of women poets, since Japanese would have been their language (the official language of educated men would have been Chinese).

    C. It probably accounts for the high percentage of love poems in the collection, since men writing poems to women would have had to write in Japanese, while their more official writings would have been in Chinese.

III. The *Man'yōshū* contains 4,516 poems by about 400 named poets and hundreds of anonymous ones.
   A. The poems are divided into three types: love poems, elegies for the dead, and miscellaneous poems (which include travel poems, poems written for special occasions, and legends).
   B. Like the Chinese, the Japanese in this collection divided the types according to whether they were written for public or private occasions.

IV. The *Man'yōshū* illustrates a uniquely Japanese aesthetic, which can be studied in Yoshido Kenkō's *Essays of Idleness* (14th century) and in Donald Keene's *The Pleasures of Japanese Literature*. Four principles discussed by both the medieval and the modern scholar are of particular interest.
   A. The first principle is the power of suggestion rather than explicit statement.
      1. Budding or fallen cherries are better than those in full flower.
      2. The crescent moon is better than the full moon.
      3. Autumn and spring are better than summer or winter.
   B. The second principle is asymmetry, which is always preferable to symmetry, (i.e., in tea services, vases, or floral arrangements).
   C. The third principle is simplicity.
      1. Houses are better unpainted than painted.
      2. Japanese food uses few spices and sauces.
      3. The scent of plum blossoms is better than that of lilacs.
   D. The fourth principle is perishability.
      1. Old pottery is better than new.
      2. Cherry blossoms are prized because their time is so short.
      3. Temples are made of wood rather than stone or brick.

V. All of these principles are evident in the poems of the *Man'yōshū*.
   A. The power of suggestion shows up in love poems, which seldom depict lovers meeting but instead deal with the yearning for an unconsummated love or the sorrow for one that has ended.
   B. Asymmetry appears in Japanese verse forms, which always have an uneven number of lines (vis-à-vis Chinese couplets, which are strung together into verses with an even number of lines).
      1. The essential verse form is the *tanka*, which has five lines of five, seven, five, seven, and seven syllables.

      2. Because of the nature of the language, Japanese poetry has never used rhyme or accents (as English poetry does) but is defined in terms of the number of syllables and line length.
      3. Even a longer form, like the *choka*, alternates lines of five and seven syllables, rounded off with two seven-syllable lines. This form died out soon after the publication of the *Man'yōshū*.
      4. Newer verse forms, like the *haiku*, are even shorter, consisting of alternating lines of five, seven, and five syllables.
  C. Simplicity is in the very nature of Japanese verse: a *tanka* has 31 syllables to work with and a haiku has 17.
  D. Perishability occurs in the principal themes of Japanese poetry: a man seeing in the mirror that he suddenly has white hair, cherry blossoms strewing the path in a garden, a lost love affair, or a cane which replaces a sword as a man's accoutrement in the twinkling of an eye.

VI. A vast majority of the poems in the *Man'yōshū* are *tankas*. Some of its most famous poems, however, are *chokas*, especially those written by Kakinomoto Hitomaro, sometimes called the Shakespeare of Japanese poets.
  A. Hitomaro is represented in the *Man'yōshū* by many public poems, written for state occasions.
  B. Hitomaro is best remembered for some of his private poems, such as numbers 220–222 in the collection: "Poem written by Kakinomoto Hitomaro upon seeing a dead man lying among the rocks on the island of Samine in Sanuki."
      1. The poem illustrates the poet's tact, love, and delicacy as he thinks about the dead man's wife, waiting for her husband to return.
      2. The final image—an anonymous drowned man lying on the shore of an island of preternatural beauty—suggests something of the fragility of the human condition and illustrates the Japanese aesthetic as defined by Kenkō and Donald Keene.

VII. The *Kokinshū*, published about 905, has a narrower range of voices, makes the *tanka* the normative verse form, and deals with a more restrictive range of emotions and situations than does the *Man'yōshū*.

- **A.** The dominant themes are the qualities of nature and the human response to them, and the emotions evoked by involvement in human affairs, especially love affairs.
- **B.** Of the 20 volumes in the collection, six are given over to poems about the seasons, and five to love.
- **C.** Despite these serious restrictions, the *Kokinshū* is full of stunningly beautiful poems.

VIII. We can illustrate some of the qualities of the collection—and some of the Japanese aesthetic discussed above—by looking at several poems by Ono no Komachi, a lady-in-waiting at the court in the 850s and 860s.
- **A.** "Autumn nights" is a poem of consummated love.
- **B.** "So much I have learned" suggests some of the difficulties involved in translation.
    1. The context in the collection and the cluster of images—called an *engo*, which functions halfway between a symbol and a metaphor—suggest that there is much more to this poem than first meets the eye.
    2. Other translators have tried to tease fuller meanings out of the poem, but in order to do so they have had to dispense with some of the compression that is the essence of the *tanka*.
- **C.** "In this forlorn state" in Japanese makes the subject of the poem the duckweed and compares the state of the poet's heart to the plant drifting downstream. At the same time, the poem suggests affinities with the picture-making qualities of Chinese poetry—a quality lost in most translations.
- **D.** "Alas! The flowers have blossomed unseen" can be read in two entirely different ways because of the ambiguity of the characters used in it, making the tiny poem incredibly rich in meaning.

IX. Because of the intense compression of Japanese poems—and the complexity introduced by the use of words that can mean more than one thing—it is probably best for those who cannot read Japanese to find several translations of each poem to try to tease out the multiple meanings of each one, and to pay attention to the translators as they explain the choices they made in translation.

Essential Reading:

The *Kokinshū*.
The *Man'yōshū*.

Supplementary Reading:

Robert H. Brower and Earl Miner, *Japanese Court Poetry*.
Steven D. Carter, *Traditional Japanese Poetry*.
Shuchi Kato, *A History of Japanese Literature 1*.
Donald Keene, *The Pleasures of Japanese Literature*.
Helen Craig McCullough, *Brocade by Night*.

Questions to Consider:

1. It has been suggested that literature always uses conventional symbols, techniques, or themes in unconventional ways, so that they strike the reader as new or strange. Can a case like this be made in these Japanese poems, which work on very small scales, or after a while do they all strike you as being the same poem, with only the difference of a word or two?

2. The *Kokinshū* has a much narrower range of voices and subjects than does the earlier *Man'yōshū*, reflecting its court origins. What is gained and what is lost for poetry by this concentration of images, themes, forms, and subjects?

Lecture Fifteen
The Tale of Genji

Scope: This lecture deals with the first novel in history, *The Tale of Genji*. After a brief review of what we know about its author, Murasaki Shikibu, a lady-in-waiting at the Heian Court in the late 10th and early 11th centuries, we focus on the novel's central character, Genji. After some reminders of differences in gender relations between the *Heian period* and our own—and of their implications for understanding the novel—we discuss some of its themes: the search for the perfect relationship, the effects of the passage of time, and the problems of desire itself, either in Buddhist terms or more generally as "a sensitivity to things." We conclude by noting that Genji is a new type of hero in our course, more like the knights in courtly medieval romance than the more militaristic heroes of earlier ages—a hero for whom taste and sensitivity count for more than prowess on the battle field.

Outline

I. Murasaki Shikibu, the author of *The Tale of Genji*, served as lady-in-waiting at the Heian court from about 1005 to about 1011.
  A. She was from a branch of the ruling Fujiwara family.
  B. All we know of her childhood is that she was so intelligent that her father wished she had been born a son, and that she learned Chinese—an achievement she later suppressed.
  C. She married in 998 or 999, bore one daughter, was widowed in 1001, and perhaps died about 1015 or 1016, her novel being written between her husband's death and her own.

II. The novel's central character is *Genji*—the son of an emperor reduced to the status of commoner, mostly to protect him from court intrigues—since his mother, although a great favorite of the emperor, has no strong family backing to protect her.
  A. He needs protection, especially from the emperor's first wife, the Lady Kokiden, a Fujiwara from the main branch of the family.
  B. He grows up splendidly and wins the hearts of everyone at court not already predisposed against him by the conditions of his birth.

1. When he is 12, he is married to Aoi, daughter of a powerful court minister. It is not a happy marriage, he spends little time with her, and she does not bear a son until some years later, after which she dies.
2. Genji is always ready to love someone who reminds him of his mother, including the Lady Fujitsubo, the wife the emperor took to replace Genji's mother, and a nine-year-old girl named Murasaki, whom he takes into his household and who eventually becomes his first (that is, his main) wife.
3. The Lady Fujitsubo makes one slip which allows Genji to make love to her. She becomes pregnant but manages to pass off her son as the emperor's.
4. Along the way Genji has affairs with many other women, including Lady Kokiden's sister, promised to the crown prince. The affair lands Genji in serious trouble.
5. At about the same time Aoi has a son and dies, and he makes love to Murasaki for the first time, after which he makes her his first wife.

C. In trouble at court, Genji banishes himself to Suma, where a priest's daughter, "the Akashi lady," is virtually thrust upon him. The affair produces a daughter.
1. When there is a change in emperors, Genji goes back to court, taking the Akashi lady with him. Their daughter will one day marry an emperor and become mother to a future emperor.
2. Despite his exclusion from succession, Genji manages to father one emperor and grandfather another.

D. Genji is now at the height of his power and influence, and he builds a great mansion for his women, divided into four courts named after the four seasons.
1. The peak of his political influence is balanced by a loss of control in his personal life, including a failure to establish a sexual relationship with Tamakazura, a new woman he brings into his mansion, and the unfaithfulness of a new wife, who will bear a son to the son of Genji's best childhood friend.
2. Genji lives to be 52, and the rest of the novel traces the careers of his flawed descendents—each of whom has some of Genji's shining qualities but is nothing like Genji himself.
3. The plot shares elements with what we might call soap opera, but it has been praised for over 1000 years because of its analysis of love and love relationships.

III. In order to understand that analysis, we need to know something about gender relations in Heian, Japan.
  A. Marriage was polygamous for aristocratic men.
   1. The first marriage was usually arranged when the boy and girl were about 12 or 13. The girl would continue to live with her parents and the boy would visit her.
   2. Second and third wives were usually given their own establishments. The husband commuted from wife to wife, perhaps stopping for liaisons along the way.
   3. Meanwhile, women waited hidden behind screens for men to call.
   4. Both parties had some freedom, but the man had considerably more, since a woman could only inspire passion, not initiate it.
   5. A woman's recourse was jealousy against a rival who kept her husband or lover from visiting, and there are numerous examples in the novel of the kind of damage such jealousy can wreak (e.g., Lady Rukojo).
  B. Sequestered women also had time, while waiting, to write, so that much of our knowledge of the life of the period comes from women's diaries, which Richard Bowring says is "a sweet form of revenge."

IV. Of the many themes that hold this vast novel together, three can be mentioned here.
  A. One of them is the search for the perfect mate, which begins in the second chapter of the novel.
  B. Initially, Genji seems to be the perfect man, but the story darkens as time passes until, at its end (as one of the novel's translators suggests), Murasaki creates in one of Genji's descendants the first anti-hero in world literature.
  C. Buddhism may color the novel's ending, tracing the effects of desire from the first violent passion of the emperor for Genji's mother to its ultimate consequences.
   1. According to the novel's translator, this is no afterthought but was built into the novel from its opening chapters.
   2. The theme, however, is not necessarily Buddhist.
   3. It may, as Japanese critics have noted, simply suggest *mono no aware,* "a sensitivity to things," which all the good characters in the novel possess and the bad characters lack; it

may also suggest the sorrow of all human existence, and its presence has made this perhaps the single most important work in the history of Japanese literature.
- **V.** Genji is a new type of hero in our course.
    - **A.** He is not a warrior; his skills are painting, poetry, fashion, and sensitivity to the needs of women.
    - **B.** These characteristics make him more like the chivalrous knight of medieval literature than the powerful fighters of earlier literature.
    - **C.** The novel contains almost 800 poems, mostly from the *Kokinshū*, used in ways that were characteristic of Chinese culture and as markers of sensibility.
    - **D.** This would change in subsequent Japanese history, but the importance of this novel in Japan suggests that it registers one important thread in Japanese culture and sensibility.

Essential Reading:

The Tale of Genji.

Supplementary Reading:

Richard Bowring, *Murasaki Shikibu: The Tale of Genji.*
Donald Keene, *The Pleasures of Japanese Literature.*

Questions to Consider:

1. In what ways is Genji responsible for what he does, given the rules of the culture in which he lives? To what extent is the fact that he seems to assume responsibility for every woman he is with a major part of what makes him an ideal male?
2. Chapter 25 of the novel contains an extended discussion of fiction, its virtues, and its liabilities. Most critics assume that Murasaki makes Genji her spokesperson in this chapter in his defense of fiction. What, precisely, is that defense? Would it work for modern works of fiction and, if so, how? If not, why not?

Lecture Sixteen
Inferno, from Dante's *Divine Comedy*

Scope: This lecture deals with Dante's *Divine Comedy,* focusing on its first book, *Inferno.* After a summary description of the poem, we discuss the structure of Dante's Hell in philosophical and moral terms, noting its debts to Aristotle, Cicero, and Virgil. Then we go on to describe the ways in which Dante's poetry makes concrete and physical the fantastic places to which he takes us, some of the fascinating characters who people those places—particularly Paolo and Francesca—and the questions about Dante's technique which the pair of lovers raises. We consider the genre of the poem and its allegorical dimensions, which allow Dante to get into the poem an encyclopedic amount of information, as well as authorizing interpretations on several different levels. We conclude by suggesting a few of the directions in which a pursuit of an allegorical reading of the poem might take us and something of the poem's inexhaustibility.

Outline

I. Dante's *Divine Comedy* is considered to be one of the greatest poems in the Western world. Despite its vastness, the poem is simply structured.
   A. A Pilgrim is lost in the woods of error and is prevented from finding his way back to the path by three fierce beasts.
      1. He is rescued by the shade of the poet Virgil, who will restore him to his right path.
      2. They will take a roundabout way, through Hell, Purgatory, and Heaven.
      3. Virgil guides him through Hell and Purgatory, and then Dante's visionary and spiritual lady, Beatrice, leads him through the nine spheres of Heaven.
      4. The poem ends with a vision of God.
   B. The Hell through which Virgil and the Pilgrim travel is a series of concentric ledges spiraling down to the earth's center. In Canto 11 Virgil explains that its topography corresponds to the ethical categories of evil as defined by Aristotle in *Ethics*.
      1. The categories are incontinence, violence, and fraud, which probably correspond to the three beasts in the woods of error.

  2. Circles two, three, and four punish sins of incontinence: lust, gluttony, avarice, and wrath.
  3. Circle Seven contains violent sinners, divided into violence against neighbors, violence against self, and violence against God.
  4. Circles eight and nine treat the fraudulent, divided into many separate categories.
  5. The icy floor of Circle Nine contains traitors against the church and state, and Satan himself is here, buried up to his waist in ice.
 C. Hell's structure is thus mostly Aristotelian—philosophical rather than theological.
  1. It also contains Christians and pagans in every circle; the only exceptions are Circles one and six, which contain the virtuous pagans and heretics.
  2. Virgil, as a representative of the best of human reason, can be the Pilgrim's guide.

II. Dante's poetry uses the ordinary and everyday to help the reader to be able to picture the fantastic and unfamiliar places to which he or she is being taken.
 A. This is a new use for the epic simile.
 B. There are hundreds—or even thousands—of epic similes in the poem.
  1. In Circle Nine the Pilgrim compares looking up at giants to looking up at a leaning tower in Bologna.
  2. The sounds of lamentation in Hell's antechamber are like sand caught in a whirlwind.
  3. The suicides in Circle Seven are trapped within trees and their voices sound like the sap that fizzes from a green log thrown into the fire.

III. Dante's hellscape is populated with some fascinating characters.
 A. Among the most famous are Paolo and Francesca in Circle Two, with the lustful.
  1. They are whirled about in a dark wind, a reminder that the state of the souls in Hell is not simply punishment but a revelation of the nature of the sin for which they are damned.
  2. Paolo and Francesca are with others whom we have met in this course, including Dido, Helen of Troy, and Paris.

- **3.** The Pilgrim calls to them, they float down to him, and Francesca tells their story, which is so moving and beautiful that the Pilgrim faints in sympathetic pain.
- **4.** She does not tell all of the details of the story, which the original reader would have known, but what she does tell generates a great deal of sympathy not only in the Pilgrim but the reader as well.

B. Many of the characters in Hell have stories to tell and many of them seem admirable or at least justified in what they did.
- **1.** This happens throughout the poem (e.g., Ulysses's story in Canto 26, Pier Delle Vigne's in Canto 13, and Farinata's in Canto 10).
- **2.** This leads readers sometimes to question whether Dante's poetry works against the moral or Christian meanings of the poem.

C. Should we be sympathizing with the damned souls in Hell? In order to answer this question, we need to consider what kind of poem this is.
- **1.** It is an epic poem, but one which redefines the epic hero as a spiritual rather than a military warrior.
- **2.** It is a comedy because it is written in a mixed style and has a happy ending.
- **3.** It is also the story of a fantastic journey.
- **4.** It is a medieval encyclopedia containing an enormous amount of what the Middle Ages believed.

IV. In order to get all of this into the poem, Dante also made it an *allegory*: an extended metaphor in which everything in the poem is equated with something outside it.

A. Medieval theologians had become very adept at reading the Bible allegorically, so that any mention of Jerusalem could refer to the literal city, the Church, the heavenly city of Zion, or the believing soul. Dante's poem functions similarly, so that the literal level (the state of souls after death) suggests other meanings, including what sin does to the sinner in this life.

B. Allegory needs a literal level, which is one reason Dante works so hard to get the reader to see, hear, feel, touch, and smell the places he visits, and also why he peoples Hell with historical characters like Paolo and Francesca. The use of concrete physicality and historical figures grounds the poem, giving it a literal level like that of the historical city of Jerusalem.

    C. The characters in Hell are placed by their locations in the elaborately structured pit, so that the reader knows why they are where they are.

        1. Once their placement has done Dante's moral and theological work for him, his characters can reveal other sides of their personalities and interests, making them far richer than traditional allegorical figures with such names as Lust, Gluttony, or Wrath.

        2. These other facets of their personalities—and the conversations they have with the Pilgrim—allow Dante to get a lot of material into his poem that is strictly extraneous to its religious theme, such as political theory or history.

    D. There are many allegorical ways to read the poem.

        1. The growth of the Pilgrim as he travels through Hell, Purgatory, and Heaven is one such reading.

        2. Another involves the monsters that guard each circle of Hell, which represent the sins punished in those circles.

        3. There are theological allegories involving the relationship among grace, divine illumination, and human reason, pictured in the relationship between the Virgin Mary, Beatrice, Virgil, and the Pilgrim.

        4. There are also complicated political allegories which involve Virgil as a representative of the Roman Empire.

V. This is an incredibly rich poem, and Dante, according to T. S. Eliot, is one of the two greatest poets in the history of the Western world—the other being Shakespeare.

Essential Reading:

Dante, *Inferno* from the *Divine Comedy*.

Supplementary Reading:

Thomas Bergin, *Dante's Divine Comedy*.

George Holmes, *Dante (Past Masters)*.

Dorothy Sayers, *Introductory Papers on Dante*.

Questions to Consider:
1. If you were to construct your own Hell along Dante's lines, what would be the general categories, and how would you rank human failings within those categories? Which modern historical persons would you place inside of each category? Would you change any of Dante's punishments?
2. Chart the changes in the relationship between the Pilgrim and Virgil as they move through Hell and Purgatory. Where does it start? How does it progress?

Lecture Seventeen
Chaucer's *The Canterbury Tales*

Scope: This lecture deals with Chaucer's *The Canterbury Tales* written 1386–1400 C.E. After a discussion of the frame Chaucer uses for his stories and some of its implications for the stories and how they get told, we deal with the poet's transitions from story to story and the groups or fragments into which the transitions divide the tales. We illustrate these generalizations with a reading of "The Wife of Bath's Tale," showing how her characterization in the "General Prologue," the prologue to her own story (in which she talks about her own five marriages), and the story she subsequently tells all fit together to create a colorful and unconventional character who would tell a story whose point is that the only happy marriages are those in which wives rule the husbands. The poet, as is his usual practice, lets us decide for ourselves how to judge this amazing woman and her story.

Outline

I. The idea of a frame story that holds together all the stories within it may have come to Chaucer from Boccaccio's *Decameron,* in which 10 people on a journey of 10 days each tell one story per day.

    A. Chaucer puts the frame story technique to far more ambitious uses.
        1. His 30 pilgrims who meet at the Tabard Inn in London plan to tell two stories each on the way to Canterbury and two stories on the way back, which would be a total of 120 stories had the poem been completed as planned.
        2. Chaucer's tales are much longer than Boccaccio's, and they are in poetry rather than prose.
        3. Chaucer characterizes his pilgrims in his "General Prologue" and then has each tell a tale that fits the character.

    B. Chaucer also provides links between the tales, featuring interaction among the pilgrims and accounting for the way in which one story leads to the next.
        1. Not all of the links are completed, even among the 22 tales Chaucer finished before his death. The links that are provided divide the tales into groups, each of which includes the links between tales.

2. Group A ("The Knight's Tale," "The Miller's Tale," "The Reeve's Tale," and "The Cook's Tale") illustrates how the links work and stresses the developing relationship among the pilgrims.
C. Each tale is an expression of the character of the teller and gains additional meaning from its context in the succession of tales.
  1. In Group A, the Reeve tells a story that gets back at the Miller, who has told a tale that the Reeve thinks is directed against him.
  2. This would presumably have been the organization of the entire collection, with links providing dynamic progressions from tale to tale.
  3. The 22 tales are conventionally divided into nine groups or fragments; links are provided within each.
D. Some critics, such as Lyman Kittredge, think that the entire collection of stories is dramatic in the sense that tellers hear other stories and then tell their own in response, and that the links are thus thematic.
  1. He identifies a "Marriage Group" of tales ("The Wife of Bath's Tale," "The Clerk's Tale," "The Merchant's Tale," and "The Franklin's Tale"), which occur in different groups but each of which responds to a story told by another pilgrim.
  2. In the collection as a whole, almost every kind of medieval story—the romance, the *fabliau*, the sermon, the animal fable, the mock epic—is represented, told by a nearly complete cross section of British society in the late 14th century.

II. "The Wife of Bath's Tale" illustrates these techniques, the connection between teller and tale, and the importance of context in the collection of stories.
  A. The Wife of Bath in "The General Prologue" is in every way larger than life: her size, her clothes, her oft-married state, the amount of the world she has seen, and her assertiveness. We also learn that she is deaf in one ear—a detail that seems extraneous but will later be explained.
  B. The prologue to her tale is longer than the tale itself. In it she tells of her five marriages, in the process attacking the medieval Church's theories about marriage and defending herself for her multiple liaisons. It also promotes experience as more educational than book learning.

1. She divides her husbands into categories of "good" and "bad" on the basis of the extent to which she could control them.
2. The first three were much older than she; she controlled them with ease and counts them as "good" husbands. The last two were more difficult, younger than she was when she married them and much harder to control.
3. The last two required much more effort on her part to win control over them, and she tells a story about how she finally managed to achieve the upper hand in her fifth and (so far) most recent marriage.
4. Her thesis in her prologue is that the only happy marriages are those in which the wife rules the husband—a shocking idea in the 14th century. It is also clear that of all of her husbands, she loved the last one (the one hardest to subdue) the most.
5. She is still a lusty woman, who has (we suspect) come on this pilgrimage partly in search of a sixth husband.

C. Her tale itself is a romance set in King Arthur's court and involves a knight who rapes a peasant woman.
1. She appeals to Arthur, who condemns the knight to death, but the women of the court intervene. They give the knight a year and a day to discover what women really want; if he finds the right answer, his life will be spared.
2. At the end of the year he encounters a loathly hag who promises to save his life if he will grant her a boon. He agrees.
3. When brought before his tribunal of court women, he tells them that what women really want is "sovereignty in love." The women judges spare his life.
4. The boon the loathly hag demands for saving the knight's life is to marry him. He reluctantly agrees. On the wedding night, she gives him a stern lecture on the nature of true virtue and nobility, and she ends by giving him a choice: she can be stunningly beautiful, but he will always have to worry about her faithfulness to him; or she can remain as she is but promise absolute dedication to him.
5. He turns the choice over to her, and when she asks whether he is granting her sovereignty in the marriage and he tells her that he is, she becomes a dazzlingly beautiful woman who says that she will also always be faithful to him.

        6. She has educated a knight about women and in the process has also shown that what is good for her is also good for him. They live happily ever after.
   D. The Wife of Bath ends her story by asking Christ to cut short the lives of all husbands who will not be ruled by their wives; the ending reminds us of the complex character that is the Wife of Bath.
       1. She seems in some ways a proto-feminist, demanding recognition of the female point of view in marriage and the values of experience as a teacher—vis-à-vis the book-learning of men.
       2. As always, Chaucer lets us make up our own minds about the Wife of Bath and her story.
III. The narrative strategy of the frame impacts the stories in *The Canterbury Tales*.
   A. The frame allows a certain distance between the author and tellers and between the author and the tales themselves.
   B. The frame gives readers some room for interpretation, an idea which is a great step forward in the art of storytelling.

Essential Reading:

Chaucer, *The Canterbury Tales*.

Supplementary Reading:

Helen Cooper, *Oxford Guides to Chaucer: The Canterbury Tales*.
Derek Pearsall, *The Canterbury Tales*.

Questions to Consider:

1. In some of the most famous tales in this collection, how do the connections between the character as given in "The General Prologue," the prologue to the tale itself, and the context provided by the links between tales help us to understand the intimate connections Chaucer has arranged among character, context, and tale?
2. How does the frame of this collection of stories manage to put distance between the author, the tellers of the stories, and the tales themselves? Does it allow an interpretive space for the reader to make up their own mind about what they are reading?

Lecture Eighteen
1001 Nights

Scope: This lecture deals with the *1001 Nights*. After a brief account of the unusual origins of the book, we discuss its frame story and some of the ways in which the frame influences narrative technique, especially vis-à-vis Chaucer's frame technique in *The Canterbury Tales*. We then put *1001 Nights* back into its context within the great books of stories it had to draw on, particularly three collections from India. We will also look ahead to some of the ways these stories have been used in subsequent world literature, noting especially how the contemporary American writer John Barth has focused on Shahrazad in his novels and stories. We conclude by suggesting alternate ways in which the book—and particularly its frame—has been interpreted: as pure entertainment or as a manner of therapy designed to cure King Shahrayar of his misogyny and cruelty.

Outline

I. The *1001 Nights*, sometimes called the *Arabian Nights*, has no single author and grew over many centuries, collecting stories from India, Persia, Syria, Egypt, and Iraq.

    A. Many of the stories are associated with a Caliph of Baghdad—Harûn el-Rashid (r. 786–809)—giving Iraq a special place in the stories.

    B. Even his stories, however, were not written down until years (or even centuries) later; there is no single authoritative manuscript of the book, and different texts contain different stories.

II. Our interest is with the implications of the frame story for the way the stories in *1001 Nights* get themselves told.

    A. This is perhaps the most famous frame story in all of literature, involving King Shahrayar, his brother Shahzaman, and the sisters Shahrazad and Dinarzad.

        1. Having discovered that his wife is unfaithful and having assured himself that no woman can be trusted, Shahrayar takes a virgin to bed every night and then kills her in the morning, thus guaranteeing that she will be faithful to him.

2. Eventually Shahrazad, daughter of the vizier who has to find a new virgin every night, volunteers to be the next one.
3. On her night with King Shahrayar, she takes her sister with her and towards morning asks Shahrazad to tell one of her good stories, which she does. The story is interrupted at dawn when it has reached a climactic point.
4. The King spares Shahrazad for one night so that he can hear the end of the story; she finishes that one and begins another, which is similarly interrupted, and the pattern is repeated for 1001 nights.

B. The frame influences the shape of the stories which are told. What kind of story does this frame require?
1. The frame is more limiting than that in Chaucer's *The Canterbury Tales*, which had 30 storytellers, each with a varied audience for the story.
2. Shahrazad is the only storyteller here, and she has an audience of one (two, if we count Dinarzad).
3. Her job is to stretch a single story over as many nights as possible, which she does by nesting her stories—that is, embedding stories within stories, as when a character within a story tells a story, within which another character tells another story and so on, until at some point there are as many as 11 stories being told simultaneously.
4. The inside stories duplicate the theme or situation of the frame story or are at least parallel in some way.

III. The frame of *1001 Nights* is embedded in the entire history of world literature. It serves as a crossroads where many stories from the past and other cultures meet and from there are sent out into the future and the rest of the world.

A. When the Islamic Empire was at its height, Arab storytellers had access to the greatest collections of stories in the world.
1. Some scholars think that this collection originated in India and came to the Arab world via Persia.
2. India already had some collections of stories, including the *Jātaka,* the *Pañcantantra,* and the *Kathāsaritsāgara*, all of which use frames to hold together anthologies of stories.
3. In the *Pañcantantra* a wise Brahman is teaching his princely students things they need to know in order to rule wisely. He does so by means of stories, which are framed by

conversations and discussion; within individual stories characters tell other stories, so that they are nested in complex ways.
    4. The *Pañcantantra* was translated into Persian in the 6th century and into Arabic in the 8th century, after which it made its way into Syria, Hebrew, and eventually most of Europe. It provided stories for *1001 Nights,* Boccaccio, Chaucer, and even some Grimm Brothers fairy tales.
  B. From *1001 Nights* these stories make their way into the rest of the world.
    1. They were translated into French in the 18th century and became part of an Oriental craze that lasted in Europe throughout the century; 19th-century children grew up with these stories.
    2. Marcel Proust, at the end of *Remembrance of Things Past,* makes an allusion to Shahrazad that he knows his readers will recognize.
    3. Bits of the book run through Leopold Bloom's mind on his day in Dublin in Joyce's *Ulysses,* and the book provided a lifelong inspiration for the Argentinean writer Jorge Luis Borges.
    4. John Barth, the American fiction writer, has centered a great deal of his work on Shahrazad and *1001 Nights* in such works as *Chimera* and *Tidewater Tales,* focusing on narrative structure in ways that make storytelling and playing with nesting techniques into the very subjects of the books.
  C. All of these references suggest once again that literature is a cross-cultural process that borrows and learns not just across language and geographical boundaries, but across temporal ones as well.
IV. Of the many ways in which *1001 Nights* can be read, two are worth mentioning here.
  A. The first way is to read it as a wonderfully entertaining book, gathering some of the best stories of the world into one place.
    1. There is every kind of story here: romantic, edifying, moral, bawdy, and tragic; and the genres include anecdotes, animal fables, fairy stories, and serious stories about love and deception.

- **2.** The stories are entertaining enough to save Shahrazad's life and to allow her to live happily ever after with King Shahrayar; they certainly can entertain us as well.
- **B.** The second way to read the book is as a lesson in maturity; Shahrazad, in the process of telling her stories, neutralizes Shahrayar's misognyny and ruthlessness and helps him grow up.
    - **1.** Some of the stories, like "The Merchant and the Demon," seem to parallel Shahrazad's own situation and give storytelling a redemptive quality.
    - **2.** Shahrazad is also perhaps teaching Shahrayar new patterns of response that, according to critic Fedwa Malti-Douglas, substitute "extended and continuous desire and pleasure" for the "immature male pattern of excitement, satisfaction, and termination." The new pattern continues desire from night to night in a way that combines sexual and textual issues.
    - **3.** The Indian collections we previously discussed already noticed the parallels between sexuality and storytelling; John Barth develops these in his work with Shahrazad.
    - **4.** In this reading Shahrazad becomes the wise woman who initiates a man into maturity and sophistication.
- **C.** *1001 Nights* reflects another development in the sophistication of the art of storytelling that parallels Chaucer's achievement but does so in a different way.
    - **1.** The book shows us how frames can function.
    - **2.** The frames require stories to become more artful, especially in terms of nesting.

Essential Reading:

1001 Nights. Also titled *The Arabian Nights.*

Supplementary Reading:

Robert Irwin, *The Arabian Nights: A Companion.*

Fedwa Malti-Douglas, *Woman's Body, Woman's Word.*

Questions to Consider:

1. Do any of the nested stories in the collection achieve John Barth's ideal condition, in which the climax of the innermost story triggers the climax of its container story and so on, setting off a series of climaxes like a string of firecrackers? Which ones achieve this, and how are the stories structured so as to achieve this effect?

2. Does there seem to you to be a consistent world view, morality, or ethical stance that runs through the stories of *1001 Nights* and holds them together, or are the stories simply good stories whose purpose is pure entertainment?

Lecture Nineteen
Wu Ch'eng-en's *Monkey*

Scope: This lecture treats Wu Ch'eng-en's 16th-century novel, *Monkey* (or *Journey to the West*). We begin by talking about the rise of the novel in China as a vernacular and popular genre and notice similarities with the rise of the novel in other cultures. After a brief account of the historical germ at the center of the book, we describe the mythic elements that were added to the story over a thousand years of oral transmission, and then describe its basic plot: that of a Chinese monk on a journey to India, accompanied by fabulous creatures, the most important of which is Monkey, one of the great creations in literature. We notice some analogues in the folklore and mythology of other countries, and we conclude by noting the extent to which the diverse materials of the novel are shaped and controlled by Buddhist and/or Taoist thought.

Outline

I. The novel is a late-comer among the literary genres in every country. It uses *vernacular*, or nonclassical, language, is written in prose, and is intended for a popular rather than a learned audience.

    A. Classical and vernacular Chinese in the 16th century differed perhaps as English in the King James Bible differs from modern English.

    B. The novel, when it emerged in China in the 16th century, was written in the vernacular—the equivalent of similar books in other cultures, such as the *Jātaka, 1001 Nights,* and Boccaccio's *Decameron.*

II. The story at the heart of *Monkey* had a long history before becoming a novel.

    A. It was presumably written by a retired public official, Wu Ch'eng-en, in the 16th century, although the attribution is not absolutely secure.

    B. The story originally was about a Buddhist monk (Hsuan-tsang) in the 7th century who traveled to India to acquire more Buddhist texts. His journey lasted from 627–45, and he spent the rest of his life translating what he brought back.

1. The original accounts of the trip, written by the monk and one of his companions, are sober documents about a difficult journey.
2. Once appropriated by storytellers, the account grew for about a thousand years, exchanging the identifiable geography of the original account for fantastic lands, populated by monsters and demons, where very unusual things are likely to happen.
3. The monk's name had been changed to his honorific, Tripitaka, and his human companions had been replaced by animals who were also divine shape-shifters: Monkey, Pigsy, Sandy, and a white horse—the last two of which are really dragons.
4. Monkey had become its central character, so Arthur Waley in his translation called it *Monkey: Folk Novel of China*.

III. The plot is full of fantastic adventures, mythic beings, animal spirits, fearsome battles, monsters, and miraculous deliverances.
   A. Its first seven chapters deal with Monkey, hatched from a rock by the sun. In his quest for immortality, he storms heaven, is finally subdued by Buddha himself, and imprisoned under a mountain for 500 years.
      1. Towards the end of this 500-year period, Buddha sends the *bodhisáttva* (Kuan-yin) to Earth to help humans acquire more scriptures for the East. She enlists Monkey as her first companion to the yet-undisclosed pilgrim.
      2. Monkey agrees in exchange for forgiveness of some of his bad karma, and he waits under the mountain for the pilgrim to free him.
      3. Kuan-yin also enlists Pigsy, banished from heaven for a serious error and now working on a farm; growing more pig-like in appearance as time passes. He has no vocation for a spiritual quest, he gets easily discouraged, and he functions primarily as a comic foil to the pilgrim, Tripitaka, and Monkey.
   B. The novel then recounts the birth and early life of the man who will become Tripitaka, the pilgrim and nominal leader of the quest for scriptures.
      1. The story of his birth and early years is extraordinary, as befits one who will grow up to be a hero; as a baby, he was tied to a

plank and sent down a river in a way reminiscent of the stories of Sargon the Great and Moses.
2. After other adventures of an equally astounding nature, Tripitaka is given his charge, introduced to his companions, and they set off for India.
3. The novel is full of incident but at the end, after a safe return home, all five pilgrims are canonized and Tripitaka achieves full Buddhahood.

IV. Monkey is one of the great creations of world literature.
  A. He has antecedents in the trickster gods of many mythologies; the animal fables of Aesop; many Indian collections; the *1001 Nights*, Chaucer's tales of Chanticleer, Pertelote, and Reynard the Fox; and the monkey warrior of the Indian epic, the *Ramayana.*
    1. He is always still a monkey: curious, arrogant, brash, and willful.
    2. He is also a monkey with the kind of supernatural powers we associate with comic-book heroes (e.g., he can shift his shape).
    3. Because of his intelligence and resourcefulness, he becomes the actual leader of the quest—although he gets the pilgrims into almost as many scrapes as he gets them out of, thanks to the nature of his character.
    4. During the battle in heaven, he pursues a general through a bewildering series of disguises as animals, reminiscent of "The Porter and the Three Ladies" (not covered in Lecture Eighteen) in the *1001 Nights*.
    5. Monkey is a satirical hero as well; he also despises pomposity, stuffiness, and arrogant authority, and very much enjoys a chance to challenge and disrupt them.
    6. He has never lost his appeal as a folk hero in China, and writers as recent as Maxine Hong Kingston and Gerald Vizenor have used aspects of Monkey in their own contemporary novels.
  B. Tripitaka likewise has multiple antecedents.
    1. He is still a character out of folklore and in some measure the saintly monk of history.
    2. In the 1000-year folk tradition he has become a disciple of Buddha banished from heaven for 10 incarnations and 81 ordeals.

3. This is his tenth incarnation, and he has achieved such purity that he has never lost a drop of semen, so that his flesh and/or his semen can bestow immortality—which makes him vulnerable to attack by demons of both sexes and makes the job of his guardians that much more difficult.
4. Tripitaka is an ordinary mortal on a perilous quest, whiny and worried and discouraged by all obstacles—which forces Monkey in another way to become the real leader of the expedition.
5. The multiple antecedents and analogues incorporate many other stories and situations from other traditions; we recognize bits of the Hamlet story, Oedipus, the *Oresteia*, the Minotaur, and Moses and the Egyptian sorcerers, among many others.

V. Part of the achievement of the novel is to hold these diverse elements together intellectually with concepts derived from Buddhism.
   A. The keystone of the novel's thought is the Heart Sutra, which Tripitaka is given and which is meant to remind him that the world is illusion and that attachment to the world and the senses is the great obstacle to freeing oneself and seeing Buddha in the Western Paradise.
   B. Tripitaka keeps forgetting its precepts, however, and must constantly be reminded of them by Monkey, who himself illustrates other aspects of Buddhist thought.
      1. Monkey, via his experience and training, has achieved some measure of discipline by the time the pilgrims set off on their journey.
      2. He is still, however, a monkey, so the bodhisáttva gives Tripitaka a cap which, once placed on Monkey's head, cannot be removed. Tripitaka is also given a spell which can tighten the cap, causing great pain.
      3. The cap is a metaphor for mental discipline—whether Buddhist or Taoist—which keeps the mind and attention focused.
      4. Monkey is the one traveler most dedicated to the quest, having to overcome the trepidation of Tripitaka and the sensuality and sloth of Pigsy, and be responsible for bailing all of the pilgrims out of innumerable scrapes.

5. In this way he is a kind of Virgil to Tripitaka's Pilgrim or Sancho Panza to Tripitaka's Don Quixote, except that this Sancho Panza is the real leader of the quest.
   6. In spite of its comic tone and many adventures, the book maintains a religious focus.
C. Some critics have asserted that the entire novel is structured so as to undercut the illusion of reality with gentle mockery and satire, making this a "Buddhist comedy." Monkey's new name, after his initial training, is "Awareness of Vacuity" or "Emptiness."

Essential Reading:

Wu Ch'eng-en, *Hsi Yu Chi* (*Monkey*, or *Journey to the West*).

Supplementary Reading:

C. T. Hsia, *The Classic Chinese Novel: A Critical Introduction.*

Anthony C. Yu, "Introduction" to *Journey to the West.*

Questions to Consider:

1. Frequently in the novel, the pilgrims get involved in an adventure which requires a great deal of energy and resourcefulness, only to discover after it is over that the whole event was being orchestrated by a higher power. Given what you have decided is the main theme or point of the novel, what purpose do these events fulfill? For whose benefit are they staged? Who learns anything from them?
2. Hsia, in his *The Classic Chinese Novel,* points out a central paradox involving the bestowal of Buddhahood on Tripitaka at the novel's end; "a bestowing which is granted precisely because he has done nothing to earn it: to consciously strive for Buddhahood would have again placed him in bondage." How does this final paradox reinforce others throughout the book? In what way is the entire novel based on a tension between its story and its theme?

Lecture Twenty
The *Heptameron*

Scope: In this lecture we look at Marguerite of Navarre's *Heptameron*. After considering the influence of Boccaccio's *Decameron* on the work and comparing it with Chaucer's *The Canterbury Tales* and *1001 Nights,* we consider the way the collection's frame affects its 72 stories, concentrating on how the transitions between stories characterize the 10 storytellers. Marguerite's collection is different from earlier anthologies in that she insists that all of her stories are true and rhetorically plain, and she provides an equal number of male and female storytellers to focus on her themes of rape, seduction, and infringements of the marriage code in aristocratic Europe. We will consider the story of Amador and Florida and its context to illustrate our generalizations and to suggest that in the book Marguerite is both contributing to the "Quarrel about Women" in the Renaissance and carving out a space for female narrative in literature.

Outline

I. Marguerite of Navarre, sister of King Francis I, was a patron of literature in the French Renaissance who personally commissioned a translation of Boccaccio's *Decameron*, which inspired her own book; she died before she could match Boccaccio's 100 stories.

   A. Like Chaucer's, her book is an incomplete work, consisting of 72 stories.

   B. Like *1001 Nights,* her book has no definitive edition, and its textual history is as interesting as that of the Arabian work.

II. Like Chaucer and the *1001 Nights*, Marguerite provides a frame for her stories: a group of 10 aristocrats trapped by floods in a monastery for 10 days decide to tell stories to each other to pass the time until they can return home.

   A. Like the *Decameron,* the *Heptameron*'s frame is a disaster—a flood instead of a plague.

   B. A character in the frame says that they can complete a version of the *Decameron* that Marguerite was writing for the French court.

C. In some manuscript versions, a theme is provided for the storytellers each day, as it is in Boccaccio's book.

III. The *Heptameron* is also like Chaucer's *The Canterbury Tales* in that the storytellers are characterized sufficiently enough that we can see the connections between teller and tale.
   A. Each story is followed by a general discussion by the 10 storytellers, so that we get to know them very well.
   B. The storytellers tell their stories in response to others' stories, as they do in Chaucer, so that the entire work becomes an extended dialogue.

IV. There are unique features of Marguerite's book as well.
   A. In the *Heptameron,* all stories must be true. Historians have validated parts or all of about 20 of the stories so far.
   B. The stories must be told in the plain style, without rhetorical adornment.
   C. Marguerite's tellers are evenly divided: five men and five women, all from the same aristocratic class (like Boccaccio's young people) but bringing different perspectives to the questions raised by the stories (like Chaucer's pilgrims), making for lively and interesting debates.

V. The overriding themes of the stories are love, sexuality, and the abuses of the clergy.
   A. The clergy theme is not introduced for its own sake; rather, Marguerite, a correspondent of Erasmus and Rabelais, agreed with them that the Catholic Church's insistence on celibacy for the clergy implied the inferiority of marriage and of women—a subject also treated by the Wife of Bath in *The Canterbury Tales*.
   B. The themes of the book touch on the "Quarrel about Women" in the Renaissance: their status, identity, subjectivity, and place in a patriarchal culture. The themes are not so much about love as about rape, seduction, incest, and other infringements of the sex and marriage codes in aristocratic Europe.
      1. Rape and seduction are frequent themes because many of the stories involve lovers who are from different classes and cannot marry, which may lead to violent explosions of repressed feelings.

    2. Platonic, courtly love can also serve as a cover for physical attraction, tempting lovers into thinking that they are safer than they really are, as in Dante's story in *Inferno* about Paolo and Francesca.
VI. Parlamente's story in the collection brings both motifs together.
    A. The story is about Amador and Florida, who try to be platonic lovers but whose story ends in one attempt at seduction and one of rape on Amador's part—either an indication that he was never what he seemed or that he is the victim of repressed sexuality.
    B. Modern critics (e.g., Patricia Francis Cholakian) see the story as transitioning from a chivalric romance into a story from a woman's point of view about women's struggles and choices.
        1. Florida has to make a lonely and difficult choice between love and duty, as so many heroines will in future literature.
        2. In the process of telling her story, Marguerite is carving out a space for women to tell their own stories from their own point of view.
    C. The context of the story heightens these themes.
        1. The story is told in reaction to another story about a lover who kept his love at a Platonic level but died of frustration.
        2. This leads to a number of different opinions on the meaning of the story.
    D. In the discussion following Parlamente's story, there is lively disagreement about its meaning, divided partially along gender lines.
        1. What emerges in the debate is that honor for men means dominance and conquest, while for women it means (narrowly) chastity and (more importantly) managing to maintain personal integrity.
        2. For women, the matter is even more complicated by the fact that their own sexual desire is likely to be misread by men as a sign of moral laxity, causing every woman truly in love to be tugged in two different directions simultaneously.
        3. In terms of narrative, the conflict can suggest two different endings to either of the stories discussed here.
VII. Other critics (e.g., Betty J. Davis) have focused less on the stories than on the relationships among the storytellers and have come to similar

conclusions. Parlamente and her husband, Hircan, make an interesting example of how complex relationships among tellers can be.
- **A.** They are married, and their marriage seems a viable one.
- **B.** They disagree, however, about the question of sexual morality: she condemns adultery, while he feels that pleasure should be taken whenever it is available.
- **C.** There are oblique references to affairs that Hircan has had, which Parlamente treats with what Davis calls a "mechanism of denial."
- **D.** In this way, the relationships among the storytellers replicate the relationships treated in the stories themselves.

VIII. The *Heptameron* is full of the kind of complexities we encounter in good literature all the time.
- **A.** Every story is capable of multiple interpretations, depending on listener or reader perspective.
- **B.** The *Heptameron* anticipates modern fiction in that it demands our awareness of who is saying what to be able to make our own judgments about meaning.
- **C.** The readings we have given the text in this lecture are fairly new ones teased out by feminists over the past three decades.

Essential Reading:

Marguerite of Navarre, *Heptameron.*

Supplementary Reading:

Patricia Francis Cholakian, *Rape and Writing in the Heptameron of Marguerite de Navarre.*

Betty J. Davis, *The Storytellers.*

Questions to Consider:

1. As you read these stories and notice the interaction that occurs among the tellers between tales, try to decide whether attitudes about women, marriage, sex, adultery, and the clergy divide up strictly along gender lines, or whether there are characters who cross over to help defend points of view largely put forward by the other gender. If there are any such crossover characters, do their stories support their complicated positions on the central questions of the collection?

2. Who are the most chauvinistic of the men among the group at the monastery? Does the narrator undercut them in any way, or are their points of view allowed to stand without authorial contestation? What rhetorical points does the narrator make in treating these characters the way she does?

Lecture Twenty-One
Shakespeare

Scope: The subject of this lecture is Shakespeare. After a brief account of drama in other cultures, we consider Shakespeare's place in English drama, focusing on his use of language. We treat the ways in which characters are individualized in Shakespeare's plays by their speech patterns, and then we treat some of the other ways Shakespeare uses language and some of the contributions he has made to modern English—including invented words, phrases that have made their way into common parlance, and his metaphoric habit of thinking. We also consider Keats's idea of negative capability as a way of illustrating Shakespeare's personal reticence in the plays, which may take up many different issues, but always allows the audience to make up its own mind; this, in part, accounts for the universality of the plays. The generalizations of the lecture are illustrated with an examination of the famous "Tomorrow" soliloquy from *Macbeth*.

Outline

I. Almost every culture has invented or reinvented drama, many of them prior to the Elizabethans and Shakespeare.

A. The Greeks, whose tragedies we looked at in Lecture Seven, were the first, as early as the 5th century B.C.E.

B. India had its Golden Age of drama in the 4th and 5th centuries (the Gupta period), featuring Kālidāsa, who is sometimes called the Shakespeare of Indian theater.

C. Chinese drama emerged in the 13th century, and in Japan Nō drama flourished two centuries before Shakespeare.

D. Shakespeare's own drama had a long prehistory in England.

   1. The origins of English drama were probably dramatized readings of the Gospels during Mass, which led to the *mystery* and *morality plays*.

   2. English drama also had strong roots in village festivals, which mocked town dignitaries and officials.

   3. This purely native tradition produced some interesting—if relatively undisciplined—plays, but it was given shape and

structure by the rediscovery of Plautus, Terence, and Seneca during the Renaissance.
   4. The "university wits," including Christopher Marlowe, absorbed this classical influence at Cambridge and then came down to London to write plays a few years before Shakespeare began his career.

II. No treatment of origins, however, can account for the achievement of Shakespeare, which in many ways defies ordinary categories. Perhaps the best way to get a sense of his greatness is to do so through a consideration of his language.
   A. Each of Shakespeare's many characters speak in individual accents and rhythms.
      1. Shakespeare seems to have understood each of his characters well enough to know what it would be like to see the world through their eyes; every speech is not just in character, but a revelation of character.
      2. John Keats, a Romantic poet, said that Shakespeare had *negative capability*: the ability to empty out one's own ego enough to be able to become a character in a play.
      3. Shakespeare's range of characters is extraordinary: from the pidgin English of Caliban to the philosophical language of Hamlet—and everything in between—there is a virtually complete cross-section of people in his world throughout his plays.
      4. Doctors, sailors, statesmen, soldiers, lawyers, and many others have written books showing that Shakespeare must have been one of them, because he always gets the language of every profession right.
   B. Shakespeare could do this in part because of his amazing vocabulary and his delight in language.
      1. When he could not find the right word, he invented or redefined one.
      2. He also made hundreds of expressions proverbial, so that most of us quote Shakespeare several times a day, even if we do not recognize the source of the expression.
   C. Words had a lot to do on the Elizabethan stage, which had no scenery or artificial lighting, so that words had to set the scene and the atmosphere. An audience in Elizabethan England went to *hear*

a play, not to *see* one (the root of the word "audience" is *to hear*).

    D. Shakespeare also had a metaphoric habit of mind, which means that his plays are full of amazing, brilliant, and illuminating comparisons.

III. Shakespeare's personal reticence—a part of his negative capability—is responsible for the objective point of view taken by his plays.
    A. After 400 years of intense scrutiny, we still know almost nothing about Shakespeare's personal life and beliefs.
        1. In his plays, points of view are expressed by individual characters, but in the context of the entire play, individual points of view tend to be balanced by those of other characters. *As You Like It* is a wonderful debate about the values of the *pastoral*, without the playwright endorsing any single one of them.
        2. This is one of the characteristics of his plays that have made them nearly universal, since they are so open-ended that each age and individual is free to interpret them.
    B. Jorge Luis Borges, the Argentinean short story writer, in a tribute to Shakespeare entitled "Everything and Nothing," suggests that Shakespeare shares with God the ability to be "many and no one."

IV. As an illustration of Shakespeare's gift for language, we can consider *Macbeth* and its most famous soliloquy, the "Tomorrow" speech.
    A. Macbeth, like many Shakespearean tragic protagonists, is thrust into a role that he cannot comfortably play: that of a cold-blooded regicide. He is, as the actor Ian McKellen says, "a murderer with a conscience."
        1. Macbeth is partly aware of this before the murder of King Duncan, and assured of it afterwards.
        2. Macbeth spends the rest of the play trying to kill his conscience, but he also knows that in doing so he will be giving up everything that ordinarily makes life worth living: friends, feasts, loyalty, and love.
        3. It is at this point, immediately following the death of his wife, that Macbeth delivers his famous "Tomorrow and tomorrow and tomorrow" soliloquy.
    B. The speech itself incorporates in both sound and metaphor Macbeth's sense of eternal recurrence and utter pointlessness.

1. Life for him has no substance: it is a "walking shadow," a "poor player," a story told by an idiot.
   2. Perhaps no bleaker speech has ever been uttered in drama.
   3. What Macbeth has done to himself in trying to be more than he is helps to make him a hero in the Elizabethan sense of the word, despite all the terrible things he has done.
- **C.** Macbeth still matters to us because he is utterly and ruthlessly honest with himself about what he has done and become; Shakespeare's words allow us to be inside his soul.
- **D.** No one in the history of English drama has ever had this magnificent combination of language and the ability to see life as a whole. Shakespeare deserves his place as the best poet and dramatist in our language.

Essential Reading:

Shakespeare's plays.

Supplementary Reading:

Maurice Charney, *How to Read Shakespeare.*

Edward Quinn, *How to Read Shakespearean Tragedy.*

Philip Schwyzer, *Archaeologies of English Renaissance Literature.*

Stanley Wells, *Shakespeare: The Writer and His Work.*

Questions to Consider:

1. Pick a character from a Shakespeare play who has only a single (or at least a very infrequent) appearance. What can you tell about him or her simply from the way he or she uses words? Then put the character back into the context of the entire play and try to see how language characterizes the individual and how their actions in the play reinforce and validate the way that character speaks. What does this tell us about Shakespeare's negative capability as defined by John Keats?
2. It has been asserted by critics that the primary difference between Macbeth and Lady Macbeth is that he has an imagination which she entirely lacks. How does this difference work itself out in the play?

Lecture Twenty-Two
Cervantes's *Don Quixote*

Scope: This lecture deals with Cervantes's *Don Quixote*. We begin by defining the novel as a genre that attempts to reflect the real world in which we live. The contrasting genre in Cervantes's time was the *romance*, which could include the fabulous and which was usually about knights-errant. Don Quixote represents the romance perspective on events, while his squire, Sancho Panza, represents the novelistic perspective. The contrasting points of view raise questions about the way we read both books and reality and the ways in which they read us as we read them. The framing techniques of the novel reinforce this theme, which we will call *perspectivism*, the idea that all perception is conditioned by our past experiences. We conclude with an acknowledgement of the ways in which *Don Quixote* has been a seminal novel, inspiring and modeling every future reinvention of the novel in the Western world.

Outline

I. While not the first novel in history, *Don Quixote* is one of the first in the Western world and has been by far the most influential. The book is a contemporary of Shakespeare's *King Lear* (1608).

  A. A *novel* is an extended narrative in prose that gives a more or less realistic picture of everyday life. It comes from the Italian *novella*, which has as part of its definition a correspondence with the way we perceive the world (e.g., the stories of Boccaccio and Marguerite of Navarre).

  B. Its contrasting genre in the Middle Ages and Renaissance was the romance, which was also a prose narrative but which could include the fabulous (e.g., The Wife of Bath's Tale in *The Canterbury Tales*). The romance was the most popular literary genre of the Middle Ages.

  C. The contrast between the romance and the novel is built into *Don Quixote*.
    1. The man who becomes Don Quixote, a middle-aged poverty-stricken aristocrat, reads so many romances that it dries up his

brain; he confuses the distinction between reality and fiction and decides to become a knight-errant like the ones he has read about.
   2. Inscribed into the novel is the contrast between the romances he has read and the things that happen to him when he tries to become a knight-errant in the real world.
II. There are two perspectives on everything in the novel.
   A. There is the romance perspective of Don Quixote, who sees everything as though it is part of a knightly adventure.
   B. There is the perspective of the narrator, who reminds us that what Quixote takes for a giant is really a windmill or that an army is really a flock of sheep.
   C. It is important to remember, however, that Don Quixote is not *pretending*; he is a true psychotic, which means that he experiences reality in a different way from the narrator, the reader, and everyone else in his world.
III. After Don Quixote's first series of adventures, Cervantes gives him a squire—Sancho Panza—who is an exact opposite of Quixote in almost every way.
   A. Once Sancho has become Quixote's companion, the novelistic and romance perspectives become built into the narrative itself.
   B. This is seen in the adventure against the giant.
      1. Don Quixote insists on his vision of reality while Sancho protests that the giant is really a windmill.
      2. When Don Quixote is knocked to the ground by the windmill, he explains to Sancho that an evil sorcerer *changed* the giant into a windmill at the last moment to deprive the knight of the glory that should have been his.
IV. Cervantes published the first part of *Don Quixote* in 1605.
   A. Most of the first part is frankly comic, and scenes from this part have been mined by other authors ever since.
   B. Part I works by having Don Quixote lose touch with reality because of his reading, getting beaten up by the world around him and dragging his squire with him in the process (e.g., the misadventure at the inn).
   C. A spurious sequel by an unknown author was published in 1614, prompting Cervantes to write his own sequel in 1615, in which he

kills off Don Quixote. Part II has proven to be the more interesting part for readers and critics.

V. The second part of the novel raises a series of interesting questions which can tease the reader into or out of thought.

A. The first is the question of the values of sanity and insanity.
  1. Don Quixote is clearly mad, but he is also by far the best, noblest, and most charitable character in the book.
  2. This question is intensified as we watch the hard-headed, practical Sancho Panza begin to absorb some of the values of his addle-headed master—and become a better person for it in the process.
  3. Likewise, Quixote begins to temper some of his most rash misreadings by his association with Sancho.

B. A second question concerns the way we view the world around us.
  1. In every episode, Don Quixote and Sancho Panza are looking at the same thing, but they see it differently.
  2. In many important ways, what matters is not the thing in itself, but the reading given it by a perceiver.
  3. The way each individual reads the world is the result of all of his or her experiences across a lifetime. Quixote and Sancho read things differently because their experiences—and hence their needs—are different.
  4. Every interpretation of an object or event tells us more about the interpreter than it does about the object or event itself—which is part of what critics mean when they say that a book reads us as we read the book.

C. *Don Quixote* has been read in an amazing variety of ways by different readers in different historical periods.
  1. For the first century after it was written, it was read as a comic work about a man out of step with his contemporaries' reading of reality—a reflection of an age of social norms and values.
  2. The Romantics saw Quixote as a superior being crushed by a brutal conformist society—a reflection of Romantic values.
  3. Modern readers tend to see the work as *perspectivist*, in which Cervantes endorses neither the novelistic ("real") world of Sancho nor the romantic ("psychotic") world of Quixote; rather, Cervantes shows that the meaning of anything resides in the way we interpret it, which is in turn based on our past experiences and choices.

VI. *Don Quixote* uses frames in a different way than other framed stories we have covered in this course, such as *1001 Nights* and *The Canterbury Tales*.
  - **A.** One of the problems of the novel in its early days was that of authority.
    1. It seems true, but it is made up by someone.
    2. The question is: What, if any, kind of "truth" does it contain?
    3. Most early novels tried to make themselves feel like true stories.
  - **B.** *Don Quixote* uses some of the same techniques other early novelists would use to make the story seem true and factual, but he uses them in a tongue-in-cheek manner.
    1. The first eight chapters were presumably written by an editor who has combed records to bring this story to light.
    2. In Chapter Eight, the editor breaks off the narration, saying that he has run out of information from his archives on Don Quixote.
    3. In Chapter Nine, the editor tells an elaborate story about finding an Arabic manuscript which he buys, has someone translate into Castillian, and passes on to us.
    4. This technique gives three different points of view on each episode, reinforcing the perspectivist theme; readers also have their own angle of vision.

VII. Every time the novel has been reinvented in the Western world, it has gone back to *Don Quixote* and used different aspects for the recreation of the novel.
  - **A.** Henry Fielding borrowed heavily from *Don Quixote* in *Joseph Andrews* and said that *Tom Jones*, which incorporates parts of *Don Quixote*, was written in imitation of Cervantes.
  - **B.** Flaubert said that *Don Quixote* was in his blood from before he could even read; his great Realist novel, *Madame Bovary*, is in many ways a rewrite of Cervantes's novel.
  - **C.** Joseph Conrad, in helping to invent the psychological Realist novel, rewrote *Madame Bovary* in his *Lord Jim*, making it another child of Cervantes's book.
  - **D.** F. Scott Fitzgerald's *The Great Gatsby* is an American version of *Lord Jim,* which is an English version of *Madame Bovary,* which is a French version of *Don Quixote*.

E. Jorge Luis Borges will say that the Postmodernist novel was born in the moment in *Don Quixote* when Don Quixote himself watches copies of *Don Quixote* Part I come off a printing press in Part II.

1. This pivotal moment implies both an infinite regress and a hint that the line between fiction and reality may not be as clear as we think it is.
2. In *Don Quixote* art imitates life imitating art.

F. Every recreation of the novel ever since has gone back to *Don Quixote* for inspiration, making this perhaps the most important novel in history—at least in the Western world. *The Washington Post* chose Don Quixote as the most important novel of the millennium.

Essential Reading:

Cervantes, *Don Quixote*.

Supplementary Reading:

John J. Allen, *Don Quixote: Hero or Fool?*
Margaret Church, *Don Quixote: The Knight of La Mancha*.
Carroll B. Johnson, *Don Quixote: The Quest for Modern Fiction*.

Questions to Consider:

1. The episode of the Cave of Montesinos in Part II has always been considered a turning point in the novel, suggesting that Don Quixote is finding it ever more difficult to maintain his view of himself as a knight-errant and at the same time showing how he has been able to manufacture the illusions that have kept him going so far. Read this episode with special care, and then try to decide at precisely what point, psychologically, this occurs.
2. One of the most-admired aspects of the novel is the way in which, as the journey continues, Sancho Panza becomes more like his master and Don Quixote more like his squire. Pay particular attention to the relationship between the two as the novel progresses, and see if you can identify some of the major points at which it is clear that the two are becoming ever more like each other.

Lecture Twenty-Three
Molière's Plays

Scope: In this lecture we treat Molière, the 17th-century French comic playwright. We first review some of the principles of Neoclassicism in Europe, including common sense, universality, rationality, and social rather than individual norms. Then we describe some of the ways in which the classical heritage had been condensed into rules for Neoclassical playwrights, including *utilite et dulce* (usefulness and delight), verisimilitude, the use of type characters rather than individualized ones, and decorum. We will then recreate a typical Molière comedy, showing how in normative social contexts deviants—young girls who have read too many sentimental novels, hypochondriacs, the overly zealous in religion, misers and hypocrites—are presumably ridiculed back into conformity. We also notice some of the ways Molière manipulates this formula and his cynicism about the possibility of humans learning from experience. We conclude with a reminder of Molière's talent for writing scenes that really work on stage.

Outline

I. With Molière we are in what is usually called the Neoclassical Age (c. 1660–1770) in Western literature.
   A. The Neoclassical Age was based on the values and forms of the literature of Greece and Rome; the ancestry of Molière's plays, for example, reaches back to those of Plautus and Terence of Rome.
      1. The act of imitation did not involve slavish copying.
      2. Instead, it was an interpretive use of older writers to promote values that the period admired or needed.
   B. The values that the Neoclassical Age found in the ancient writers included a *social* rather than a *personal* orientation to nearly every issue: intellect, reason, balance, symmetry, order, and restraint.
      1. This age had just emerged from a century and a half of bloody religious wars, fought over interpretations of the Bible and featuring the primacy of the individual conscience.
      2. So this age was looking for values based on reason, empirical evidence, and common sense, along with group rather than individual norms.

3. It was an age that sought for universals—those things that were true for all people in all times and places; it rejected the odd, the eccentric, and the subjective.
4. The approved values were thus rationality, restraint, conformity to social norms, and common sense.
5. They were also suspicious of the passions: anger, love, and even hilarity.
6. There was not much love poetry in this age; even Molière's comedies push the lovers aside to make room for other concerns (unlike Shakespeare, who makes lovers the center of his comedies).

II. The age also produced a series of rules to be observed while imitating classical literature. We will briefly consider four of them.
   A. The first rule is *utilite et dulce* ("usefulness and delight"), which decreed that literature teaches useful lessons via entertainment and pleasure.
      1. One of the favorite such techniques in the period was *satire*: using laughter to bring deviants and eccentrics back into normative belief and values.
      2. Molière himself expresses this view in his preface to *Tartuffe*.
   B. The second rule is *verisimilitude*; hence, literature must be lifelike so that connections with real life can easily be made. A corollary of this rule was *the principle of the unities*, which specified that a play must treat no more than 24 hours of elapsed time, must occur in a single setting, and must have a single plot.
   C. The third rule made character *types* rather than individuals normative, to make them as widely applicable as possible.
      1. Molière's plays are full of such types, which go back to classical drama.
      2. Some examples are the jealous older husband of a young wife, the tricky servant, the miser, the hypochondriac, the braggart soldier.
   D. The fourth rule is that of *decorum*.
      1. Comedy should ridicule folly and deal with contemporary settings, characters, and language.
      2. Tragedy should punish vice and deal with old stories about noble characters in noble language.

III. In following these rules, Molière's comedies are relatively formulaic. In each, a deviant or eccentric is treated satirically in order to bring him back into line with normalcy.
   A. This is in stark contrast to the comedies of Shakespeare, in which the deviant lovers are generally valorized at the expense of their corrupt social, political, and legal context; in Molière, that social order is normative.
   B. In an early one-act play, *The High-Browed Ladies*, two young women who have read too many romances expect to be wooed in ways they have learned from their reading. Their wooers bring them back into line with social norms by tricking them into thinking that their valets are the wooers and then exposing their error, teaching them their useful lesson.
   C. In *The Imaginary Invalid*, a hypochondriac is ruining his family's life (and his daughter's love life) with his excessive concern for his health. He is the deviant who needs to be brought back into line.
   D. In *Tartuffe*, Molière deals with a much more controversial topic: a man who is excessively religious and uses his religion to tyrannize his family. Molière had to rewrite it three times to get it past the authorities and onto the stage.
      1. The central character is Orgon, who turns to religion as a way of controlling his family and maintaining his importance.
      2. The play suggests that one can be *too* religious, which offended a great number of people.
      3. In each Molière comedy, there is one character who expresses the social norm. In this one it is Cléante, who describes the proper and socially acceptable way of being religious; this idea also offended many people.
   E. In *The Miser*, a man disrupts his family life with his excessive avarice.
IV. While Molière uses a basic plot, like Shakespeare, he is capable of amazing variations on the same essential structure.
   A. In *The Misanthrope*, a man named Alceste, becomes irritated by the hypocrisy and social glibness of his circle.
   B. He wants people to be honest and to always tell each other the absolute truth.
      1. As always, the social order wins over the deviant individual.

    2. In this play, Molière works a variation on a theme by allowing us more sympathy with the misanthrope, Alceste, than is usual, so that we feel ambivalent about his defeat at the play's end.
V. Molière also turns out to be somewhat cynical about the possibility of curing his deviants and eccentrics.
    A. So many of his plays need miracles, royal intervention, or some other suspension of ordinary laws of cause-and-effect in order to bring about the happy ending.
    B. If anyone learns anything from a Molière comedy, it has to be the audience, which can see its own flaws in his stage characters and go to work on them.
VI. Molière spent virtually his entire life in the theater, and he has an absolutely unerring sense of what works on stage and what is funny.
    A. From the smallest exchange of lines to more extended dialogue to stage business and the structure of entire plays, his touch is unerring.
    B. In *The Miser,* a dialogue occurs between the miser and his son in which the miser talks about his gold, and the son thinks that he is talking about the son's fiancée.
        1. The dialogue makes perfect sense to both of them, even though they become increasingly exasperated with each other's obtuseness.
        2. The audience, which knows what is going on, finds the exchange amazingly funny.
    C. Molière consistently controls humor in all of his plays. No one has ever mastered the theater as well as he.

Essential Reading:
Molière, the comedies.

Supplementary Reading:
W. D. Howarth, *Molière: A Playwright and His Audience*.
Robert McBride, *The Sceptical Vision of Molière*.

Questions to Consider:

1. Is it easier to see, having read and studied the comedies of Molière, why this age would have read *Don Quixote* as a comic work about a man out of step with his society? In what ways would the story of Don Quixote have made a good plot for one of Molière's comedies? How do you think he would have treated Quixote? Like his miser, his imaginary invalid, or like Alceste?

2. What kinds of characters are his lovers in his plays? Are they similar from one play to another? Are they of interest as characters in their own right, or are they intentionally bland, making good contrasts with the main business of the plays? Are they interesting comic characters?

Lecture Twenty-Four
Voltaire's *Candide*

Scope: Voltaire's *Candide* is the subject of this lecture. *Candide*'s subtitle is *Optimism*, and we begin with an account of that popular 18th-century philosophy, which asserted that "this is the best of all possible worlds." We then recount Voltaire's rejection of Optimism, based especially on the Lisbon earthquake of 1755. *Candide*, a prose fiction rather than a novel, is a debate about the validity of "the-best-of-all-worlds" hypothesis, with Dr. Pangloss defending the idea and Martin the pessimist attacking it. The book in many ways, including in its tidy structure, is a refutation of Optimism. In exploring the book's last chapter, we consider the three key items in an alternative world view: the metaphor of the mice on the galley, the lessons of the contented Turkish farmer, and Candide's resolve that "we must cultivate our garden." We conclude by suggesting some important and still-provocative questions raised by the book.

Outline

I. Voltaire is an important figure in the Neoclassical Age.
  A. He was a voluminous author in many genres.
  B. He was a perpetual critic of the French government and the Catholic Church.
  C. He was later heralded as someone who had prepared the way for the French Revolution.

II. The subtitle of *Candide* is *Optimism,* a popular 18th-century theory that asserted that "this is the best of all possible worlds."
  A. Optimism argues that since God is both omnipotent and benevolent, he necessarily created the best of all worlds.
   1. Certain conditions in the world—famine, flood, earthquakes, disease—are necessarily a part of this best of all worlds, each promoting some greater good of which we, from our limited perspectives, might be unaware.
   2. The theory was generated in its most complex form by the German philosopher Gottfried Leibniz, but it was adopted,

simplified, and endorsed by a wide variety of 18th-century theorists, including Christian Wolff and Alexander Pope.

   B. Voltaire himself was an Optimist in his early years, but he found it increasingly difficult to square the immense amount of suffering in the world with the theory.
      1. He abandoned the theory altogether after the Lisbon earthquake on November 1, 1755.
      2. *Candide* is his explicit refutation of the theory.

III. *Candide* is a prose fiction, not a novel.
   A. It has too much coincidence in it to be entirely plausible.
   B. Its characters are not fully developed in novelistic ways.
   C. It is extremely unlikely that its protagonists could have endured all that they do and still survive, even though many of the events in the book did actually happen to someone.
   D. The book owes debts to other genres, however.
      1. It is partly a *picaresque* story, in which a protagonist travels from place to place getting in and out of events that are not tied together very tightly in terms of cause and effect.
      2. It is a satire on human efforts to comprehend and explain life.
      3. It is partly an Oriental tale, like some of those from the *1001 Nights*, which had recently been translated into French.

IV. The spokesman for Optimism in *Candide* is Dr. Pangloss, who tries to find the necessary reason for *everything* in the universe.
   A. At the outset, Pangloss is the tutor of young Candide, and he teaches a reduced and satirical version of Leibnitz's theory. He teaches not only about the best of all possible worlds, but tries to work out the specific way in which everything in the world serves some greater good.
   B. When Candide is kicked out of the Baron's castle for being caught kissing Cunegonde, the Baron's daughter, he gets to test Pangloss's theory out in the world.
   C. Pangloss continues to reappear to reaffirm the Optimist theory.
   D. Partway through the book, Candide acquires a companion, Martin, who says that he is a *Manichean* who believes that the earth is a battle ground between the forces of good and evil. Martin pessimistically argues that this may be the worst of all possible worlds.

V. *Candide* has a very tidy structure that reflects its satirical nature:
   A. Its 30 chapters are symmetrically arranged.
      1. Ten chapters occur in the Old World.
      2. Ten chapters occur in the New World.
      3. The last 10 chapters return to the Old World.
   B. In a world as random and chaotic as the one in which Candide lives, the artful symmetry seems another misguided human effort to impose an order than cannot possibly reflect reality.

VI. At the book's end the theory of Optimism has been pretty thoroughly exploded. The last chapter of the novel suggests a new theory to put in its place.
   A. A dervish that Candide and his companions visit tells them that the purposes of creation are none of their business, and that mice on a galley should not even ask whether they are comfortable or not.
   B. A Turkish farmer tells them that working his own land keeps him from the three great human evils: boredom, vice, and poverty.
   C. So the little group goes back to its farm, where Candide keeps repeating that "We must cultivate our garden."
   D. While this last chapter can be read in a variety of ways, several items need to be kept in mind.
      1. The mice-in-the-galley metaphor suggests that the universe was not made for us; therefore any speculations we make about its purpose and nature will be as foolish as mice speculating on the purpose or nature of the galley in which they happen to be.
      2. Work can keep us from speculating too much and getting ourselves tangled up in useless hypotheses about why we are here and what we are supposed to be doing.
      3. "Cultivating our garden" is the metaphor for whatever work we do, and it will prevent us from worrying too much about good and evil or whether this is the best of all possible worlds.

VII. Beyond natural disasters, *Candide* contains a lot of *human* cruelty and indifference to others' suffering, the origins of which are a little harder to pin down.
   A. About midway through the book, Candide and his servant discover Eldorado, a utopia in South America.

1. Candide, however, is not content there, and he leaves to return to Europe with the wealth from Eldorado.
   2. Does a hostile environment—like the one in Europe—produce the cruel, greedy, prideful human nature we meet there, while a friendlier environment produces kinder people, as it seems to do in Eldorado?
   3. Is human nature instead as fixed as the predatory habits of a hawk, as Martin suggests?
   4. Much of the suffering in the book is produced not by nature's attacks on people, but by people's attacks on each other.
   5. So whose fault is this? And what can be done about it, if anything?
B. Questions like these remind us that *Candide* is really a debate about ideas—a philosophical tale in which the intellectual debate is more important than characters or plot. These questions still resonate today.

Essential Reading:
Voltaire, *Candide*.

Supplementary Reading:
Robert M. Adams, *Candide, or, Optimism: A Fresh Translation, Backgrounds, and Criticism*.

Haydn Mason, *Candide: Optimism Demolished*.

Questions to Consider:
1. Some of Candide's lowest points in the book are caused not by natural events but by human cruelty and/or indifference. In what way is that a separate theme from that of Optimism? To what extent is it integrated into the questions about the nature of the universe we live in?
2. What, exactly, do you understand Candide to mean when he says that "We must cultivate our garden"? If he means it as a metaphor (and not as a literal garden), how would it translate into your life?

Timeline
(Lectures 13–24)

C.E.

618–907	T'ang Dynasty in China.
629	Buddhist monk Tripitaka travels to India.
c. 699–761	Wang Wei.
701–62	Li Po.
712–70	Tu Fu.
750	Muslim capital established in Baghdad.
c. 759	The *Man'yōshū*.
786–809	Caliphate of Harûn el-Rashid in Baghdad.
c. 905	The *Kokinshū*.
c. 1022	*The Tale of Genji*.
1271–95	Marco Polo travels to China.
14th century	Earliest surviving manuscript of *1001 Nights*.
1321	Dante's *Divine Comedy*.
1348–50	The Black Death in Europe.
1353	Boccaccio's *Decameron*.
1386–1400	Chaucer's *The Canterbury Tales*.
c. 1450	Guttenberg's movable-type printing press.
1492	Columbus's first voyage to the New World.
1517	Protestant Reformation begins in Europe.

1550	Wu Ch'eng-en's *Monkey*.
1558	Marguerite of Navarre's *Heptameron* published.
1571	Battle of Lepanto between Spain and the Turks.
c. 1600	Shakespeare's plays.
1605	*Don Quixote*, Part I.
1611	The King James Bible.
1615	*Don Quixote*, Part II.
1664	Molière's *Tartuffe*.
1751	First edition of French *Encyclopédie*.
1755	The Lisbon Earthquake.
1759	Voltaire's *Candide*.
1789	Beginning of the French Revolution.

Glossary
(Lectures 13–24)

allegory: An extended metaphor in which characters and objects inside a narrative are equated with meanings that lie outside them. In simple allegory an abstraction is usually personified and named after the abstraction—e.g., Lust, Charity, or Anger—and then has to behave in accordance with the dictates of the abstraction. As noted in Lecture Sixteen, Dante uses allegory in a much more complicated way to suggest a variety of meanings which lie outside the narrative of the *Divine Comedy*.

anti-hero: A protagonist of a novel or play whose attributes are generally the inverse of those considered heroic by his or her culture. He or she can either be the object of satire or a criticism of the values of the culture in which he or she appears.

bodhisáttva: One who in Buddhism has achieved the status of a Buddha but who elects to return to earth to help others in their quest for salvation from the cycle of birth and death; or one who is well on the way to ultimate enlightenment but still has several lives to live through to finish the journey.

carpe diem: Literally meaning, "seize the day." The phrase comes from the Roman poet Horace, and it has been generalized to refer to any literary work that advocates the enjoyment of the present moment, since the future is uncertain, and death awaits us all.

choka: A Japanese verse form of indeterminate length, alternating between five- and seven-syllable lines and ending with two seven-syllable lines. It does not deliberately rhyme.

decorum: Appropriateness of style, character, and action to a particular genre. In the Neoclassical period, there were many rules governing decorum in a work, including the ideas that a comedy should ridicule folly, feature contemporary settings and characters, use ordinary language, and end happily. Molière follows the rules of decorum to the letter and uses them to write brilliant comedies.

engo: A word cluster in a Japanese poem which has metaphoric resonance. For example, "blossom," "flower," "fade," and "color" in a poem by Ono no Komachi in Lecture Fourteen suggests that something is being compared to a flower.

fabliau: A humorous story, French in origin, usually about middle- or lower-class characters, often bawdy in nature, and which frequently involves trickery of one sort or another. In Chaucer's *The Canterbury Tales*, the tales told by the Miller, Reeve, Summoner, Merchant, Shipman, and Manciple all belong to this genre.

frame: A narrative structure which contains within it other stories, making the stories themselves "stories-within-a story." The device allows characters within the frame to tell the narratives, thus distancing the author from the tales themselves and from the characters who tell them. In this unit of our course, Chaucer, the *1001 Nights,* and Marguerite of Navarre make the most compelling use of frames, but they occur in other works as well.

Genji: A generic title for one born in the imperial succession but made a commoner by the bestowal of a surname.

haiku: A Japanese verse form of three lines, the first and third containing five syllables and the second line seven syllables. It is really the first three lines of a *tanka*.

Heian period: The period in Japanese history when Heian was its capital city, 794–1185. During most of this period the emperor was controlled by the powerful Fujiwara family.

Jātaka: A collection of stories of the 550 lives through which Gautama Buddha passed before being born as Prince Siddhārtha in 563 B.C. Its final version was achieved as late as the 4th century C.E., but many of its stories are much older. It is written in the Indian dialect of Pali, and its stories are framed by discussions between the Buddha and his followers. Some of the stories found their way into later collections, including the *1001 Nights.*

Kathāsaritsāgara: The most famous collection of Sanskrit stories, this one (whose title translates as *Ocean of the Rivers of Story*) dates from the 11th century, although most of its stories are much older. The collection has a double frame, and the technique of nested stories within stories is typical. It exercised a great influence on the *1001 Nights,* and it inspired the title of Salman Rushdie's book, *Haroun and the Sea of Stories.*

Manicheanism: An early Christian heresy, derived probably from Persia, which posits that all of history is a struggle between two deities (one good and one evil), making every human heart and conscience a battle ground. Martin in Voltaire's *Candide* claims to be a Manichean; he certainly is a pessimist.

maya: Illusion in Hindu and Buddhist thought.

mystery play: A medieval religious play whose plot is taken from a Scriptural story. It grew out of liturgical drama and was generally performed at festivals by trade guilds.

mono no aware: A Japanese phrase which translates as "a sensitivity to things." Some Japanese critics assert that this is the ultimate value and meaning of *The Tale of Genji*.

morality play: A dramatized allegory in which abstract virtues and vices appear in personified form, usually fighting over a human soul. *Everyman* (c. 1500) is the best-known example in English.

negative capability: A critical term devised by John Keats, the Romantic poet, to describe Shakespeare's ability to empty out his own ego to become fully the character he created. The character thus becomes an independent creation, not simply a manifestation of some aspect of its creator.

novel: An extended narrative, usually in prose, which in its earliest manifestations in virtually all cultures purports to give a realistic representation of people, manners, and life by avoiding the conventions usually associated with poetry or drama and substituting for them a depiction of the world "as it really is." Wu Ch'eng-en's *Monkey* is an exception to this tendency toward realism, but *The Tale of Genji* and *Don Quixote* are novels by this definition.

Optimism: An 18th-century philosophical theory, generated by the German philosopher Gottfried Leibniz, which in its simplified and popularized form in the period came to be known by its slogan, "This is the best of all possible worlds." The theory is satirically described and refuted in Voltaire's *Candide*.

pastoral: A genre of literature dealing with shepherds and country life (the Latin word for shepherd is *pastor*). The genre is based on subject matter rather than form, so it may occur in poetry, prose, or drama. In part, it set city living against country living and examined the values of each. Shakespeare's *As You Like It* is a pastoral comedy.

Pañcatantra: A collection of stories from India dating from the 2nd or 3rd centuries, featuring frame stories for each of its five books and nested stories within stories. Some of its stories and perhaps some of the techniques of the *1001 Nights* probably were inspired by this book.

persona: Literally, a mask. In literary criticism, the term is used to define a second self created by an author whose voice we hear in the poem or story. In Lecture Thirteen Li Po's *persona* is described as madcap and reckless—that of a "fallen immortal." It is his voice that we hear in most of Li Po's poems.

picaresque: A 16th-century Spanish story gives this genre its name. It refers to a kind of story, usually about a somewhat lovable rogue, who travels from place to place getting into and out of scrapes. The *picaro,* in playing pranks on local authorities, gives the author opportunity for satire. The episodes of a picaresque story are generally loosely connected: the *picaro* simply leaves one place and winds up in another. *Don Quixote* owes something to the picaresque tradition, as does Voltaire's *Candide.*

romance: The word derives from *Roman* and suggests its origins as a way of distinguishing this genre from those in proper Latin. In the Middle Ages the term came to be used primarily for stories about knights-errant and their adventures, which could include events and characters which violated the rules of everyday reality by using sorcery, magicians, and other fabulous events. "The Wife of Bath's Tale" in Chaucer's *The Canterbury Tales* is a romance, and Cervantes's *Don Quixote* parodies the genre.

tanka: A Japanese verse form of five lines. The first and third lines contain five syllables, the second, fourth, and fifth lines contain seven syllables. It does not deliberately rhyme but may do so inadvertently.

type character: A character who embodies the most important distinguishing characteristics of his group or class (e.g., a miser or a braggart soldier in classical drama). Neoclassicism advocated the use of type characters rather than sharply individualized ones in order to make its art more universally applicable. Molière makes skillful use of type characters in his plays.

utilite et dulce: Literally, "usefulness and sweetness." This was one of the precepts of Neoclassicism that literature can teach via pleasure: a story, a beautiful poem, or an exciting play can hold our attention while the artist inculcates in us things that will help us live better and happier lives.

verisimilitude: The appearance of truth. This was a precept of Neoclassical literature, demanding that what happens in literature should be plausible in terms of our ordinary experience of life. The rule in drama, as in the plays of Molière, included the rule of the unities of time, place, and action, meaning that events in a play should cover no more than 24 hours of elapsed time, should be set in one location, and should exclude all subplots to concentrate on the main story line.

Biographical Notes
(Lectures 13–24)

Cervantes, Miguel de (1547–1616): The man who wrote *Don Quixote*, which may be the most important novel in history, led an eventful but largely unsuccessful life. He fought at the Battle of Lepanto in 1571—the battle which freed the Mediterranean from Ottoman control—and received three wounds, one of which paralyzed his left hand for the rest of his life. On his way home, he was captured by Turkish pirates and held for an impossibly high ransom given his circumstances; it was many years before the ransom was actually collected, by which time the chance to use the glory of Lepanto for personal advancement had long passed. He wrote voluminously, but nothing much by way of income accrued from his efforts, so in 1587 he took a position as a commissary for the Armada that would invade England the next year. His accounts failed to balance, and he was thrown into prison until about 1603. He made little personal profit from the two parts of *Don Quixote* (1605, 1615), but he did fulfill his lifelong dream of becoming a famous writer and had the satisfaction of knowing at his death that it was one of the most popular books in all of Europe.

Chaucer, Geoffrey (c. 1340–1400): He was a public servant for most of his life, serving as a soldier in the Hundred Years War in France, carrying out diplomatic missions to Italy, serving as a member of Parliament from Kent, and holding down the positions of Controller of Customs at the Port of London and Clerk of the King's Works. Poetry was always for him an avocation, even though it seems to have been his first real love. He is the author of many other works besides *The Canterbury Tales;* the most important of these is probably *Troilus and Criseyde*, a long poem drawn from post-Homeric Greek legend which has been treated as the first novel in English. He helped to make English a language for poetry (as Dante and Petrarch had done for Italian) and is thus sometimes called "The Father of English Poetry." He was the first poet buried in Westminster Abbey in what became, because of his presence there, "The Poets' Corner."

Dante Alighieri (1265–1321): Born in Florence, Dante received a good education in the standard classical and medieval works of his age. By 1295 he was deeply involved in the political life of his city, and when his party was defeated, he was banished in 1302, never to return to Florence. He lived the rest of his life wandering around Italy, living with other people, a detail which he poignantly remembers in *Paradiso,* where he remembers how salty someone else's bread tastes and how hard it is to go up and down someone else's stairs. In exile, however, he wrote some of his most important works, including *Il Convivio* (*The Banquet*), *De vulgari eloquentia* (*The Eloquent Vernacular*), *De monarchia* (*On Monarchy*), and the *Divine Comedy*. He also, before his exile, had written *La vita nuova* (*The New Life*), which strings together via a biographical framework 31 symbolic poems in praise and love of his idealized mistress, Beatrice. He died in Ravenna.

Kakinomoto Hitomaro (late 7th–early 8th centuries): The most important poet in the *Man'yōshū*. Nothing is known of his life except what can be inferred from his poems. He is responsible for many long poems in the collection and hundreds of *tanka*. Critics consider his poem on the death of Prince Takechi the most powerful in the book. He is known as the "Saint of Poetry" and sometimes called the Shakespeare of Japanese poetry.

Li Po (701–62): Born into an unimportant family, Li Po spent part of his life in unsuccessful pursuit of court office. Failing that, he recreated himself as a jester, lover of wine and women, and a good companion who could commune happily with nature by himself as well. One version of his death has him drunkenly trying to grasp the reflection of the moon in the Yellow River and drowning. It may not be true, but it is consistent with the persona Li Po created in his poems.

Marguerite of Navarre (1492–1549): The older sister of Francis I of France, she received a splendid education; when her brother became king in 1515, she became one of the most powerful women at court, advising the king and helping him bring Italian learning to France (including visitation by such famous artists as Leonardo da Vinci and Benvenuto Cellini). On the death of her first husband she became the Queen of Navarre by marrying the King of Navarre (the title was honorary only, since most of Navarre had already been annexed by Spain). Their daughter, Jeanne, became the mother of the illustrious Henri IV of France. She was a lifelong patron of writers, and Rabelais dedicated his *Gargantua and Pantagruel* to her. Most of the rest of her writings—besides the *Heptameron*—were religious or devotional in nature, with enough of what were deemed Protestant leanings that she required occasional protection from her brother.

Molière (1622–73): The stage name of Jean Baptiste Poquelin, a contemporary of Corneille and Racine in the French Golden Age of Theater during the Neoclassical period. He was the son of a prosperous middle-class family, who received a good education in expectation of a promising career, but he left behind his prospects in his early twenties to help found a theater company. Failing in Paris and accumulating serious debt in the process, his troupe went into the provinces for 12 years, where Molière polished his actor's skills and learned to write plays. When his troupe returned to Paris in 1658, he came to the notice of the king, who became his patron and protector against the attacks provoked by his plays. Over the next 25 years he wrote an amazing number of comic masterpieces (he tried his hand at tragedies, but they were unsuccessful in his own day and are a source of continuing debate in ours). When he died, after the fourth performance of *The Imaginary Invalid,* he was refused Christian burial because of his profession—still condemned by the French clergy—until the king intervened to demand a private ceremony. His death seems symbolic of a man who dedicated his life to the theater and who, perhaps more than any other playwright in Western history, absolutely mastered the crafts of writing, acting, and producing plays that are still as viable on stage today as they were when they were written.

Murasaki Shikibu (c. 973–1016): The daughter of a remote branch of the ruling Fujiwara family. She married a kinsman older than herself in 998 or 999, bore a daughter in 999, and became a widow in 1001. She served the Empress Akiko in the middle of the first decade of the 11th century; the Empress was widowed in 1011, and we lose track of Murasaki after that. Murasaki kept a diary and she wrote the first novel in history, *The Tale of Genji,* probably between the death of her husband and her own death.

Ono no Komachi (fl. mid-9th century): One of the finest poets in the *Kokinshū,* she was a lady-in-waiting at the court in the 850s and 860s. According to legend, she was both extraordinarily beautiful and cold-hearted, and she died in solitary poverty on the streets; aside from its romantic value, this story is dismissed by most critics and historians.

Shakespeare, William (1564–1616): Born in Stratford-upon-Avon, he probably attended the local grammar school. He married Anne Hathaway in 1582, and they had three children. He is first mentioned as being in London in 1592; by then he had written some plays. Over the next 20 years he produced a steady stream of plays, a book of sonnets, and two narrative poems, *Venus and Adonis* and *The Rape of Lucrece.* The Lord Chamberlain's Men was formed in 1594 with Shakespeare participating as actor, shareholder, and playwright. The company built its own playhouse, The Globe, in 1599, became The King's Men at the accession of James I in 1603, and took over Blackfriars as an indoor theater around 1609. He seems to have prospered in his profession: there are ample records of financial transactions and grain dealing, he bought a large house in Stratford in 1597 (as well as other houses and land in both Stratford and London), and purchased a coat of arms in his father's name, which allowed him to call himself a gentleman. He retired to Stratford sometime around 1612, where he died on April 23, 1616. His monument is in the chancel of Holy Trinity Church in Stratford. His plays were published by friends and theater associates in the Folio Edition of 1623.

Tu Fu (712–70): He lived during turbulent times in Chinese imperial history. He was a success neither as a courtier nor a poet in his own lifetime, and he seems to have spent his last years in perpetual wandering. Most of what we know of his life comes from his poems, which record events in such detail that historians can use them as a source for the period. His persona, in contrast to Li Po's, is that of a Confucianist who takes his responsibilities seriously. After his death he came to be revered as one of China's greatest poets, sometimes called the Shakespeare of Chinese poetry.

Voltaire (1694–1778): A pseudonym of François-Marie Arouet, he was a French satirist whose name became synonymous in his own day for sharp attacks on intolerance, superstition, and tyranny, especially as manifest in the French government and the Catholic Church. He wrote much—his collected works run to over 135 volumes—in virtually every genre of the period. Finding himself in trouble early in his life, he was exiled and spent three years in England, where he learned to admire many English things vis-à-vis their French counterparts. Thereafter he lived in many places in Europe, including a stay at the court of Frederic the Great of Prussia. He eventually built a great house for himself at Ferney (virtually on the Swiss border), making it easy to leave the country when there was a need—and there often was. Among his important writings are a six-volume *Philosophical Dictionary*, histories which pay more attention to what Voltaire called "the spirit of the age" than to the doings of monarchs and the actions of battles, an Oriental tale, *Zadig*, and perhaps his most famous work, *Candide*. He died in the midst of a triumphant return to Paris, and when the French Revolution broke out, his remains were brought to rest in the Panthéon, where he was hailed as one who "prepared us for freedom."

Wang Wei (c. 699–761): Born into an important family, Wang Wei was a successful government official. We remember him as a poet and painter (he was one of the founders of Chinese landscape painting). Wang Wei's poems display his painter's eye and always keep the reader's attention focused on what the poet is looking at. He became a Buddhist layman towards the end of his life, and Buddhist attitudes give a decided coloration to the poems of his later years.

Wu Ch'eng-en (c. 1506–82): A government official in China for his career, he was remembered as a man of wit and geniality. He wrote some poetry which has survived, and the work with which he is most associated (*Monkey,* or *Journey to the West)* was by tradition written after his retirement. He was working with materials that were by his time nearly a thousand years old, and his achievement was to weld their disparate elements into a coherent novel. The earliest surviving text is from 1592, and a later revision of Chapter 9 incorporated materials about Tripitaka's birth and youth.

Bibliography
(Lectures 13–24)

Essential Reading:

Note: Every work treated in this part of the course is available in multiple editions and translations, many of them excellent. I have listed here the ones from which my text citations were taken. In general, the best strategy is to find an edition that gives you sufficient introductory material to help orient you to the text and sufficient editorial help to understand what you are reading. If you find those things, you have found the recommended text for you.

The Arabian Nights. Jack Zipes, trans. Vol. 1: New York: Signet, 1991. Vol. 2: New York: Signet, 1999.

Cervantes. *Don Quixote.* Samuel Putnam, trans. New York: Viking Press, 1949.

Chaucer, Geoffrey. *The Canterbury Tales.* Nevill Coghill, trans. Rev. edition. Baltimore: Penguin, 1967.

Dante, *The Inferno.* John Ciardi, trans. New York: New American Library, 1954. Ciardi also has translations of the last two books of the *Divine Comedy.*

The *Kokinshū. Kokin Wakashū: The First Imperial Anthology of Japanese Poetry.* Helen Craig McCullough, trans. Stanford: Stanford University Press, 1985.

Li Po, poems. *Sunflower Splendor: Three Thousand Years of Chinese Poetry.* Wu-chi Liu and Irving Yucheng Lo, eds. Bloomington: Indiana University Press, 1975.

The *Man'yōshū. The Ten Thousand Leaves.* Ian Hideo Levy, trans. Princeton: Princeton University Press, 1981.

Marguerite of Navarre, *Heptameron.* Paul Chilton, trans. New York: Penguin, 1984.

Molière. Most of Molière's comedies have been translated into brilliant heroic couplets by Richard Wilbur. They were published mostly by Harcourt, Brace, Jovanovich, but also by Methuen and Dramatists Play Service, between 1968 and 1993. Look them up by individual play titles.

Murasaki Shikibu. *The Tale of Genji.* Edward Seidensticker, trans. Tokyo: Charles E. Tuttle, 1978.

Shakespeare, William. *The Norton Shakespeare.* Stephen Greenblatt et al, eds. New York: W. W. Norton, 1997.

Tu Fu, poems. *The Great Age of Chinese Poetry: The High T'ang.* Stephen Owen, trans. New Haven: Yale University Press, 1981.

Voltaire, *Candide, or, Optimism.* Robert M. Adams, trans. 2nd ed. New York:

W. W. Norton, 1991

Wang Wei, poems. *An Anthology of Chinese Literature: Beginnings to 1911.* Stephen Owen, trans. New York: W. W. Norton, 1996.

Wu Ch'eng-en, *Hsi Yu Chi (Monkey,* or *Journey to the West).* 4 volumes. Anthony C. Yu, trans. Chicago: University of Chicago Press, 1977–1983.

Supplementary Reading:

Adams, Robert M. *Candide, or, Optimism: A Fresh Translation, Backgrounds, and Criticism.* 2nd ed. New York: W. W. Norton, 1991. In addition to providing a very readable translation of the prose fiction, Adams also provides useful intellectual and cultural backgrounds and includes critical essays by various hands on aspects of the work.

Allen, John J. *Don Quixote: Hero or Fool? A Study in Narrative Technique.* University of Florida Monographs: Humanities 29. Gainesville: University of Florida Press, 1969. A readable account of the most important questions about the novel. In terms of its title, Allen concludes that Don Quixote is both hero and fool, a paradox that is part of why he is such an interesting character.

Bergin, Thomas. *Dante's Divine Comedy. Landmarks of Literature.* Englewood Cliffs, N. J.: Prentice-Hall, 1971. A good introduction to and reading of Dante's epic. Many of Bergin's insights were used in Lecture Sixteen.

Bowring, Richard. *Murasaki Shikibu: The Tale of Genji. Landmarks of Literature.* Cambridge, U.K.: Cambridge University Press, 1988. A readable and informative introduction to the novel, featuring both background material and illuminating analysis in a chapter-by-chapter fashion through the book.

Brower, Robert H. and Earl Miner. *Japanese Court Poetry.* Stanford: Stanford University Press, 1961. This is a comprehensive anthology with good editorial material and some interestingly different translations of some of the poems treated in Lecture Fourteen.

Carter, Steven D. *Traditional Japanese Poetry.* Stanford: Stanford University Press, 1991. An anthology of translations which also includes an extensive and very useful introduction to Japanese poetry.

Charney, Maurice. *How to Read Shakespeare.* San Francisco: McGraw-Hill, 1971. A good introduction to the conventions of Shakespeare's stage, the genres in which he worked, his own thematic concerns, and a short history of productions of his plays.

Cholakian, Patricia Francis. *Rape and Writing in the Heptameron of Marguerite de Navarre.* Carbondale: Southern Illinois University Press, 1991. As suggested in Lecture Twenty, this is a good feminist reading of the *Heptameron*, a part of the feminist recuperation of the book for modern readers.

Church, Margaret. *Don Quixote: The Knight of La Mancha.* New York: New York University Press, 1971. The book discusses the broader issues of the novel, but it also does fine and detailed readings of individual episodes. Church says that Cervantes broadened the genres in which he was working by introducing his theme of perspectivism.

Cooper, Helen. *Oxford Guides to Chaucer: The Canterbury Tales.* Oxford: Oxford University Press, 1989. An excellent guide to the textual history of the poem, a good discussion of the fragments into which critics have divided it, and stimulating readings of the individual tales.

Davis, Betty J. *The Storytellers in Marguerite de Navarre's Heptameron.* Lexington, Kentucky: French Forum, 1978. Davis largely ignores the stories of the collection to focus on the relationships among the tellers, yielding some very useful insights and helping us to understand the connection between character and tale in the stories themselves.

Holmes, George. *Dante (Past Masters).* Oxford: Oxford University Press, 1980. A very useful and readable introduction to Dante's life and all of his works, including the *Divine Comedy*.

Howarth, W. D. *Molière: A Playwright and His Audience.* New York: Cambridge University Press, 1982. A good introduction to Molière's theater and some very fine and detailed readings of individual plays.

Hsia, C. T. *The Classic Chinese Novel: A Critical Introduction.* 1968; rpt. Ithaca, New York: Cornell University East Asia Program, 1996. A thorough and illuminating account of the context for the rise of the novel in China and fine readings of individual novels.

Irwin, Robert. *The Arabian Nights: A Companion.* London: I. B. Tauris, 2004. A wonderful and entertainingly written introduction to many aspects of this intriguing book. It includes a complete history of its texts and many of its translations.

Johnson, Carroll B. *Don Quixote: The Quest for Modern Fiction.* Boston: Twayne, 1990. This is a brilliant series of essays on the novel, focusing particularly on the theme of perspectivism and on the novel's modernity. As indicated, many of the insights in Lecture Twenty-Two were borrowed from this book.

Kato, Shuchi. *A History of Japanese Literature 1: The First Thousand Years.* David Chibbett, trans. New York: Kodansha International, 1979. A survey which places both the *Man'yōshū* and the *Kokinshū* in historical as well as aesthetic contexts.

Keene, Donald. *The Pleasures of Japanese Literature.* New York: Columbia University Press, 1988. A splendid introduction to Japanese literature by one of the leading scholars of our time. His chapter on Japanese aesthetics is referred to in Lecture Fourteen, and he is cited on *The Tale of Genji* in Lecture Fourteen.

Malti-Douglas, Fedwa. *Woman's Body, Woman's Word: Gender and Discourse in Arabo-Islamic Writing.* Princeton: Princeton University Press, 1991. As the title indicates, this book's concerns are relatively general, but it contains a brilliant feminist reading of *1001 Nights*, which is our chief concern with it here.

Mason, Haydn. *Candide: Optimism Demolished.* Boston: Twayne, 1992. As with most of the books in the Twayne series, this one provides a useful introduction to *Candide* and provides a bibliography which can send the reader off in other directions.

McBride, Robert. *The Sceptical Vision of Molière: A Study in Paradox.* London: Macmillan, 1977. A study of the entire career of the playwright, focusing on his attitudes and values as they are expressed in his plays.

McCullough, Helen Craig. *Brocade by Night: "Kokin Wakashū" and the Court Style in Japanese Classical Poetry.* Stanford: Stanford University Press, 1985. This book is a companion to her translation of *The Kokinshū*, focusing especially on Chinese influences on Japanese poetry and some of the problems of translating Japanese poetry.

Owen, Stephen. *Traditional Chinese Poetry and Poetics: Omen of the World.* Madison: University of Wisconsin Press, 1985. A splendid series of essays on the way Chinese poems actually work, by a scholar who is also one of the foremost translators of Chinese poetry.

Pearsall, Derek. *The Canterbury Tales.* New York: Routledge, 1993. An excellent overview of the entire collection. Pearsall is particularly good at finding analogues and sources for the individual stories and then showing how Chaucer changed them to make them fit the characters and circumstances of his pilgrims on the way to Canterbury.

Quinn, Edward, ed. *How to Read Shakespearean Tragedy.* San Francisco: Harper and Row, 1978. A good introductory volume, by a variety of hands, on the conventions of Shakespearean tragedy. It also offers some close readings of *Romeo and Juliet*, *Hamlet*, *Othello*, *King Lear*, *Macbeth*, and *Antony and Cleopatra*.

Sayers, Dorothy. *Introductory Papers on Dante.* London: Methuen, 1954. A sympathetic reading of Dante's epic which finds a great deal of universal truth in it, by the creator of the Lord Peter Wimsey mysteries. Sayers also did a translation of the *Divine Comedy*, complete with very detailed notes, for Penguin Books.

Schwyzer, Philip. *Archaeologies of English Renaissance Literature.* Oxford: Oxford University Press, 2007. This is a brilliant series of essays exploring the ways in which archaeology and literary criticism attempt to recover the past. Its essay on Shakespeare and Donne and their use of graves and corpses in Renaissance literature is both interesting in itself and bears indirectly on the Shakespeare authorship question.

Weinberger, Eliot. *Nineteen Ways of Looking at Wang Wei.* Wakefield, Rhode Island: Moyer Bell, 1987. As mentioned in Lecture Thirteen, this book brings together 19 different translations of a four-line poem by Wang Wei and then discusses the virtues and problems of each. The book is an excellent introduction to the nuances of Chinese character-poetry.

Wells, Stanley. *Shakespeare: The Writer and His Work.* New York: Charles Scribner's Sons, 1978. A brief introduction to the life and plays of the man from Stratford, including a bibliography of important Shakespeare critics up to the time of the book's publication.

Wu-chi Liu. *An Introduction to Chinese Literature.* Bloomington: Indiana University Press, 1966. A general introduction to all of the genres of Chinese literature, cast in a historical perspective. It also gives some very fine readings of individual works.

Lecture Twenty-Five
Cao Xueqin's *The Story of the Stone*

Scope: This lecture treats Cao Xueqin's 18th-century novel, *The Story of the Stone*, about a family in decline. We begin by relating it to Western novels, then discuss the origins of the Chinese novel in storytelling and suggest that this novel solves the problem of its authority by the density of its details of everyday life. At the center of the novel is a love triangle among two very different women and Bao-yu (Pao-yu in some translations), its unconventional central character. The novel is framed by a cosmic story about a conscious stone in heaven that lives out its earthly life as Bao-yu; the cosmic frame and the everyday events of the novel throw ironic lights on each other. While the apparent intent of the novel is to suggest that in a Buddhist-Taoist perspective all earthly life is an illusion, the novel's rich involvement in the details of everyday life complicates that intent for readers.

Outline

I. The text of the novel is something of a puzzle.
   A. Cao Xueqin, its author, was born c. 1720 and died in 1763, but the novel was published in its final form almost 30 years after the author's death.
   B. During those 30 years, several manuscript versions were in circulation which had only 80 chapters.
      1. The men who published the 1792 edition (with 120 chapters) claimed that for the last third of the novel they had only edited material written by the author himself.
      2. It is the 120-chapter version that has had an enormous impact on Chinese literature, so we will treat it as a unified work without worrying much about its textual provenance.
      3. The book seems to have been a project involving several members of the family, some of whose suggestions and interpretations have survived in the early manuscript; it has always been thought of as the work of more than one hand.

II. *The Story of the Stone* is a fictionalized history of the decline and fall of the Cao family, whose general outlines have been validated by scholars.
  A. It charts the decline of a once-great family into survival in much-reduced circumstances, where it is even held in suspicion by the imperial power it had served for generations.
  B. The novel is similar to Jane Austen's novels, Proust's *Remembrance of Things Past,* and Thomas Mann's *Buddenbrooks.*
   1. Like Austen's novels, it focuses on the domestic life of an extended family and pays particular attention to the life of women of various classes within the family.
   2. Like Proust, it remembers a way of life that, for this family, has since vanished.
   3. Like Mann, it portrays the decline of a great and powerful family.

III. The Chinese novel takes its form both from storytelling traditions and from problems inherent in the novel form itself.
  A. The Chinese novel was a vernacular form vis-à-vis the classical forms of Chinese poetry and official annals.
  B. The earliest storytellers in China seem to have been Buddhists, who told stories like the ones in the *Jātaka.*
   1. By the T'ang Dynasty there were professional storytellers, some of whose story outlines have been published.
   2. These stories were told more for entertainment than for edification, and some of their techniques (like ending each episode on a note of suspense to get listeners to come back the next day) show up in the early Chinese novel.
   3. Each chapter begins with a couplet summing up its contents.
  C. The main problem with the early novel is accounting for its fictionality: Why read a story that someone has made up?
   1. By linking the novel to history, some writers (e.g., Murasaki Shikibu in *The Tale of Genji* or Cervantes in *Don Quixote*) tried to make the novel *feel* like history with the same kinds of meaning as history.
   2. Other writers (e.g., Daniel Defoe in *Robinson Crusoe*) tried to stuff the novel with so many realistic details that readers would have to assume its truth.

©2007 The Teaching Company.

- **3.** The latter is the method of *The Story of the Stone*, which is so full of the details of family life in the 18th century that it *feels* like truth; the tangents help convince the readers that the material is real. It is probably also one reason why early Chinese novels are so long.
- **4.** An exception to this is *Monkey*, which is too loosely tied to history to be historical and too fantastic to be handled in a strictly realistic and detailed fashion. It is a reminder that fantasy can carry as much truth as realistic fiction—a truth also demonstrated in *Candide*.

IV. At the center of the story is Bao-yu, pampered son of the Jia family.
- **A.** Despite his Confucian father, Bao-yu grows up sensitive, compassionate, and warm-hearted—traits which will be developed by his maturation in a garden on the family compound with the adolescent women of the family.
- **B.** His focus in the garden is a cousin, Dai-yu, who is sensitive, poetic, beautiful, and insecure (to the point of neurosis).
  - **1.** The cousins have been in love since childhood, but they always misunderstand each other.
  - **2.** Dai-yu dies on the day Bao-yu, victim of a complete nervous breakdown, is tricked into marrying another cousin: the plump, healthy, and practical Bao-chai.
- **C.** Most of the novel's story is hung on this love triangle.

V. The story of the novel is, like *Monkey*, framed by a cosmic story about a stone brought to consciousness to repair the vault of heaven.
- **A.** The stone is later carried to earth by a Buddhist monk and a Taoist priest.
  - **1.** Ages later another Taoist comes upon the stone, on which is inscribed the story of the novel.
  - **2.** Bao-yu (whose name means "Precious Jade") is the incarnation of that stone.
  - **3.** Dai-yu is also from heaven: a heavenly flower which had been watered by the stone and which has vowed to repay its kindness with a "debt of tears."
  - **4.** Everything that happens in the novel is a story within a story, which throws its events into an ironic light.
- **B.** The frame becomes even more complicated.

1. The story on the stone begins with Zhen Shi-yin, who dreams of a Buddhist monk and a Taoist priest carrying a stone, which occurs at about the time that Bao-yu and Dai-yu are passing from heaven into "The Land of Illusion."
2. Zhen Shi-yin wakes up to treasure his little daughter, who is later kidnapped and reappears in the Jia compound as the concubine of an unattractive man; Zhen Shi-yin, meanwhile, loses everything else that he has.
3. One day a Taoist priest shows up; by now Zhen Shi-yin understands the illusory nature of earthly life and goes off with the priest.
  C. The point of the frame is to remind us that everything that happens in the novel happens in "The Land of Illusion," a point which Bao-yu seems to accept at the novel's end, when he disappears forever arm-in-arm with a Buddhist monk and a Taoist priest.
VI. *The Story of the Stone* teaches the lessons of Buddhism and Taoism: detachment from the world and its desires. We have already encountered these lessons in Chuang Tzu, *The Tale of Genji,* and *Monkey.*
  A. This official doctrine and reading, however, is constantly undermined by the attention the novelist gives to the details of everyday life, making the recurrent appearances of the Buddhist and the Taoist shocks to the reader as well as to the characters in the novel.
    1. The author shows great sympathy for the lovers and the other people of his book and encourages us to be interested in them.
    2. In *The Story of the Stone* we are encouraged to adopt two perspectives simultaneously: that of life itself, with its possibilities for grief and happiness, and that of eternity, in which none of earthly life matters.
    3. Bao-yu's renunciation of life at the end of the novel is exemplary in religious terms but extremely problematic for readers, who can see how his Confucian duty to his family conflicts with his religious one to achieve detachment and renunciation.
  B. In many ways, the official ending of the book does not square with the reader's experience of it.

        1. Bao-yu's final experience with a maid named Skybright is touching, beautiful, and suggests something important about human relations.
        2. We also see the scene from the perspective of eternity, which calls into question everything that happens during it.
  C. The dual perspective makes this novel an extraordinarily rich experience for the reader.
        1. It is a Buddhist-Taoist call for renunciation, but it is also an ironic condemnation of that renunciation.
        2. It shows how only the deepest engagement in human life can prepare one for renouncing it.
        3. It is a portrayal of the power and beauty of human relationships, and a tragic love story.
        4. It is the story of the fall of a great house.
        5. It is a tribute to that moment when, in adolescence, young women are for Bao-yu the embodiments of celestial understanding.

Essential Reading:

Cao Xueqin, *The Story of the Stone.*

Supplementary Reading:

C. T. Hsia, *The Classic Chinese Novel.*

Jeanne Knoerle, *The Dream of the Red Chamber: A Critical Study.*

Questions to Consider:

1. Despite her obvious neurosis and the terrible trouble she gives Bao-yu, what makes Dai-yu so appealing as a heroine? Can she be defended in purely rational ways, or does her portrait touch both male and female readers in ways that transcend (or at least bypass) rationality?

2. Is there a villain in the novel? What or who is responsible for the rapid decline and fall of the Jia family in imperial China? Is their fall predicated on some flaw within the family itself, or is it the result of circumstance? Could adaptation on the part of the family have prevented what happened to it?

Lecture Twenty-Six
Goethe's *Faust*

Scope: Goethe's *Faust* is a new version of a story that had been told many times since the 16th century, when the historical Faustus lived. The most important changes Goethe made in the traditional story involve framing it within a wager between God and Mephistopheles (modeled on the book of Job in the Old Testament) about the merits of creation; and the nature of Faust's contract with Mephistopheles, in which he asks not for a specific good but infinite human experience. Both the wager and the contract embody the new Romantic values of infinite striving and the irrelevance of moral judgment. Both will have important consequences for future literature and thought; the idea that human nature consists not in some essence or the achievement of some particular goal or state, but rather in perpetual process and growth, comes close to the heart of the Romantic revolution in values.

Outline

I. Goethe's *Faust* is perhaps the most important work in the history of German literature, and allows us to transition from the Age of *Enlightenment* to the Romantic Movement in the Western world.

II. Goethe is universally acknowledged as a genius with an amazing breadth of accomplishment.
  - **A.** He achieved success in virtually every genre of literature.
  - **B.** He was a noted scientist, a painter, a statesman, and prime minister at the court of the Duke of Saxony.
  - **C.** Napoleon, among the many who had audiences with the great man towards the end of his life, was stunned by Goethe's erudition and the scope of his knowledge in so many fields.

III. Of Goethe's 140 volumes that were sensationally popular in his own day, the one that has had the greatest resonance through history is *Faust*.
  - **A.** The story at its core is an old one about a German scholar named Johannes Faustus who died in 1540. Faustus's story had already

been turned into literature by 1587, most famously by Christopher Marlowe in his *Doctor Faustus* around 1600.

B. In all earlier versions of the story, including Marlowe's, Faustus is damned for transgressing some boundary or literally selling his soul to the devil.

C. Goethe worked on his version of the story for about 60 years, making it a lifetime interest (he finished the last part just before his death, and it was published posthumously). Fragments of the work were published in 1790; Part I was published in 1808; Part II was published in 1832.

D. Goethe's version is a *closet drama* (or "poetic drama"): a drama written in dramatic form but not intended for the stage (e.g., Milton's *Samson Agonistes* or Shelley's *Prometheus Unbound*).

IV. The changes to the story Goethe made in the first scenes of his play suggest profound shifts in sensibility in the late 18th and early 19th centuries. These shifts mark the transition from the Enlightenment to *Romanticism*.

A. In virtually all earlier versions, the primary contract is between Faust and Mephistopheles. Faust gives his soul to Mephistopheles in exchange for some specific gift (e.g., wealth or power) for a specified number of years.

B. In Goethe's play, the primary contract is a wager between God and Mephistopheles about the value of creation; this occurs in a frame prologue set in heaven.

    1. Mephistopheles says that creation is a bad job and that humans are the worst part of it.

    2. For Mephistopheles, humans are mostly animal but cursed with the gift of reason, which keeps them perpetually frustrated and unhappy. He says that he does not even enjoy tempting them very much, since they are such easy prey.

    3. God offers Faust as his justification for creation and for human beings, and gives Mephistopheles permission to tempt Faust from the primal source (what he should be as a human being).

    4. The scene is based on the book of Job in the Old Testament, but here its terms are very different: If Mephistopheles can

corrupt Faust, he demonstrates that creation was a mistake. If God wins, he demonstrates that it has value.
- **C.** The play then shifts to Faust's study, where we find Faust depressed, frustrated, and on the verge of suicide.
  1. Faust has doctorates in everything and still knows nothing; he wants experience, not knowledge.
  2. Faust seems to illustrate everything that Mephistopheles says about humans in his wager with God.
  3. When Mephistopheles appears in Faust's study, they eventually work out the terms of the contract: Mephistopheles will keep providing Faust with new human experiences until the point at which Faust is content with what he has and where he is, after which Mephistopheles can have his soul.
  4. Faust wants not some specific good but infinite human experience, with each experience becoming the springboard for the next.
- **D.** This contract marks the transition from the Enlightenment or Neoclassical Age to that of Romanticism.
  1. It marks the end of an age of empirical knowledge and rationality and the beginning of one of limitless aspiration, subjectivity, and the desire for transcendence.
  2. It also rejects morality as the basis for judging a protagonist, since Faust is asking for *all* experiences, perpetual growth, and *all* possible actions; whether these experiences and actions might be considered good or evil is not part of the contract, nor does God expect that it should be.
  3. Sir Kenneth Clark, in *Civilisation,* suggests that Faust is the human version of Goethe's theory of will in plants, which strive to keep growing until they die.
  4. The terms of Faust's contract are active versus passive, not good versus evil.

V. The rest of the play—both Parts I and II—are about Mephistopheles trying to find the ultimate moment for Faust. Part I is primarily concerned with Faust's affair with Margaret (or Gretchen), but in Part II his experiences become more abstract and allegorical. Beyond the adventures themselves, there is much to consider.
- **A.** In the play, Goethe uses almost every verse form known to German poetry in his day, and he manages to match style with content in virtually every scene.

1. Faust's opening soliloquy is done in the style of Hans Sachs (1494–1576), whose verse form was the most popular one in German at the time Faust lived; the technique anticipates Joyce's use of styles in the chapter in the obstetric hospital in *Ulysses*.
2. There is a good deal of satire in the play.
3. Part II becomes increasingly allegorical, so that each episode is also about something besides itself.

B. At the heart of the play, however, are the wager and the contract between God and Mephistopheles, both of which suggest an important change in sensibility.
1. Historically, humans were thought of as having some changeless or eternal essence, which it was their duty to achieve.
2. Against this Goethe posits perpetual motion, striving, ambition, and the desire to *become*, not *be*.
3. We still live in the wake of that shift, believing in growth, process, and development, even if we are not always sure what we are trying to grow up to be.

C. The darker side to this idea is that if personal development is the primary human goal, then a consideration for others may become secondary.
1. Faust leaves a trail of victims of his own drive for experience behind him in the two parts of the play.
2. As God makes clear in the prologue, he does not hold that against Faust; it is the striving for experience that counts.

D. From this wager and contract will come a mixed progeny: transcendentalism, hero worship, Nietzsche's idea of the "superman" and its contribution to fascism, and Raskolnikov in Dostoevsky's *Crime and Punishment*.
1. What also emerges is an alternative to the idea that possessions are the goal of human life.
2. With all of Faust's chances, he never chooses personal wealth or power; for him, the pursuit of experience is an end in itself.

Essential Reading:

Goethe, *Faust*, Parts I and II.

Supplementary Reading:

T. J. Reed, *Goethe.*

Jane K. Brown, *Goethe's Faust: The German Tragedy.*

Questions to Consider:

1. It has been said that in Part I, if Faust abandons Gretchen, the story is her tragedy; if he does not, it is his. In terms of his contract with Mephistopheles, how would this be true?

2. In theory, this should be an infinite play: As long as Faust keeps wanting new experiences, Mephistopheles has to keep providing them. Since Faust is saved at the end of Part II, we have to understand that he never stops striving. So why does he die? What leads Mephistopheles to think that he has finally defeated Faust and won his wager with God?

Lecture Twenty-Seven
Emily Brontë's *Wuthering Heights*

Scope: This lecture deals with Emily Brontë's *Wuthering Heights*. After reviewing some of the essential differences between the values of the Enlightenment and those of Romanticism, we trace some Romantic motifs in this novel: the idea of a supernaturally powerful passion; elements of the Gothic; Heathcliff as a *Byronic hero*, created by and modeled on Lord Byron, the Romantic poet; and the values and powers of nature. Most of these occur in the novel's first half; the second half is more like the novels of Jane Austen and anticipates the *Realist novel*. The other forward-looking aspect of the book is its complicated point of view: Stories are nested inside each other, and everything we know we learn from characters within the novel, not from an omniscient author. In fact, the author virtually vanishes from the story, another anticipation of the techniques of *Realism*. The complex point of view also complicates an interpretation of the story.

Outline

I. *Wuthering Heights*, perhaps the 21st century's favorite 19th-century novel, was first published in 1847.
   A. Most people probably know the story more from the 1939 film version than the book.
      1. The movie is purely more Romantic than the book.
      2. It makes the ghosts of Catherine and Heathcliff (mere suggestions in the novel) more decidedly real by allowing audiences to see them.
   B. The book is Romantic only in its first half; its second half is more like a Jane Austen novel or—as some critics have suggested—a Realist novel of the future.

II. The first half of *Wuthering Heights* is full of Romantic values.
   A. Romanticism's followers generally repudiated the values of the Enlightenment.
      1. Where the Enlightenment valued reason, empirical evidence, common sense, objectivity, social norms, and universal values, Romanticism valued intuition, passion, and subjectivity.

2. Where the Enlightenment found its core values in reason, Romanticism found them in the processes of the natural world.
3. Where the Enlightenment found satisfaction in adapting to the great machine of the universe, Romanticism sought transcendence in order to merge with the great powers of the universe.

B. The strength of the passion of Catherine and Heathcliff, which can destroy both of them and perhaps continue on beyond death, would have been considered impossible or absurd by Enlightenment thinkers.
1. At best, the lovers would have been considered a warning against allowing passion to overwhelm rational control.
2. Here, however, they are given center stage, and their passion is at least partially endorsed.

C. The Romantics were willing to admit the supernatural into their works, and in *Wuthering Heights* the supernatural appears in ghosts who may or may not be real—including the ghost of Catherine (who appears to Lockwood) and the ghosts who are said to roam the heaths at novel's end.
1. The ghosts are part of the trappings of the *Gothic novel*.
2. The Gothic novel is a popular Romantic genre which sets stories in exotic and mysterious settings (e.g., Ann Radcliffe's *The Mysteries of Udolpho* and Mary Shelley's *Frankenstein*).

D. Heathcliff himself is a Romantic figure—a Byronic hero based on the life and protagonists of Lord Byron, the Romantic poet: moody, passionate, superior to other human beings and (either through having committed some unforgivable crime or through satiation) isolated from other people.
1. He is absolutely autonomous and free.
2. Therefore, he is therefore irresistible to other people—especially women.

E. The values of nature are endorsed in the novel's first half.
1. Wuthering Heights is a real farmhouse set on the wild moors, and they are the natural habitat of Catherine and Heathcliff.
2. The civilized and cultured world of Isabella and Edgar Linton, Thrushcross Grange, is removed from nature.
3. Heathcliff's name suggests his association with nature, while Edgar and Isabella's names suggest a level of refinement that cuts them off from direct contract with the natural world.

    F. All of these values are the ones Catherine betrays when she marries Edgar Linton to use his money to help Heathcliff. In the process she first destroys herself and then Heathcliff.

III. The second half of the novel is quite different from the first half.
    A. At the novel's end, peace has been made between the two houses.
        1. Catherine, the daughter of the original Catherine and Edgar Linton, will marry Hareton Earnshaw, who has inherited both Thrushcross Grange and Wuthering Heights from Heathcliff.
        2. Catherine and Hareton will go to live at Thrushcross Grange, and Wuthering Heights will be closed down.
    B. In a symbolic way, this is perhaps the closing down of the wild passions and dreams of Romanticism and a step on the way to the Realist novel.

IV. The technical aspect of the book that has intrigued readers and critics is its point of view.
    A. *Point of view* in fiction is the angle of vision from which the story is presented to us.
        1. The forms of point of view are third-person omniscient, third-person limited, and first-person limited.
        2. In the early days of the novel, the normative point of view was third-person omniscient (e.g., *The Tale of Genji, Monkey, Don Quixote,* and *The Story of the Stone*); the omniscient point of view was authorized by Henry Fielding in *Tom Jones*.
    B. The story of Catherine and Heathcliff is narrated by a visitor from London named Lockwood, who hears the story from Nelly Dean, a servant at Wuthering Heights since childhood.
        1. Lockwood goes back to London and then returns to hear of Heathcliff's death and the impending marriage of Hareton Earnshaw and Catherine Linton—and also Nelly's skeptical report of the ghosts that roam the moors.
        2. Nelly incorporates into her story letters and bits of narrative from Catherine, Heathcliff, and other characters within the story; Lockwood comes upon a few bits of material on his own.
    C. What is missing is an omniscient authority, or author, to help us evaluate what happens.
        1. The perspectivism seen in *Don Quixote* has become the method of *Wuthering Heights*.

      2. Every event in the story comes to us from someone's point of view, and many of the events are given to us in multiple versions from multiple perspectives; how do we decide which, if any, version is the true one?

      3. The author's disappearance is a trait of the modern novel.

V. The characteristics of the novel's two principal narrators further complicate interpretation.

    A. Lockwood is a fashionable fop who is totally out of his depth in trying to understand a character like Heathcliff, whose capacity for love and hate is so much greater than his own.

    B. Nelly Dean is a conventionally religious woman, practical and commonsensical, who dislikes disorder, illness, and vagary.

      1. We have to take into account her values and the possible influence they might have on the way she tells the story.

      2. Nelly is also a participant in the story she tells, and her decisions influence the events that occur, so that her version of the story could well be to reassure herself—and to gain Lockwood's endorsement—that she did the right thing, despite the tragic outcome of the Catherine-Heathcliff story.

      3. At the end, Nelly and Lockwood agree that the story has a happy ending: Hareton will marry Catherine, reason and the conventional will triumph over passion, and Jane Austen will inherit the world of Lord Byron.

    C. In terms of narrative, the reader becomes aware by the novel's end that Lockwood and Nelly, with their limited perspectives, have flattened out and rationalized a story that may be far bigger and more mysterious than either of them realizes.

    D. The artfully manipulated point of view thus allows Brontë to tell not one story, but two: the Lockwood/Nelly Dean version and the one that the reader is allowed to glimpse between the lines of theirs.

VI. The book is thus both a great Romantic piece of literature and an indication of the direction that narrative will take in the age of the Realist novel that comes close behind it.

Essential Reading:

Brontë. *Wuthering Heights*.

Supplementary Reading:

Graham Holderness, *Wuthering Heights. Open Guides to Literature.*

J. Hillis Miller, *Fiction and Repetition.*

Questions to Consider:

1. While reading the novel, how do you go about deciding whether Nelly is a reliable narrator or not? What might she be trying to cover up or how might she be telling the story in such a way as to justify her own actions and judgments?

2. If Emily Brontë had provided us with an omniscient narrator, what are the most important ambiguities in the tale that you would like him or her to explain? If we assume that these ambiguities are deliberate on Brontë's part, what might be some of her reasons for wanting to tell the story this way?

Lecture Twenty-Eight
Pushkin's *Eugene Onegin*

Scope: Pushkin lived during the Westernization of Russia, which included the influx of such European literature as the *sentimental novel* and Romantic poetry. Pushkin's *Eugene Onegin* is a commentary on much of that literature. It has as its central character another Byronic hero, but one from whom the narrator distances himself and whose story ends in defeat. The form of *Onegin*, which Pushkin called "a novel in verse," also owes a great deal to Byron's *Don Juan* in its complicated poetic stanza and a narrator who tells his own story as he tells his fictional one. It parodies the endings of the sentimental novel. *Eugene Onegin* turns out to be a meditation on the relationship of life and art, which can be explored in several directions. In its detailed recreation of a specific moment in Russian history, it—like Brontë's *Wuthering Heights*—anticipates the Realist novels that would learn from it.

Outline

I. Alexander Pushkin is usually considered Russia's national poet—like Dante and Shakespeare in Italy and England, respectively.

    A. He helped to create the modern Russian literary language, as Dante did for Italian and Shakespeare for English.

    B. In his short life (which was nearly as sensational as Byron's) he wrote a great deal of brilliant literature.

        1. Modern Russians are more likely to know more about Pushkin and his works than any other Russian writer.

        2. As with Shakespeare, many lines from Pushkin's poems have become proverbs.

        3. Pushkin provided material for operas to a series of great composers, particularly Tchaikovsky, who set "The Queen of Spades" and *Eugene Onegin* to music.

II. Pushkin lived during a period of Westernization in Russia, when European influences were encouraged and European ideas, philosophy, art and architecture, manners, and literature were all available for Russian adaptation.

- **A.** In literature, the sentimental novel, in vogue in Europe, came to Russia. In these novels, feeling replaced events as the major components of the novel.
- **B.** Also influential were the works of French rationalists like Voltaire.
- **C.** The most important influence on Pushkin came from the works of Lord Byron, who was an influence on Goethe and Brontë.
    1. In 1818, towards the end of his life, Byron began work on what many consider his greatest masterpiece: *Don Juan*, a narrative poem.
    2. By Byron's death six years later he had completed six sizable cantos.
    3. The first two were published in 1819, and they inspired Pushkin to begin work on *Eugene Onegin*.

III. One of the greatest debts that Pushkin's poem owes to Byron is that its protagonist is something of a Byronic hero: handsome, graceful, wealthy, and jaded from too much pleasure at an early age.
- **A.** When Onegin inherits a country estate, he moves there, where—for lack of better company—he makes friends with a Romantic poet, Lensky, who is in love with a neighboring family's daughter, a girl named Olga.
    1. When Onegin meets Olga, he also meets her older, bookish sister, Tatyana, who falls immediately in love with Onegin and—having read a lot of sentimental novels—sends him a letter the next day offering herself to him as his wife.
    2. After a time Onegin tells Tatyana that he cannot love her and warns her to be more careful with her affections in the future.
    3. A disagreement between Onegin and Lensky precipitates a duel in which Onegin kills Lensky; after a time, Onegin returns to St. Petersburg.
- **B.** At a party, he sees an amazingly beautiful woman enter the room. It is Tatyana, with whom it is now Onegin's turn to fall hopelessly in love.
    1. After Onegin pursues her for months, she confronts him but upbraids him for wanting her for the wrong reasons.
    2. Tatyana is now married and although she confesses that she still loves Onegin, she will remain faithful to her husband.
    3. Onegin, stricken, is still standing where Tatyana left him when her husband enters the room, and the poem ends.

4 In one way, this is a kind of comeuppance for a Byronic hero, who gets a taste of his own medicine.

IV. Pushkin's debt to Byron includes verse form and tone as well as a sketch of the protagonist.
- **A.** Byron, despite his Romanticism, admired the wit and formal brilliance of 18th-century poetry.
- **B.** In *Don Juan,* he used a complicated verse form called *ottava rima.*
  1. *Ottava rima* rhymes *ababbcc*, a difficult form in English, which is a rhyme-poor language.
  2. Byron plays with the difficulty by setting up some perfectly outrageous rhymes (e.g., "river" with "Guadalquivir").
- **C.** *Eugene Onegin* resembles *Don Juan* in many ways.
  1. It was written over a period of some years and published a canto or two at a time.
  2. Its narrator is, like Byron, the central character of the poem—a witty, charming, urbane companion with whom we enjoy spending time.
  3. Pushkin calls his installments "Chapters" instead of "Cantos," since he called this "A Novel in Verse," suggesting that despite his reservations about Romanticism (reservations he also shared with Byron), Pushkin appreciated the Romantic willingness to blend genres together to create new ones.
- **D.** Pushkin invented the *Onegin Stanza* for this poem, which rhymes *AbAbCCddEffEgg*, in which the capitalized letters stand for *feminine rhymes* (two-syllable rhymes with unaccented final syllables) and lowercase letters stand for *masculine rhymes* (stressed on the final syllable). Vladimir Nabokov says that the 14-line stanza allows four lines for the content, the final couplet for a summary, and the middle eight lines for conversation with the reader.
- **E.** Like Fielding's *Tom Jones* and Byron's *Don Juan,* the reader's primary relationship in *Eugene Onegin* is with the narrator, not the characters.

V. Pushkin's poem is about many things, of which we can note a few.
- **A.** It is about the inexorability of time, as it operates on both his characters and on the narrator himself, reminding all of them that time gives no second chances.

1. This is not as depressing as it might be, because the poem itself is witty, wholesome, and joyful.
2. In the end this reconciles us to the human condition rather than alienating us or pushing us towards despair.

B. The poem is also about the relationship between art and life.
1. The work, full of poetic virtuosity, keeps reminding the reader of the medium itself, not just the story being told, which is appropriate for a poem whose central character is its poet.
2. Every character in the poem has been shaped in one way or another in Don Quixote-like ways by his or her reading: Tatyana has read many sentimental novels, Lensky has read German and English Romantic poetry, and Onegin has read a great deal of Byron.
3. This theme is made explicit in the scene in which Tatyana browses in Onegin's library, noting the books he has read and the markings he has put in them, and she ends up wondering if he has a real character or if he is simply a pastiche pasted together out of modern literature.
4. The poem thus asks about the extent to which world views and character are determined by literary and cultural stereotypes and how adequate these stereotypes are for dealing with experience.

C. Pushkin tries to move the world of art away from literary stereotypes towards the actual world by using many of the techniques—especially in regard to setting—that would later characterize the Realist novel.
1. Pushkin takes characters and situations from Byron and sentimental novels and locates them in a real St. Petersburg.
2. At the end of the poem the real world intrudes on its Romantic plot.

Essential Reading:

Pushkin, *Eugene Onegin.*

Supplementary Reading:

John Bayley, *Pushkin: A Comparative Commentary.*
A. D. P. Briggs, *Alexander Pushkin: A Critical Study.*

Questions to Consider:

1. How attractive and/or sympathetic is Eugene Onegin to you as you read the poem? Does your sympathy wax and wane from episode to episode, or can you identify a more or less constant level of sympathy? What devices of Pushkin can you identify as designed either to draw you into Onegin's life or to push you back a bit from it?

2. Consider in your own life or in those of some people you know the impact of cultural stereotypes in determining character, values, beliefs, and behavior. Pushkin thought that the integration of these stereotypes into our lives disables us from real experience. To what extent could the same case be made for our own stereotypes, wherever they come from?

Lecture Twenty-Nine
Flaubert's *Madame Bovary*

Scope: We begin with a definition of Realism in literature, including its standards of truth, its avoidance of authorial intrusion, and its focus on contemporary life and manners. Flaubert's *Madame Bovary* is used to illustrate Realism in the novel: it is an ordinary story about ordinary people told with detachment and objectivity, but it also manages to convey Flaubert's critical attitude toward the bourgeoisie in provincial France, including some passages of brilliant satire. It likewise conveys the Realist idea that character and circumstance are destiny. Flaubert is also a superb artist who manages to turn the characters and items in Emma Bovary's world into symbols which haunt the mind long after the book is read. This is thus the prototypal Realist novel which is also a nearly perfect work of art. Final judgment about Emma is left to the reader, but she has had an impressive progeny in later literature.

Outline

I. Realism in art and literature is a rejection of the values of Romanticism, and it is associated with the rise of the middle class, the Industrial Revolution, and a new faith in science.

   A. Realists meant to depict the real world truthfully.

   1. They dealt with contemporary life, avoiding Romantic exoticism and interest in the past, as Manet was doing in painting.
   2. Standards of truth were those of science (i.e., rejecting Romantic idealizing and spiritual or emotional norms).
   3. The method of the Realist was to be objective and inductive, like a scientist working in a laboratory
   4. In terms of narrative strategies, the Realist author tried to evaporate himself or herself out of the book, making it seem an unmediated vision of the world. Flaubert said that an author should be like God in the universe: present everywhere but visible nowhere.

   B. In writing about the contemporary world, Realists inevitably wrote about the middle class, of which many Realists—including

Flaubert—were critical, disapproving of the manners, values, smugness, and complacency of the bourgeoisie.
   C. Realists wanted their work to be more inclusive than that of the Romantics, so it had to include the trivial, the low, and the sordid.
II. Flaubert's *Madame Bovary* illustrates all of these Realist principles.
   A. It is an ordinary story about ordinary people in two provincial French towns in the middle of the century.
      1. Emma Bovary grows up reading sentimental and romantic novels which fill her head with expectations that her marriage fails to fulfill.
      2. She drifts into adultery and debt, and when the debts are called in, she commits suicide by taking arsenic.
      3. Her husband dies a short while later, and her daughter, Berthe, is sent to live with an aunt, where she works in a cotton mill.
   B. The story is told with detachment, objectivity, and with sufficient detail to give a picture of life in a provincial French town in the 1840s.
      1. A passage from Chapter 9 of Book I shows Emma, bored and impatient, watching her husband, Charles, eat his dinner.
      2. In *Mimesis*, Erich Auerbach analyzes the passage to demonstrate Flaubert's "impartial, impersonal, and objective" presentation while at the same time giving us insights about Emma that she cannot have about herself.
      3. This is the kind of seriousness in the treatment of ordinary people that Auerbach says was prepared for by the story of the denial of Peter in the New Testament.
III. Flaubert's critical attitude toward the bourgeoisie is apparent in the novel through his treatment of the village priest and the local pharmacist, who turn out to be partly responsible for the disasters that overtake Emma and Charles.
   A. Flaubert treats some of the characters satirically.
      1. The village priest is so busy that he cannot begin to understand what Emma says to him.
      2. Homais, the village pharmacist, is so full of himself and his enlightened thinking that he could never understand what bothers Emma.
   B. Perhaps Flaubert's most stunning bit of satire occurs during a local agricultural fair, during which Rodolphe, Emma's first real lover,

seduces her. By interweaving the fair, with its concern for animals and manure, with the seduction, Flaubert manages to make a telling commentary on the beginning of Emma's first adulterous affair.

  C. Despite these indications of Flaubert's attitudes, *Madame Bovary* is still presented in an extremely detached and objective way.
    1. The novel can be seen as either immoral (as it was accused of being by the French government, which took Flaubert to court) or moral (which his lawyer argued at the trial).
    2. The fact that the novel can evoke such disparate responses illustrates its objectivity.

  D. The novel is probably neither a defense of adultery nor a judgment on it but a Realist novel about a woman who dreams, acts, and dies.
    1. After Emma's death, Charles tells one of Emma's lovers, Rodolphe, that no one is to blame—that fate is responsible for what happened.
    2. The Realists understood fate to be a combination of character and environment, and that seems to be true in Emma's case.
    3. The book in fact can be understood as a laboratory experiment which asks what happens if this particular woman is placed in these particular circumstances.
    4. The result, while not an illustration of fate as something that works from outside, is as inevitable as if it were, and it illustrates the power of character and environment—their inexorability—for the Realists.

IV. *Madame Bovary* is made up of a series of brilliantly depicted scenes, each of them done in the precise and abundant detail befitting a Realist writer, for whom environment is partly responsible for what happens to a protagonist.

  A. There are many stunningly good scenes in the novel: Emma's wedding, an evening at a ball in the neighborhood, the agricultural fair, Emma's first ride in the forest with Rodolphe, the scene where she first experiences the excitement of being an adulteress, and many others.
    1. One scene happens when Emma meets Léon, a former flame, at an opera in Rouen.
    2. The description of the events of the next day, when Léon and Emma meet at Rouen Cathedral and then take a mad cab ride

back and forth across the city, is brilliantly done; the author does not need to tell us what happened, since the details of the scene make that perfectly clear.

B. Flaubert managed to turn many of the precise details of setting and environment into symbols.
1. Emma, already bored with her marriage, throws her dried-up wedding bouquet into the fire piece by piece, and watches the pieces, like black butterflies, sail up the chimney.
2. The sound of the stable boy's wooden leg as he walks by becomes a symbol of Charles's medical incompetence, since it was his bungled effort to correct the boy's clubfoot that led to gangrene and the necessity for amputation.

V. *Madame Bovary* is the first full Realist novel in our course.

A. Emily Brontë and Alexander Pushkin had elements of full Realism in their works, but the former is still a Romantic story while the latter makes the narrator its central character and calls a lot of attention to its own medium. This is true of all of the other novels we have treated in this course as well.

B. Once it was established, the Realist novel became part of the mainstream; most novels published today are still in that tradition.

C. What sets Flaubert's novel apart from most other Realist novels is its artistry, which has been partly responsible for its immense legacy as well.

VI. Despite the objectivity and impersonal narrative strategies, readers will still wind up having to decide what to make of Emma.

A. Emma Bovary is a female Don Quixote or Mephistopheles' grasshopper in *Faust;* but her dreams can be seen as silly.
1. She is, however, the only one who thinks that there must be more to life than she experiences in her drab environment.
2. Readers need to decide about her for themselves—especially given Flaubert's famed objectivity in presentation.

B. Emma Bovary has had an immense progeny, from the first readers of the book (especially women readers) through multiple generations of literary Emmas created by authors including Kate Chopin, Sinclair Lewis, Willa Cather, and John O'Hara.

Essential Reading:

Flaubert, *Madame Bovary*.

Supplementary Reading:

Victor Brombert, *The Novels of Flaubert*.
Anthony Thorlby, *Gustave Flaubert and the Art of Realism*.

Questions to Consider:

1. It has been suggested that if there is a "villain" in this novel, it is Homais, the pharmacist. What, if anything, is villainous about him? What parts of Emma and Charles's disasters is he responsible for? Is he deliberately villainous? What do you think Flaubert is saying about Homais and the kind of character he represents in French provincial life in the mid-19th century?

2. Flaubert's criticism of petty bourgeois life is pretty astringent and pretty general—but not all-encompassing. Who are the genuinely good characters in the novel? What is it about them that distinguishes them from most of the others and allows them to escape being painted by Flaubert's satirical brush?

Lecture Thirty
Dostoevsky's *Notes from Underground*

Scope: Dostoevsky has been called a fantastic Realist, whose interest is in the psychology of characters in heightened emotional and spiritual atmospheres. His *Notes from Underground* illustrates this as well as provides a transition to his later works. The novel is a Swiftian satire, using an unattractive protagonist to illustrate problems with certain ideas—as Swift does in "A Modest Proposal." The ideas whose negative impact is described came to Russia in two waves of Westernization: utilitarian Utopianism and a vague Romantic humanitarianism. The book illustrates what happens to a man who has absorbed them: He becomes a vicious anti-hero who does spiteful things to others and to himself in order to maintain the one value without which, for Dostoevsky, one cannot be human—free will, even if it is exercised in self-destruction. We conclude with a consideration of the Underground Man as a prophet of new and disturbing tendencies in modern life.

Outline

I. Dostoevsky is a writer in the Realist tradition (called the "Natural School" in Russia), which flourished during the mid-19th century. He began his career as a Realist with *Poor Folk* in 1846.

   A. *Poor Folk* is an *epistolary novel* consisting entirely of letters written by its characters.
   1. The epistolary novel was a popular genre in the 18th century.
   2. Letters have played important roles in such nonepistolary works as *Eugene Onegin* and *Madame Bovary*.

   B. *Poor Folk*, in true Realist fashion, gives realistic descriptions of the suffering of poor people in St. Petersburg in the 1840s.

II. Dostoevsky was arrested for sedition in 1849, was nearly executed, and spent four years at hard labor in Siberia and six more in the army stationed on the Chinese border. When he returned to St. Petersburg in 1859, his ideas had undergone a radical transformation.

   A. He came back with a belief that Russian Christianity could save the world from materialism, utilitarianism, and the economic doctrine of enlightened self-interest. According to his new theories,

human beings, though fallen, are free to choose between Christ and evil.
- **B.** The idea of free will preoccupies him for the rest of his career.
    1. Socialism, whose advocacy had landed him in trouble in the first place, now looked pernicious to Dostoevsky, both for its atheism and for what he saw as its denial of freedom.
- **C.** He also altered some precepts of Realism, in which he had written his first books.
    1. He came to think that Realism paid too much attention to surface detail.
    2. He wanted to concentrate on human character and psychology, especially in moments of crisis, in which ultimate truths are likely to be revealed.
    3. Like a later Realist, Henrik Ibsen, Dostoevsky found his material in sensational stories in newspapers and focused on moments of emotional and spiritual intensity—a practice some critics call *fantastic* or *sensational Realism*.
    4. Nothing that happens in a Dostoevsky novel is impossible, but everything always happens in this heightened atmosphere that makes his books different from those of other Realists.

III. *Notes from Underground* (1864), under-appreciated in its own day, has gained in stature ever since, both as an introduction to the four great novels that Dostoevsky would write over the next 16 years (*Crime and Punishment*, *The Idiot*, *The Possessed*, and *The Brothers Karamazov*) and as prophetic of both the malaise of humanity in a standardized and mass-produced world and the needs of humans for freedom and humanity, even at the cost of personal suffering.
- **A.** The first section is the confession of an unpleasant man who explains why he chooses to live like a mouse.
- **B.** The second section contains two connected stories about events that happened to the Underground Man 20 years earlier.
- **C.** In a footnote to the first section, the author explains why a character like this *has* to exist in Russian society. The footnote also separates the author from the Underground Man, making the Underground Man a *persona*, created by the author to tell his own story.
- **D.** As we discover in the novel, the Underground Man was formed by a wave of "-isms" that entered Russia from Europe in the past half-

century—optimism, utilitarianism, utopianism, liberalism, and Socialism—all of which have in common the ideas that human nature is essentially good and that science and technology will create a utopian world, as long as we are all willing to pursue rational self-interest.
- **E.** The second section deals with Romantic sentimentalism and humanitarianism.
- **IV.** The tricky part of reading *Notes from Underground* is that the criticism of these ideas comes not from one who rejects them but from one who accepts them all—and then turns out to be a reprehensible character *because* he accepts them.
  - **A.** This fits the book in the tradition of first-person satires like Daniel Defoe's *The Shortest Way with Dissenters* and Jonathan Swift's *A Modest Proposal*, both of which have unattractive or dull characters arguing for positions against which the authors are opposed. This requires from the reader an ability to read between the lines, upside-down, and backwards to find what the author is really saying.
  - **B.** In the Underground Man, Dostoevsky is creating a *parody* of all of these "-isms," showing what happens to one who tries to live by them.
- **V.** The Underground Man shows us that his impulses are in conflict with each other.
  - **A.** He is sick and refuses to go to a doctor; when he was a civil servant he would tyrannize petitioners, even though he is not a vindictive man.
    1. In both cases what would be his natural or normal desire (to see a doctor, to be nice to the petitioners) is blocked by what he calls "spite."
    2. These conflicts prevent him from being anything—a hero or an insect; instead, he is a perfectly characterless man, which he suggests that any self-conscious Russian in the 19th century would have to be.
  - **B.** The Underground Man insists that once one has accepted "the laws of nature"—the ones forming the core of the "-isms" that came to Russia from the West—one cannot be a free agent.

1. If everyone acted entirely on the basis of enlightened self-interest, everyone would be incapable of performing an irrational act; the result would be a utopia.
2. The Underground Man insists that there is no evidence in history to suggest that humankind is even *capable* of such enlightened self-interest.
3. What is always left out of such equations is free will: the right to choose, even if it means choosing against one's own happiness.

C. The symbol for the future utopia is the Crystal Palace, built in London in 1851 and used as a symbol of future happiness by Chernyshevsky in *What Shall We Do?* (1863)—to which Dostoevsky's novel is a response.

D. The Underground Man's point is that if everyone behaved purely according to the laws of enlightened self-interest, everyone would be exactly alike and would cease to be fully human.
1. To be human is to *choose*, and history is full of stories about people who had everything and still did repulsive things because they were bored (e.g., Cleopatra).
2. The Underground Man is not defending suffering for its own sake or as an end in itself; sometimes it is the only way that we can know that we are alive, fully conscious, and fully *human*.

E. In the tenth section of the first part of the novel, the Underground Man says that if he could find another way to assure himself of his freedom, he would gladly choose it.

F. This section of the book was badly mangled by the censors, but it hints at what was to become Dostoevsky's way of salvation in future novels: the teachings of and submission to Christ.

VI. The second section of the novel satirizes Romanticism.

A. It tells the story of the Underground Man's relations with Liza, a prostitute whom he—in an effort to establish his absolute superiority over her—hypocritically convinces of the horror and misery of her life.
1. She unexpectedly takes him up on his offer to rescue her, humiliates him by catching him in a squalid and absurd argument with his servant, and winds up comforting him.

2. Triply humiliated, he takes her sexually in brutal fashion and then pays her for her services. She leaves his flat, leaving the money behind.
- **B.** The satire is directed against a vague Romantic humanitarianism which allows people to feel superior by dreaming Faustian dreams of helping humanity but always in the abstract.
    1. The Underground Man spends much of his time in his mouse hole reading Romantic literature and dreaming Quixotic or Bovary-like dreams of saving the world.
    2. Confronted with a situation in which he might actually be able to help someone (since she has believed the Romantic clichés he has given to her) he recognizes that their roles are reversed: she has become the Romantic heroine and he the one who needs saving.
    3. He feels some remorse at what he's done but decides that suffering will be good for her.
    4. At the end of the novel, the Underground Man returns to his solitude.
- **C.** Liza's capacity for selfless love will be the alternative to the egocentric and self-destructive efforts of the Underground Man in future Dostoevsky novels. It cannot, however, save the Underground Man in this one.

VII. *Notes from Underground* is important in three major ways.
- **A.** It suggests the direction of Dostoevsky's fiction over the next two decades. The Underground Man and Liza suggest characters in *Crime and Punishment* and *The Brothers Karamazov*.
- **B.** The novel seems prophetic of the increase in violence and carnage in contemporary cities.
    1. We live in a world much closer to the ideals of a utopia than Dostoevsky did.
    2. Some of this is reflected in the Underground Man's desire to deliberately violate the laws of enlightened self-interest, just to prove that he is still alive and human.
- **C.** In terms of the course, Dostoevsky has taught us another way to tell a story: inside-out and backwards, using a persona that we have to take ironically.

Essential Reading:

Dostoevsky, *Notes from Underground.*

Supplementary Reading:

Joseph Frank, *Dostoevsky: The Stir of Liberation, 1860–1865.*

Michael R. Katz, ed. *Notes From Underground: A Norton Critical Edition.*

Questions to Consider:

1. The first episode in the second section (the one treating the disastrous farewell party attended by the Underground Man) is not mentioned in any detail in the lecture. How does it fit into the rest of the novel, particularly the second section, which deals with Romantic humanitarianism? What does it contribute to the overall themes or suggestions of the book?

2. In what really important ways is *Notes from Underground* a necessary preparation—for both author and reader—for the better-known novels, such as *Crime and Punishment* and *The Brothers Karamazov*, that follow it?

Lecture Thirty-One
Twain's *Huckleberry Finn*

Scope: Mark Twain's Realism is part of American Regionalism, growing out of the westward movement and the contrasting ways of life on the Atlantic seaboard and west of the Appalachians. Twain began as a regional humorist, and regional values—honesty, humor, truthfulness, and the integrity of the common man—carry over into *Huckleberry Finn*, whose protagonist is a regional character in conflict with the civilizing forces of the towns along the Mississippi. The great moments of the novel occur when Huck's "corrupt conscience," shaped by the values of shore society, conflicts with his "honest heart," formed by his relationship on the raft with the runaway slave, Jim. In the first two-thirds of the book, Huck obeys his heart, suggesting Twain's optimistic view that humans can transcend their environment and training. But the last third of the book, when Tom Sawyer rejoins Huck, suggests a more pessimistic vision—closer to the negative one that informs Twain's later writing.

Outline

I. American Realism began in a movement called *Regionalism*, which in the arts described life west of the Appalachians, while the East Coast was still dominated by Romanticism.

   A. So much of American literature during this period was idealized, spiritual, hopeful, sentimental, and expressive of faith in a benign natural order and a benevolent deity.

   B. Mark Twain (Samuel Langhorne Clemens) was born in Missouri on the Mississippi, and he got his start in literature as a Regionalist, describing a kind of life that seemed to have little in common with that on the eastern seaboard.

   C. Regionalist literature described a life that was crude, primitive, colorful, and often funny in contrast to the settled certainties of the established eastern writers.

   1. Twain's own experiences—printer, soldier, newspaper writer and editor, steamboat pilot, prospector—were in the places where Regionalism grew up.

  2. The pen name he adopted—Mark Twain—came from a call telling a riverboat pilot how deep the water was and has a regional ring to it.
- **D.** Twain's two names suggest the divided consciousness of a Regionalist who came to live in the East and became a contributor to *Atlantic Monthly*. He in fact was more responsible than any other writer for bringing Regionalism into the mainstream of American letters.
    - **1.** He began writing in the Regionalist tradition of Artemus Ward and G. W. Harris in pieces like "The Notorious Jumping Frog of Calaveras County," which made his national reputation.
    - **2.** In it and many other early pieces, Twain contrasts the Eastern establishment view with that of the regional, vernacular character. The humor resides in the tension between the two, and it marks the considerable distance between views of life in the two parts of America.
    - **3.** Twain's work insists that if eastern literature is prettier, then Western literature is more honest; it refutes eastern respectability and sentimental moralizing.
    - **4.** Twain's work is also a declaration of democracy and the values and integrity of the common individual, at which point American Realism comes into line with European Realism.
    - **5.** Henry Nash Smith traces these two voices and their development across Twain's early career: especially *Roughing It* and *Life on the Mississippi*.

II. In *The Adventures of Huckleberry Finn* Twain allows the vernacular, regional character to tell his own story—as opposed to *The Adventures of Tom Sawyer*, in which a genteel authorial voice with an omniscient point of view tells it.
- **A.** The opposing point of view—that of conventional gentility—is represented generally by the towns along the banks of the Mississippi, peopled with such characters as the Widow Douglas, Miss Watson, and even Tom Sawyer himself.
- **B.** Huck carries the values of conventional shore society inside him, so that all the major conflicts in the book—between convention and rebellion, respectability and individuality, shore and raft, official and regional values—are located in the head of a 12-year-old river rat.

III. Twain wrote the book in fits and starts over a seven-year period, and it seems to have grown on him during its writing.
  A. He seems to have started by wanting to take Huck on a trip down the Mississippi on a raft, revisiting places Twain himself knew very well.
   1. Then he added Jim, a runaway slave, for whom it makes no sense to be going *down* the Mississippi, deeper and deeper into slave territory (the novel is set in the 1840s).
   2. With Jim added, Twain seems to have decided that he would have them float down the Mississippi only to where the Ohio joins the Mississippi, and then have them canoe *up* the Ohio into free territory.
  B. Twain, however, did not know the Ohio River, and so he has Huck and Jim miss Cairo (where the two rivers join) in a fog and keeps them going south. Then, not knowing what to do, he has the raft destroyed, sends Jim and Huck off in opposite directions, and sets the novel aside for two years.
IV. What also seems to have happened is that Twain discovered a much deeper relationship between Huck and Jim than he had anticipated.
  A. In Chapter 15, Huck plays a trick on Jim, and Jim is so hurt that Huck wishes that he had never played the trick. He says that he humbled himself to Jim, for which he has never been sorry.
  B. In Chapter 16, when Jim tells Huck that he plans on buying or stealing his wife and children out of slavery, Huck is appalled, and he decides to turn Jim in.
   1. As Huck is leaving in the canoe to do so, Jim calls out to him that Huck is the only real friend he has ever had, and Huck is suddenly not sure whether he wants to turn him in or not.
   2. When he has a chance to turn Jim in, he deflects it and then asks himself if he would feel better if he had done the "right" thing. He decides that he would not, and since he is probably damned anyway, from here on he will simply take the easiest way out, not worrying about the morality of his decisions.
   3. This is a great moment in the novel: Huck's conscience, trained by shore society, tells him that slaves are property and that it is his duty to turn Jim in. Huck believes that helping Jim is wrong, but he does it anyway, transcending his training and—at this point in the novel—suggesting that a good heart can defeat a diseased conscience.

©2007 The Teaching Company.

V. The next section of the novel, written two years later, is in part a satire on shore society.
  A. This is the point of the episode in which Huck spends time with the Grangerfords, involved in a feud with the Shepherdsons.
  B. It continues in the scenes in which two con-men, calling themselves the King and the Duke, commandeer the raft and thus keep it heading south.
    1. They spend their time exploiting the religious sentimentalism, the greed, and the craving for social approval on shore.
    2. In doing so, they highlight what Henry Nash Smith calls "the community of saints" (Huck and Jim) aboard the raft.
  C. Perhaps the greatest moment in American literature happens in Chapter 31, when the King and the Duke have turned Jim over to the authorities for the bounty on runaway slaves.
    1. If Huck is to stick by Jim, he will have to defy the law, not just evade it, as he would have to have done in Chapter 16.
    2. At first, he decides to turn Jim in but then, in a magnificent moment, chooses to defy the law—and hence go to hell, as he really believes he will—to help Jim escape, suggesting that people *can* outgrow their training and still listen to their pure hearts.
    3. This is the beginning of many American stories, including Hemingway's stories about Nick Adams, in which young people leave home to try to outgrow what they have been taught and which they instinctively know is wrong. As Hemingway himself said, this moment is the beginning of all modern American fiction.
VI. Twain again laid the novel aside for a time, and when he came back to it, he finished it in a way that no one has liked very much.
  A. Huck finds Jim a prisoner on the Phelps farm, where he is joined by Tom Sawyer, who orchestrates an escape for Jim full of contrived details that come from books but which do not advance the cause of Jim's freedom.
  B. Eventually, Tom announces that Miss Watson has died, freeing Jim in her will, thus making all of this a game.
    1. We understand Tom Sawyer's part in this: this is just the way he is.

- **2.** What we do not understand is Huck's part: why is Huck so willing to go along with Tom Sawyer's outrageous plots? What has happened to the relationship he had with Jim on the raft, when he was willing to go to hell rather than abandon Jim?
- **C.** By the novel's end, Huck becomes Sancho Panza to Tom's Don Quixote again—a sidekick, whose moral growth on the trip down the river seems to be forgotten.
    - **1.** The ending raises all manner of questions about what happens in the book: does Huck grow and change or not? Can an individual learn to transcend what he or she has been taught or not?
    - **2.** The ending has been considered an artistic failure by some; by others, a deliberate artistic decision by Twain, who by the time he finished the book did *not* believe that we can transcend our experience, that we always carry with us our shore values.
- **D.** Twain's final views on what he called "the damned human race," foreshadowed at the end of *Huckleberry Finn*, are captured in late stories like "The Man Who Corrupted Hadleyburg" and "The Mysterious Stranger." They also show up in the Colonel Sherburn episode in *Huckleberry Finn*, suggesting that by the end of his life Twain had lost his faith in regional values and had come to believe that character and circumstance *are* our fate, which we can never transcend—a point we have already encountered in *Madame Bovary*.
- **E.** The ending of the novel has raised many questions, which you will need to decide for yourself as you read it.

Essential Reading:

Mark Twain, *The Adventures of Huckleberry Finn*.

Supplementary Reading:

Hamlin Hill and Walter Blair, eds. *The Art of Huckleberry Finn*.
Henry Nash Smith, *Mark Twain: The Development of a Writer*.

Questions to Consider:
1. Hamlin Hill suggests that the final hoax of this book is on the reader. How would that work? What, precisely, is the hoax? If it is a hoax, what has Twain fooled us into thinking? Does the hoax seem deliberate on Twain's part?
2. In the Grangerford parlor there is a basket of artificial fruit—prettier than real fruit but chipped so that the chalk underneath shows. In what way is this a symbol specifically of the Grangerfords, the Shepherdsons, and, more generally, of all of the shore life depicted in the book? What aspects of shore society are satirized in the long Peter Wilks episode?

Lecture Thirty-Two
Dickinson's Poetry

Scope: After a brief consideration of the anomaly of Emily Dickinson's life and the writing of her verses, we consider the habitual techniques that characterize her tough-minded and unflinching poetry: the use of common meter stanza form, her use of dashes instead of conventional punctuation, and a difficult syntactical and grammatical density. We then read and analyze four of her poems which illustrate both these technical items and her habitual way of refusing to settle for easy answers, making every poem an individual quest which reaches a different conclusion. All four poems are about death and the possibility of a life after death, and they range in tone from hopeful to ambiguous to despairing. We conclude by placing her work in the context of the Romantics, the Realists, and future Modernist poets.

Outline

I. Emily Dickinson is somewhat of an anomaly in American literature. She does not belong to any school or tradition, unless we consider her an early Modernist, along with Walt Whitman, Thomas Hardy, and Gerard Manley Hopkins.

   A. Emily Dickinson, born into a prominent family in Amherst, Massachusetts, from an early age withdrew into the seclusion of her family house for reasons we still do not understand. Early critics and biographers (mostly male) assumed that she was reacting to a thwarted or failed love affair.

   B. Modern feminists tend to think that the withdrawal from ordinary life was a deliberate choice by an artist, along the lines of Jane Austen, Emily Brontë, or Christina Rossetti—a way of having what Virginia Woolf would call "a room of one's own."

II. Dickinson's production of poetry increased as she withdrew from the world.

   A. In the 1860s she wrote a series of letters to someone she called her "Master," but since we have only drafts of the letters, we do not know if they were ever sent—or, if they were, who answered them.

1. The "Master" letters coincided with her most productive period of writing.
2. In 1862 she sent four poems to Thomas Higginson, who had written an article in *Atlantic Monthly* containing advice to young poets; he advised her not to publish yet, and she did not.
3. Only seven of her poems were published during her lifetime.
   B. After her death, over 1,700 poems were found in various places and written on various media, all over the house.
   1. Selections of her poems were published in 1890, 1891, and 1896, but disagreements between the families who were executors of the poems kept them from being published *in toto* or even having them all located in the same place.
   2. In 1960, Thomas Johnson brought out the first complete edition of her poems, so that Dickinson studies have had only about half a century to assimilate her body of work.

III. Like her life, Dickinson's poetry is outwardly placid, simple, even deceptively childlike. Her poems are also tough-minded and full of integrity, refusing to take conventional attitudes or to smooth over difficult questions.
   A. Poem #241 is a kind of position paper for Dickinson, laying out her preference for truth, however painful, to taking the easy way out.
   B. She demonstrates in her poems the same kind of integrity and independence that caused her to refuse to yield to the Great Revival that was sweeping across New England when she was a young girl.

IV. Most of Dickinson's poems—including #241—are written in *common meter*, made up of alternating lines of iambic tetrameter and iambic trimeter and usually rhyming *abcb*.
   A. English is an accentual language; an accent helps to define any word's proper pronunciation.
   B. Tŏ-dáy is a natural *iamb*: an unaccented syllable followed by an accented one.
   1. A line of iambic tetrameter is made up of four iambs, and a line of iambic trimeter of three iambs.

- **2.** A common meter stanza metrically looks like this: ˇ ´ ˇ ´ ˇ ´ ˇ ´ / ˇ ´ ˇ ´ ˇ ´ / ˇ ´ ˇ ´ ˇ ´ ˇ ´ / ˇ ´ ˇ ´ ˇ ´. The rhymes fall at the end of the second and fourth line.
  - **3.** Most greeting cards use this stanza—the easiest one to write in English—and many nursery rhymes use it as well.
- **C.** It is also called common meter because many Protestant hymns are written in this stanza form.
  - **1.** Dickinson's #241 can be sung to the tunes of "Belmont" ("The Lord's My Shepherd") and "St. Anne" ("Our God, Our Help in Ages Past"), among many others.
  - **2.** The Romantics had revived the use of common meter, as Coleridge did in his "The Rime of the Ancient Mariner."
- **D.** Dickinson complicates this seemingly simple stanza form in a variety of ways.
  - **1.** She uses dashes instead of conventional punctuation marks, and the dashes are often rhetorical in nature; the best way to read the poems are aloud, using the dashes as pauses.
  - **2.** She capitalizes words for emphasis—the way we might use italics.
  - **3.** She compresses syntax and grammar to make her poems dense and imagistic.
  - **4.** The combination of these techniques, because they tend to complicate meaning, makes her poems open-ended, raising as many questions as they answer. They also require some work from the reader.

V. Four of her poems can illustrate these generalizations.
- **A.** Poem #214, a response to a Ralph Waldo Emerson poem, suggests that the only heaven we can be sure of is the emotional intoxication that can come from a close observance of and participation in the details of nature.
- **B.** Poem #348 is about the way nature always reminds us of our own transience. Spring actually *hurts* the poet by reminding her that while it always renews itself, she is another year older and that much closer to death.
- **C.** Poem #216 is wonderfully ambiguous in its consideration of the question of whether we in some ways live beyond our own deaths. The poem faces up to its questions, but it can provide us with no final answers, either optimistic or pessimistic.

- **D.** Poem #449 is a response to John Keats's "Ode on a Grecian Urn."
    1. It is ambiguous in its consideration of the value of living and dying for some large abstraction outside ourselves, whether that be Beauty or Truth.
    2. We cannot be sure of what it is that does not survive our deaths.
- **VI.** From her hermitage in Amherst, Dickinson participated in some of the great literary movements in the world outside.
    - **A.** With Faust, Heathcliff and Catherine, and Lord Byron, she is a Romantic rebel, daring to think and say things in her poems that would have greatly shocked those in her immediate world. As one critic has said it, she was a Romantic hero in an upstairs bedroom.
    - **B.** With Flaubert, Emily Brontë, and Ibsen, she is a recorder of the constraints on women in the 19th century; contemporary feminists have thus discovered in her a kindred spirit.
    - **C.** Her poems seem very *modern* to us, not only in their questioning of conventional and accepted beliefs (which she shares with an early Modern poet like Thomas Hardy), but in their reliance on metaphors and images to communicate their meaning (which she shares with Ezra Pound, H. D. [Hilda Doolittle], and T. S. Eliot).

Essential Reading:

Emily Dickinson poems.

Supplementary Reading:

Paula Bennett, *Emily Dickinson: Woman Poet.*
Bettina Liebowitz Knapp, *Emily Dickinson.*

Questions to Consider:

1. As you read the poems of Dickinson, does any settled, recurring, or consistent set of values, beliefs, or attitudes suggest itself to you? Could you make a map of her mind on the basis of the poems, or is each poem so entirely unique, self-starting, and self-generating that each has to be considered on its own, without reference to her other poems?

2. As you read the poems, what explicit statements, images, or metaphors suggest to you the awareness of Dickinson as a woman who was, as modern feminists claim, keenly aware of the constraints under which 19th-century women lived? How could we tell, if we did not know who had written these poems, that it was a 19th-century woman? How could we infer her attitude about the place of women in her world, both from what she says and from the way she says it?

Lecture Thirty-Three
Ibsen and Chekhov—Realist Drama

Scope: We begin by finding in drama the elements of Realism we have seen in earlier lectures on the novel. Henrik Ibsen's contribution to Realist drama was to bring onto the stage contemporary people and such sensational issues as corrupt politics and journalism, venereal disease, and the oppression of women—the subject of *A Doll's House*. He left the *shape* of drama intact, however, using the formula of the "well-made play." Chekhov changed the form of drama to match its new Realist content. *Uncle Vanya* is a play which seems plotless: it has no central character, individual story lines bump into each other in ways that disturb all of them, and after an anti-climactic culmination, everyone is pretty much where they were at the beginning—simulating the texture of everyday life. Ibsen and Chekhov between them created a new kind of drama for the great playwrights who followed them.

Outline

I. We have already encountered Realism in fiction in this course; here we turn to Realism in drama.

   A. Realism's tenets include a faithful representation of contemporary life, a rejection of Romantic idealism and subjectivity, an inclusiveness that includes the low and the mean, and a critical attitude toward the bourgeoisie.
   1. Earlier Realists had also stressed the importance of environment in shaping individual character.
   2. That aspect received new emphasis from Charles Darwin's *The Origin of Species* (1859), which argued that adaptation to environment is what causes changes over time.

   B. When applied to drama, these tenets suggest a truthful depiction of the contemporary world, a focus on the middle class, an objectivity that mimics the stance of a scientist in a laboratory, and an emphasis on the shaping influence of environment.

   C. In drama it also produced a new set of stage techniques.

1. A *proscenium arch stage* suggests an actual setting in which the opening is the fourth wall, through which the audience gets to oversee life as it is lived by the characters on stage.
2. Asides and soliloquies are abandoned as unrealistic.
3. Exposition has to be done naturally: A maid explains to a newly arrived guest what has been going on, or an old friend shows up who needs to be caught up on what has happened since they left.
4. Middle-class drawing rooms are meticulously recreated on stage, down to the bric-a-brac on the end tables.

II. Henrik Ibsen of Norway invented this new kind of drama, recreating himself from 1877 on with such plays as *The Pillars of Society* (1877), *A Doll's House* (1879), and *Ghosts* (1881), which very slowly made their way onto mainstream stages.

A. No respectable theater would touch these plays because they all attacked pillars of middle-class life—marriage, family, church—as oppressive, hypocritical, and life-crushing.

B. *A Doll's House* is about a woman who comes to realize that no one has ever taken her seriously as a person; she ends the play by leaving her husband and children in an effort to find herself.
1. Years later, when a women's rights organization in Norway gave Ibsen an award, he said that his interest was not specifically in *women's* rights but in *human* rights.
2. In all of his plays, characters struggle to free themselves from the "dead hand of the past"—that is, from tradition, custom, conventionality, and respectability, all of which stifle and kill the present moment.
3. Torvald and Nora are equally victims of this dead hand of the past, reacting to environmental pressures that help to make them what they are—symbolized by the stuffy Victorian drawing room in which the action takes place.
4. As Ibsen grew older he, like Mark Twain, became increasingly skeptical of humans' ability to transcend their environment and training. In this play he still believes that they can, which is one reason for its impact in its own day and on the modern stage.

III. Ibsen created modern drama by changing its content, bringing onto the stage contemporary issues including the oppression of women, corrupt politics and journalism, and even venereal disease.

- **A.** He used for his new kind of drama the conventional formula of the well-made play which was current all over Europe in his day.
- **B.** The *well-made play* begins with a late point of attack, just before the crisis, and then fills in the background that explains the crisis, so that we move backwards in knowledge as we move forwards in time; we always receive the last piece of necessary information just before the climax occurs.
    1. *A Doll's House* is a perfect illustration of the formula of the well-made play, climaxing on the night of a holiday party in which Nora has danced the tarantella, by which time the audience perfectly understands all that has led up to the moment when Nora walks out the door.
    2. Ibsen revolutionized drama's content but kept its form. For modern audiences, the form of drama makes Ibsen's plays seem sometimes a bit creaky, too full of coincidence and perhaps too theatrical to be entirely like real life.

IV. Anton Chekhov completed the Realist revolution in drama by making the form of drama match its content, bringing theater as close to ordinary life as it had ever been.
- **A.** Chekhov thought that all drama falsified life by forcing it into the genres and stage conventions that were permissible on European stages.
    1. All drama had to be either comic or tragic, neither of which captures what it feels like to live an ordinary life or to spend an ordinary day.
    2. Chekhov's goal was to let life be the determiner of form, rather than the other way around.
- **B.** *Uncle Vanya* (1900) illustrates Chekhov's method.
    1. A group of characters on a country estate keeps half a dozen plots in motion, all of which are at cross-purposes and are mutually incompatible.
    2. There is no single central character; like life, this play is an *ensemble* event, with each character trying to make himself or herself its central character—and failing, because all the other characters are trying to do the same thing.
    3. There are multiple plots, some of which cancel each other out.
    4. The climax of the play is anticlimactic; at the end, the characters are all back where they were when it started.

    5. Eric Bentley says that the difference between an Ibsen and a Chekhov play is that in Ibsen's plays a secret is slowly revealed that indicates that what everyone believed all these years was not really so; in Chekhov's plays what everyone believed all these years is confirmed, even though no one wants to believe it.
    6. The ending of *Uncle Vanya* is neither comic nor tragic, and its life seems simply to go offstage to continue as it had been before the play started and while we were watching it.

V. Realism comes to drama in Ibsen's introduction of contemporary and sometimes sensational material that he got from newspaper stories, and in Chekhov's manipulation of the *form* of drama, making its trajectory more like that of ordinary life.
    A. Between them they prepared the way for a period of great drama in the Western world.
        1. Their descendents include George Bernard Shaw, Arthur Miller, Tennessee Williams, and Eugene O'Neill.
        2. Their achievements stimulated the reactions of innovative playwrights like Luigi Pirandello and Bertolt Brecht.
    B. In many ways what Nora does in *A Doll's House* is as revolutionary as what Faust does in his play and what Catherine Earnshaw does in *Wuthering Heights*. The Realist Movement takes these grand gestures out of the cosmic realm and locates them in the Victorian drawing room.

Essential Reading:

Anton Chekhov, *Uncle Vanya*.
Henrik Ibsen, *A Doll's House*.

Supplementary Reading:

Robert Brustein, *The Theatre of Revolt*.
Richard Gilman, *Chekhov's Plays*.
Richard Hornsby, *Patterns in Ibsen's Middle Plays*.

Questions to Consider:

1. What happens to Nora after she leaves home at the end of *A Doll's House*? In other words, if you were to write another act, how would it go? Does she make it in the world outside her house? What happens to her? What happens to her husband and children? Does she ever return home? What are her chances of succeeding at what she says she wants to do when the play ends?

2. Take individual characters in Chekhov's *Uncle Vanya* and follow each one's plot through the play, looking for the ways in which each plot has its own integrity and pattern. Then notice the places where the stories intersect. What happens when they do? How do the plots tend to neutralize each other, and in what precise ways? What is that one thing each character learns?

Lecture Thirty-Four
Rabindranath Tagore's Stories and Poems

Scope: We begin by suggesting that 20th-century literature is more *international* than it has ever been in history—a point which Tagore's introduction of the Western short story into Indian literature illustrates. We then define the modern short story along lines laid down by Chekhov as a short fiction in which interior events are more important than exterior ones, and traditional plot gives way to significant internal adjustments. Tagore promotes internationalism in both politics and religion, and we find this syncretistic quality in both his poems and his stories. His Realism is of a psychological nature, but its subjects—contemporary problems in Indian villages—he shares with Ibsen, whose influence he acknowledges. "Punishment," the one story we look at in detail, is about the oppression of women in traditional Indian society, featuring a strong female protagonist who reminds us of Ibsen's Hedda Gabler.

Outline

I. In the 20th century we are closer to having a truly "world" literature than we ever have been, as a host of factors—political, technological, economic—allowing influences to flow from country to country and culture to culture in ways that would have amazed our ancestors.

II. Rabindranath Tagore appears at a moment in literary history when the short story—a popular genre as long as there has been literature—had been reinvented by several writers, the most important of whom is Anton Chekhov.

    A. Most earlier short stories had been little novels which, because of their limited length, depended more on plot and external action than psychological issues and characterization in their development.

        1. Chekhov transfers the main action from the external to the internal world, from outside events to mental processes that happen *inside* a character.

      2. This had already been anticipated in the stories of Nathaniel Hawthorne and Tolstoy, but Chekhov made the internal world the focus of the short story and thus recreated it.
      3. In a Chekhov story called "Gooseberries," nothing really happens; the point of the story is the happiness of the farmer and the troubled thoughts of his visiting brother.
      4. Virginia Woolf in "Modern Fiction" says that Chekhov made the short story "spiritual," by which she means "internal" or "psychological"; she did not admire fiction that emphasized the external world.

  B. In these ways Chekhov was a major influence on the other writers who contributed to the recreation of the short story: James Joyce, Sherwood Anderson, Ernest Hemingway, and Katherine Mansfield among them.

  C. Chekhov also maintained an objective point of view in his stories, insisting that an author's attitudes and ideas had no place in literature.
      1. The author's job is to describe as accurately as they can what people do and say, and to stay out of the way while doing so.
      2. We can see this as part of the removal of the writer from their work that we have already noticed in other Realist writers.

III. At the end of the 19th century colonialism was at its height, so that European influences permeated and modified local literary traditions; Tagore is at a crossroads in all this.

  A. India had been under English influence since about 1600, so that by the time India became an independent country (1947), English had become more or less the common language of the country. Many modern Indian writers use English in their works.

  B. India had its own rich literary traditions reaching back 3,000 years, but in Tagore we have an Indian writer using a Western literary form: the short story. Tagore was influenced by the Realists Chekhov, Turgenev, Shaw, and Ibsen.

  C. Since the height of European influence on non-Western cultures coincided with the Realist Movement, most of the earliest Western-type literature from these cultures is in the Realist mode. The literature is about middle- or lower-class characters, describes contemporary life, uses a more or less objective point of view with minimal authorial intrusion, and includes some social criticism.

- **D.** Rabindranath Tagore illustrates all of this, writing Realist stories about people who exploit the caste system, suppress women, and benefit from the sufferings of the poor.
- **IV.** Tagore was educated in India and Europe and, like Goethe, was something of a universal man: poet, novelist, dramatist, essayist, teacher, musician, and painter.
  - **A.** He founded a school that became a university, wrote the words and music for 2,000 songs (two of which became the national anthems of India and Bangladesh), and directed his erudition and talent toward international understanding and cultural synthesis.
    1. He supported Mahatma Gandhi but cautioned against too much nationalism and too little internationalism; he saw Gandhi as the perfect union of the East and the West.
    2. In a short story, "Broken Ties," Tagore sends his protagonist through a period of Western influence, then through a period of mysticism, guided by a swami, and to a final reconciliation of the two through the guidance of a young widow who teaches the protagonist how to blend the spiritual and the physical.
  - **B.** In religion, too, Tagore was syncretistic, combining elements of Hinduism, Buddhism, and Western religions into what he called "the deity of life," in which the divine advances and retreats into and out of ordinary life, nature, and other people.
    1. This is illustrated in a poem about a would-be ascetic who keeps missing signs of God that are all around him.
    2. In "Flute Music," a man running away from an arranged marriage finds signs of the divine on a horrible street, which is suddenly the world of Vishnu.
  - **C.** Tagore is also a wonderful story teller, as he demonstrates with "The Hungry Stones"—full of substantive and informative allusions to *1001 Nights*.
    1. This story also suggests the division within every modern Indian: half colonized British and half Indian.
    2. "The Hungry Stones" is a nested story.
- **V.** Some of Tagore's fiction takes up the problem of the oppression of women, particularly in rural villages. That is the subject of his story, "Punishment."

A. In the story a man accuses his wife of killing her sister-in-law, a murder that was really committed by the woman's husband.
   1. The man, Chidam, instinctively blames his wife, Chandara, based on his training as a man, even though he very much loves his wife (who very much loves him in return) and knows very well that she is innocent.
   2. She is so indignant at the false accusation and the kind of betrayal it implies that she refuses to defend herself, insisting in court that she is guilty, even when the two brothers both confess to the murder in an effort to save her life; she is eventually executed, refusing to see her husband before she dies.

B. The title of the story is thus ironic in that it is finally about Chandara's punishment of her husband for instinctively valuing a brother above a wife.
   1. The husband's reflexive way of thinking is very traditionally Indian, reflected in an episode in the *Mahabharata*.
   2. Against the weight of all that tradition, Chandara can oppose only her life.

C. While the story treats its events in a psychological way (we have it mostly from Chandara's point of view), it deals with some of the same social issues that Realist writers deal with in the West.
   1. In a way, the story is about how societal norms are internalized until they seem part of us, even when they run counter to our desires or needs.
   2. The problem is exacerbated by its lower-class protagonists, who have no other place than marriage in which to wield their power.

D. The story is finally Chandara's story: a story about an unconventional woman—like Catherine Earnshaw, Nora Elmer, or Hedda Gabler—willing to sacrifice happiness or even life to make a point that needs to be made.

Essential Reading:
Rabindranath Tagore poems and stories.

Supplementary Reading:
Kalpana Bardhan, *Of Women, Outcastes, Peasants, and Rebels.*
Mary Lago, *Rabindranath Tagore.*

Questions to Consider:

1. In what ways do you see parallels between the situations of Nora in *A Doll's House* and Chandara in "Punishment"? Are the modes of analysis by the two authors similar? How important is the environment in explaining the situations and attitudes of the characters in the two works? In what other ways can you see the influence of Realism in the West on this short story?

2. Why is it important in "Punishment" that the first person on the murder scene is Ramlochan Chakravarti, who is described as "a pillar of the village"? What would have happened if the first person on the scene would have been another landless worker? Would the results have been the same?

Lecture Thirty-Five
Higuchi Ichiyō's "Child's Play"

Scope: The Realist Movement came to Japan in its enforced Westernization after 1853. The writer who came closest to embodying its spirit, Higuchi Ichiyō, however, had virtually no access to Western literature and ideas. Her model was a 17th-century writer, Ihara Saikaku, who wrote stories about merchants and other city people in Osaka. He was Ichiyō's favorite writer, and she uses many of his techniques in her stories, including locating them in and around the red-light district of Edo (now Tokyo). The story that we consider here, "Child's Play," is about the Indian summer of children who live in and near the pleasure quarter, on the verge of having to assume adult responsibilities, set against a backdrop of adults whose avarice, subservience, and hypocrisy makes the children's inevitable transition a sad one. We consider the excellent aspects of the story itself and conclude by locating Ichiyō in the larger international Realist Movement.

Outline

I. Japan's second recreation of itself dates from 1853. Along with so much else that came to the country from the West came the Romantic and Realist movements, which Japan assimilated and remade in its own image in record time.

II. Higuchi Ichiyō, however, came to her Realism via a Japanese, not a Western, route.
   A. In her brief schooling, she was trained primarily in classical Japanese literature, like *The Tale of Genji*, and classical Japanese poetry. She did not read her first works of Western literature until she was already writing the story that made her famous, "Child's Play."
      1. Japanese reviewers of her story called her a Naturalist and associated her with the traditions of Zola, Ibsen, and Chekhov, assuming that she had been influenced by Western writers.
      2. As in the work of the Realists, she deals with poor people who live on the edge of the pleasure quarter of Edo (now Tokyo)

and who serve the courtesans and wealthy patrons in what we might think of as a very civilized red-light district.
- **B.** Ichiyō's point of view, however, suggests that she is not working in the Western Realist tradition.
  1. While Realism tried to evaporate the author out of the work, she is a chatty and friendly presence in her story.
  2. She guides us through the pleasure quarter at the story's beginning and stops to talk directly to us many times throughout the story.
- **C.** Her model was Ihara Saikaku, a 17th-century writer partly responsible for the creation of a popular literature in Japan that paralleled those in China and in the West.
  1. He wrote novels about life in and around the pleasure quarter of Osaka (then the most important city in Japan), whose characters are ordinary people, whose plots are more picaresque than tightly organized, and whose narrator provides wry and witty comments along the way.
  2. A complete edition of his works had been published in 1894, and from her diary we know that Ichiyō read all of them and admired them greatly.
  3. Like Ihara Saikaku, Ichiyō's Realism is a matter of dealing with ordinary people who live in areas of the city that had never played a part in classical Japanese literature.
  4. Ihara Saikaku also made liberal use of type characters, or *caricatures*, which subordinate all personal qualities to one generalized defining one. Saikaku's merchants, wives, courtesans, and his people of the street are all in some ways typed or caricatured. Ichiyō borrowed this technique from him as well but used it in a different way.

III. "Child's Play" is about children in and around the pleasure quarter in the last moments of childhood, before they are required to assume adult responsibilities.
- **A.** "Child's Play" central character is Midori.
  1. Midori's sister is the most sought-after courtesan in the red-light district, and Midori has already been sold to the same establishment.
  2. By the story's end, when she begins to menstruate, Midori is ready to assume a role comparable to that of her sister.

3. Her childhood infatuation with Nobu, the son of a Buddhist priest in the poor district bordering the pleasure quarter, leads nowhere; she becomes a courtesan and he goes off to study to become a Buddhist priest.

B. Midori's best friend, Shota, grandson of the neighborhood pawnbroker, assumes his part in the family business; in the future, if he wants to see Midori, he will have to pay for the privilege.

C. Ichiyō's use of type characters and caricatures is confined to the adults in the story and can be illustrated with her portrait of Nobu's father, the Buddhist priest.
1. Nobu's father is fat, married, addicted to eating eels, and his activities include more economic ones than religious ones.
2. He even sets up his attractive daughter in a tea stand and sends his wife out during festivals to hawk mementoes. To call him "his holiness" is splendidly ironic.
3. All adults in the story are caricatured in this way, including "Groveling Tetsu" and Shota's skinflint grandmother.
4. The point of the technique is to suggest that there is no innocence in the adult world; all innocence is in the world of the children, and it is doomed.

D. The children in the story are not caricatured but are treated as individuals and with real tenderness by the narrator. This is especially true of the relationship between Midori and Nobu.
1. They had noticed each other in a way beyond that of childhood playmates only a short while before the story takes place.
2. Both, however, are so inexperienced at their feelings that they are awkward and shy in each other's presence.
3. In a crucial and wonderfully symbolic scene, when Midori tries to help Nobu when he is stranded outside her house in a driving rain, neither quite knows what to do or say, and at the end, a piece of expensive fabric is left in the mud as a symbol of what might have been and will never be.
4. When Nobu leaves for the seminary, he seems to have left a paper narcissus on Midori's doorstep, which she treasures—again because of what might have been in a different place and time.

- **IV.** As Robert Lyons Danly reminds us, the Japanese title of the story is "Comparing Heights" and alludes to a poem from the Japanese novel, *Tales of Ise* by Ise Monogatari.
    - **A.** The poem tells a story of children growing up together and winding up as man and wife, living happily ever after. The point of the allusion is sad and ironic; it suggests what might have been in a different time and place.
    - **B.** Louisa May Alcott's *Little Women* was written just 27 years before this story, and in it growing up is a promise, not a threat.
        - **1.** The virtuous girls are awarded fine husbands or careers, and the excitement of first love is the reward for being willing to leave the world of childhood.
        - **2.** In "Child's Play," Midori's beauty and intelligence will be rewarded with customers; her own experience of first love does not matter, and her passage to adulthood is painful and terrifying.
- **V.** Japanese critics hailed Ichiyō as their representative of the Realist Movement. In a way, that was an accurate assessment, despite the fact that her models were not Flaubert, Dostoevsky, Ibsen, or Chekhov but a Japanese writer of the 17th century.

Essential Reading:

Higuchi Ichiyō, "Child's Play."

Supplementary Reading:

Robert Lyons Danly, *In the Shade of Spring Leaves: The Life and Writings of Higuchi Ichiyō, a Woman of Letters in Meiji Japan.*

Donald Keene, *Dawn to the West.*

Questions to Consider:

1. In what time of year does this story occur? How is the season symbolic of the story's subject and theme? How does Ichiyō manage to incorporate details of the season into the story as symbols of what is going on in the human realm?

2. Think about the portrait of Nobu's father in this story in relation to the portrait of the monk in Chaucer's *The Canterbury Tales*. What *should* the Buddhist priest and the monk look like? How *do* they look? In what ways are their portraits similar and different? Is there satire involved in either or both of the portraits? In what ways are the *tones* of the portraits similar or different? What is the function of the portrait in each of the larger works in which it appears?

Lecture Thirty-Six
Proust's *Remembrance of Things Past*

Scope: In the book *Remembrance of Things Past*, Marcel Proust rejects Realism and recreates the novel. The subject of *Remembrance of Things Past* is time, which its protagonist will try to defeat. We look at the narrator's sense that his "self" is a serial succession, not an "I" enduring through time. Outworn selves are not lost but survive in the unconscious. The narrator distinguishes between voluntary and involuntary memory, the latter retaining the *whole* of an experience in unconscious depths; the problem is how to retrieve it. For the narrator, the solution comes in the famous madeleine episode, in which a town in which he spent his childhood summers is restored to him in its entirety by the taste of cake dipped in lime tea. The importance of this novel for the future of literature is incalculable: It shifts attention from the external to the internal world and changes the way everything is done in fiction, from characterization to plot. What fiction after Proust will try to do is to capture life *as we experience it*, rather than as it is prepackaged by omniscient narrators.

Outline

I. The first word in the novel is *longtemps* ("for a long time") and the last is *temps* ("time"), so the novel is in many ways about time: about the time in which Proust lived, the time in which he wrote the novel, the effects of the passage of time, and the enemy the protagonist hopes to defeat by finishing the book.

    A. Time and the havoc it wreaks on everything is a standard theme in literature.
        1. Here, as in most cases in literature, this kind of voice is a lament.
        2. It is an *elegiac* novel, a heroic battle fought against time.
    B. The novel is a search for some absolute that can oppose the flow of time. The protagonist will try many things—friendship, romantic love, ideas—all of which turn out to be subject to time themselves.
        1. Even the self, which we think of as enduring across time, changes from day to day.

       2. This is an idea which may derive from Henri Bergson's concept of time as duration, and we will encounter it again in Pirandello; here, it is the theme.
       3. For Proust, our old selves live on in the subconscious, returning in dreams, so that waking up each morning, having spent the night with other selves, we need to recover our current identities.
       4. While we are asleep we have access to levels of memory usually blocked by our conscious mind, and we can be any self we have ever been. Waking, we have to reorient ourselves to *this* room and *this* self.
       5. Inside each of us is something permanent and unchangeable that cannot be destroyed by time; hence the title of the book, which in French means *In Search of Lost Time*.

II. In the novel Proust distinguishes between two kinds of memory: voluntary and involuntary.
    A. *Voluntary memory* is that of the conscious mind, the memory of the intellect, which is what we use when we are awake, and which the boy in the story uses to remember events from his boyhood in Combray.
       1. Voluntary memory is good at remembering things that happened routinely or extraordinary events.
       2. The boy can remember typical summer evenings at Combray or one particular night when a most extraordinary thing happened and he wound up having his mother spend the night in his room with him.
       3. The narrator knows that there is more to his memories of Combray than this, but this is all that his voluntary memory can retrieve.
    B. *Involuntary memory* retains *all* of our experiences.
       1. It is, however, normally inaccessible to the conscious mind.
       2. In the famous madeleine and tea episode, the taste of the cake dipped in lime tea suddenly and unexpectedly restores the entire memory of Combray; a sensation, linked to a similar one in the past, can restore a part of the past.
       3. If a restored memory like this one can be translated into art, then it can be preserved from the erosion of time. If a novel can make the past and all the selves that lived through it timeless, then time can be defeated.

    4. Thus the madeleine episode suggests the point of the entire novel.
III. *Remembrance of Things Past* has been one of the most influential novels in all of literature. It also recreates the way stories get told and fiction is made.
  A. Proust's novel can be read as a portrait of life in France before World War I, as Tolstoy described life in Russia in the early 19th century, or Balzac did for life in France in the 1830s and 1840s.
  B. For Proust, however, a work like that misses the whole point of literature.
    1. The Realist novel had tried to give an objective account of the world the way a scientist might give it; Henry James had insisted on the importance of point of view, that every story is *someone's* story, which needs to be built into fiction.
    2. Realist stories, however, are still stories—abstracted, intellectualized, made into neat structures—that is *not* the way we experience reality, which is more like what Virginia Woolf calls "an incessant shower of innumerable atoms."
  C. In most novels, when a new character is introduced, we get a portrait of that character, who is then set into action in the novel.
    1. That is not how we come to know people; our knowledge builds up slowly over many years and experiences. The portrait is the *end* product, not its start.
    2. There are no character portraits in Proust; rather, we come to discover things about his characters as the novel moves, slowly adding items into our general portrait over the book's 3000 pages.
  D. The same is true for plot. Our lives do not fall into tidy plots; rather, it is only in retrospect that we look back over experience and try to impose some linear and causal structure on it.
  E. In both cases, we have intellectualized and generalized our experience, and that is the product of voluntary memory—which means that by that time we have lost the most important parts of it.
IV. What Proust (and also James Joyce and Virginia Woolf) were trying to do is to get into fiction the texture of experience itself—"real" life before it has been packaged and structured by the intellect.

A. Underneath our habits and clichés, our "true life" goes on. It is this "true life" which Proust took upon himself to explore and illuminate.

B. It takes Proust's protagonist 3,000 pages and a lifetime of experience to figure out how to recover his own lost time and then turn them into this novel.

   1. This recovery will not happen until the very last chapter.

   2. Along the way, Proust redefined the modern novel, which can never be quite the same again after him.

Essential Reading:

Marcel Proust, *Remembrance of Things Past*.

Supplementary Reading:

Wallace Fowlie, *A Reading of Proust*.

Terence Kilmartin, *A Reader's Guide to Remembrance of Things Past*.

Questions to Consider:

1. Proust argues that we often rush to make a character portrait of someone we know, and then when we see that person, it is to the sketch that we carry around in our heads that we refer. How often and with which characters in *Remembrance of Things Past* does this occur, either for the narrator, for other characters in the book, or even for us, the readers? How inadequate, for example, is both the narrator's and the reader's first idea of the character of Swann? How does that work for other characters, and how does it validate Proust's new way of doing characterization in the novel?

2. Using Swann as your subject, notice how often in the first book Marcel will stop to tell us something that he did not learn until much later, giving us two views of Swann simultaneously. At how many other junctures in the novel, and concerning how many critical points, does Proust use this technique?

Timeline
(Lectures 25–36)

1644–45	Manchus conquer China; Ch'ing Dynasty established.
1789	French Revolution begins.
1792	120-chapter version of *The Story of the Stone*.
1808	Goethe's *Faust,* Part I.
1815	Battle of Waterloo; end of Napoleonic Era.
1823–30	Pushkin's *Eugene Onegin*.
1832	Goethe's *Faust,* Part II.
1847	Brontë's *Wuthering Heights*.
1848	Revolutions across Europe; Marx and Engels's *Communist Manifesto*.
1854	The Treaty of Kanagawa opens Japan to the rest of the world.
1856	Flaubert's *Madame Bovary*.
1859	Darwin's *The Origin of Species*.
1864	Dostoevsky's *Notes from Underground*.
1879	Ibsen's *A Doll's House*.
1884	Twain's *Huckleberry Finn*.
1890	Posthumous publication of some of Emily Dickinson's poems.
1893	Tagore's "Punishment."
1895	Higuchi Ichiyō's "Child's Play."
1900	Chekhov's *Uncle Vanya*.
1913–27	Proust's *Remembrance of Things Past*.

1914–18 .... World War I.
1915 .... Einstein's General Theory of Relativity.
1918 .... Bolshevik Revolution in Russia.
1920 .... Gandhi becomes leader of the Indian independence movement.

Glossary
(Lectures 25–36)

anti-hero: A protagonist of a novel or play whose attributes are generally the inverse of those considered heroic by his or her culture. He or she can either be the object of satire or a criticism of the values of the culture in which he or she appears. The Underground Man is something of both in Dostoevsky's *Notes from Underground*.

Byronic hero: Named after the English poet, Lord Byron, the figure was largely his invention and it was also largely modeled on himself. A Byronic hero is always striking in appearance, passionate, superior to other human beings, isolated from community either by having committed a great sin or by being jaded and sated with pleasure. He relies entirely on himself for his actions, compromising with neither other people nor God, and the absolute freedom this stance gives him makes him irresistible to other people—especially to women. Bits of the Byronic hero show up in Goethe's *Faust* (Goethe much admired the figure created by Byron), and more than a little bit in Emily Brontë's Heathcliff in *Wuthering Heights*. The best-known American example is probably Captain Ahab in Melville's *Moby Dick*.

caricature: An exaggerated type character, in which one or only a few qualities of a character are made to define him or her, all other qualities being subordinated to the selected ones. It is generally used for satire, but it is put to different use in Higuchi Ichiyō's story, "Child's Play," where it is used to define the adult world vis-à-vis that of the children.

closet drama: A play, usually in poetry, that is designed to be read rather than acted, either because staging would be too demanding or because the verse is better treated as literature than as drama. The 19th century was the great age of closet drama and is most closely associated with the Romantics—although there have been examples in other times and movements. Goethe's *Faust* is a closet drama in this course.

common meter: Also called common measure, this is a stanza form consisting of alternating lines of iambic tetrameter and iambic trimeter, which usually rhymes *abab* or *abcb*. In Protestant hymnals the measure is designated "C. M."

Enlightenment: An intellectual movement in the 18th century in Europe which celebrated reason, the scientific method, empirical evidence, and common sense. It included within it deism, a belief in progress and democracy, and it opposed restraint, superstition, intolerance, authoritarianism, and revealed religion. Neoclassicism (see Lectures Twenty-Three and Twenty-Four in Part II of this course) was a literary manifestation of the Enlightenment.

epistolary novel: A novel made up entirely of letters written by one or more characters. Samuel Richardson is usually credited with inventing the genre in his *Pamela, or Virtue Rewarded* in 1740. It achieved the height of its popularity in the 18th century, but Dostoevsky's first novel, *Poor Folk*, used it as late as 1846. It generally fell out of favor in the 19th century and after, but it may account for the importance carried by letters in some of the works in this course (e.g., *Eugene Onegin* and *Madame Bovary*).

feminine rhyme: A rhyme of two syllables, the first stressed and the second unstressed. "Waken" and "forsaken" are feminine rhymes, with the accent in both cases falling on the penultimate syllable.

Gothic novel: A novel in which mystery, suggestions of the supernatural, and horrors are the chief elements. It came into being in the 18th century (Horace Walpole's *The Castle of Otranto* is usually considered the first) and was a popular form during the Romantic period in England, Europe, and America. Perhaps its most famous examples are Ann Radcliffe's *The Mysteries of Udolpho* and Mary Shelley's *Frankenstein*. In our course there are Gothic elements in Emily Brontë's *Wuthering Heights*.

iamb: A metrical unit (foot) consisting of one unaccented syllable and one accented one (˘´); thus, a line of iambic pentameter consists of five iambs, a line of iambic tetrameter of four, and a line of iambic trimeter of three such feet.

Onegin stanza: Modeled more or less on the *ottava rima* used by Byron in *Don Juan*, this verse form was invented by Alexander Pushkin for his *Eugene Onegin*. It is a 14-line stanza which rhymes *AbAbCCddEffEgg*, with the capital letters indicating feminine rhymes (two-syllable rhymes with unaccented final syllables). It is an extraordinarily complicated verse form in any language, and it has proven a powerful challenge to translators of Pushkin ever since.

ottava rima: A stanza of eight iambic pentameter lines rhyming *abababcc*. It is, as the name suggests, an Italian form, presumably invented by Boccaccio but used extensively by Tasso and Ariosto. It has been used by several English poets—namely Spenser, Milton, and Keats—but was made famous by Byron's use of it in his *Don Juan*.

parody: A work which generally ridicules or criticizes some other work by imitating either its substance, form, or style and then exaggerating the aspects of form or style that are being criticized, or carrying to extreme lengths the implications of its substance. Dostoevsky in *Notes from Underground* parodies Western ideas by having his Underground Man adopt them and then show what a wreck his life has become because of them.

persona: Literally, a mask. In literary criticism, the term is used to define a second self created by an author whose voice we hear in the poem or story. In Dostoevsky's *Notes from Underground,* the story is told in the first person but not in Dostoevsky's voice. The Underground Man is Dostoevsky's persona in the book.

point of view: In fiction, the angle of vision from which an author presents his or her story. A writer who knows everything about everyone in a story (he or she can, for example, present a dialogue between two characters in which he or she knows what is going on inside both of their heads) is called an *omniscient* narrator. A writer who confines his or her point of view to that of a single character (so that the reader never knows any more about what is happening than that one character does) is using a *limited* point of view. An omniscient author can also address his or her readers directly, as Henry Fielding famously does in *Tom Jones.* A limited point of view can be either third-person or first-person; in the latter case the narrative is told by someone from within the story itself—someone who may be telling either his or her own story or someone else's. Emily Brontë uses nested first-person accounts to create part of the complexity of her novel. An *omniscient* point of view in which the author never speaks in his or her own voice, but tries to disappear from the narrative to make it seem objective, is sometimes called a scenic point of view. It will be a hallmark of Realist fiction, beginning in our course with Flaubert's *Madame Bovary.*

proscenium arch stage: As used in today's parlance, the proscenium arch is located over the front of the stage; if there is a curtain, it hangs from the arch. It became normative in theaters built during the Realist period in drama (and after). It was designed for a box set which includes three walls; the fourth wall is the proscenium arch itself, which is treated as a wall by actors on stage, who act out their drama as though unaware that a voyeuristic audience is peering in through the fourth wall, watching their lives unfold. The proscenium arch stage is imperative for Ibsen plays and useful for those of Chekhov.

Realism: A term used in art and literature for a philosophical approach that began as a conscious movement in the mid-19th century. The movement rejects the values of Romanticism, avoiding the exoticism and idealizing of the past that typified that movement. Instead, it embraces objectivity and a faith in science. In terms of narrative strategies, the Realist author tried to evaporate himself or herself out of the book, making it seem an unmediated vision of the world.

Realist novel: A subset of the general Realist movement in all of the arts that began in the second half of the 19th century. It was a reaction against Romanticism (as Romanticism had been a reaction against the Enlightenment), and for our purposes in this course, its identifying characteristics include empirical standards of truth modeled on those of science; an objective, detached point of view, simulating that of a scientist in a laboratory; the avoidance of authorial intrusion into the novel, making it seem like an unmediated picture of reality; subject matter chosen from the contemporary world, which in effect means a focus on the middle class; and an inclusiveness that permits dung heaps as well as clouds. Its slogan was truthfulness in depicting the real world, but since many other writers in other literary movements have aimed at that as well (e.g., verisimilitude in Neoclassical literary theory), it is perhaps useful to think of the movement as distinguished by the narrative strategies just listed.

Regionalism: In literature, the quality of a work which connects it to a particular locale or geographical region, including that region's habits, speech, history, and values. There have been regional works in the literature of every culture, but in America Regionalism had particular meaning, since it distinguished between the conventional (and largely Romantic) literature of the Eastern seaboard and that of the life on the farms, rivers, and mining camps of the West. In that way, as in the case of Mark Twain, Regionalism became part of the basis for Realism in American literature.

Romanticism: A movement in the late 18th and early 19th centuries which reacted against virtually all of the values of the Enlightenment and Neoclassicism. Its values included a revived interest in the medieval, a love of nature, individualism, the imaginative and the free (as opposed to the reasonable and the structured), subjectivity, cultivation of the emotions, and a restless aspiration for union in love or with nature or God, culminating in a desire for transcendence. Goethe, Brontë, and Pushkin are the best representatives, in various ways, of Romanticism in this course.

sentimental novel: A novel in which feeling is given primacy over thought as a desirable guide to conduct or as a mark of distinction in a protagonist who can feel more deeply than other characters. The subgenre was more or less invented by Samuel Richardson in his *Pamela, or Virtue Rewarded* (1740), but it was developed and refined by Jean-Jacques Rousseau's *Julie, or the New Eloise* (1761) and by Goethe's *The Sorrows of Young Werther* (1774). It had its vogue in theater and poetry as well. It is a model that stands behind Pushkin's *Eugene Onegin* up to the very end, when what we expect as a sentimental and moving reunion of lovers is disappointed by the intrusion of the real world on the artificial one of sentimental fiction.

vernacular: The native language of a locality or region or the common everyday speech of a people, as opposed to the literary language. In a general way, in the West, the first definition applies, as in French or German as opposed to Latin; in the East the second definition is pertinent, as in vernacular Chinese as opposed to classical Chinese.

well-made play: The term applies to plays, popular in the 19th century, which feature a plot based on a hidden secret which is revealed at the play's climax; action which, while it moves forward, continues to reveal the past in a symmetrical way, so that the further the on-stage action advances, the further into the past the audience (and the characters on-stage) are able to see; and a climax which occurs the moment that the secret from the past is brought into the on-stage present. The genre is most associated with Eugene Scribe, a French dramatist, but it became normative in theaters across Europe in the 19th century. Ibsen directed more than 20 well-made plays in Christiana during his time there, and he retained many features of the form in the Realist plays he began writing later in his career.

Biographical Notes
(Lectures 25–36)

Brontë, Emily (1818–48): The daughter of a curate in the Yorkshire moors, Emily and her two sisters (Charlotte and Anne) and one brother were raised by an aunt after the early death of their mother. They spent their childhood reading everything they could get their hands on and creating and writing about imaginary lands that were the scenes of lurid events. Aside from a brief period at school and a short stint as a governess, Emily spent her entire life in and near her home. She and her sisters published a volume of poetry (under the male pseudonyms of Currer, Ellis, and Acton Bell), which garnered no attention, and Emily's one novel, *Wuthering Heights*, was published under the pseudonym Ellis Bell in 1847. It shocked its early readers and reviewers, but over the years it has become arguably the most popular 19th-century English novel. Emily succumbed to the family illness of tuberculosis within a year of its publication.

Byron, George Noel Gordon, Lord (1788–1824): The most influential English poet in the world during the Romantic period, particularly in regard to the creation of the Byronic hero, which is discussed in Lectures Twenty-Seven and Twenty-Eight. His life, after a suppressive childhood and the somewhat unexpected inheritance of a title, was the stuff of which legends are made. He was strikingly handsome, and women competed with each other for the honor of seducing him, although there is by now ample evidence that he had an equal taste for boys. After a brilliant commencement to a literary and social career, he exiled himself from England partly because of an affair with a half-sister that produced a child and partly (most of his biographers now think) because of other even—in those days—less savory sexual activities. He spent the rest of his life abroad, dying of a fever contracted while training troops he had raised at his own expense for action in the Greek Wars of Liberation. He was the most widely read poet of his day, by all levels of society, and his own personal legend and poetry merged to create a great sensation across Europe and America. The Byronic Hero was his ultimate legacy to literature, treated seriously by writers and thinkers from Goethe to Bertrand Russell and beyond.

Cao Xueqin (c. 1715–63): We know almost nothing about his early years; by tradition he was towards the end of his life a schoolteacher and a painter. He had been born into an important family in Nanking, a member of the Manchus who had overthrown the government in 1644. His grandfather supervised the compiling and editing of the T'ang Dynasty poetry collection and served the emperor in a variety of functions. In 1722, for a variety of reasons, a new emperor withdrew his support from the family, and in the political purges that followed, the Cao family disappeared from public records and the family members by repute lived in relative penury thereafter. It has always been understood that the events of *The Story of the Stone* recapitulate in some manner the decline and fall of the family, although the precise relation of history to fiction remains extraordinarily elusive.

Chekhov, Anton (1860–1904): A grandson of serfs, Chekhov studied medicine in Moscow, helping to support his bankrupt family by writing sketches for newspapers and magazines. He received his medical degree the same year (1884) as the publication of his first collection of short stories. He began writing plays in the mid 1880s, and his first success as a playwright came with the production of *The Seagull* in 1898 at the Moscow Art Theater, under the direction of Constantin Stanislavsky. He continued to practice medicine and worked tirelessly for improvement of life for the poor in Russia. He is remembered for his brilliant short stories and his four major plays: *Three Sisters* (1901), *The Cherry Orchard* (1904), *The Seagull*, and *Uncle Vanya* (1899). He suffered from tuberculosis most of his adult life, and he died of it in 1904.

Dickinson, Emily (1830–86): Born into a prominent family in Amherst, Massachusetts, that was influential in founding Amherst College, she spent almost her entire life in the family house. She briefly attended Mount Holyoke College, but when she returned home, except for a few visits to Washington and Philadelphia while her father was in Congress, she withdrew more and more into the inner recesses of the family house, by the end of her life seeing hardly anyone. Her two passions were gardening and poetry, and they seem to have fulfilled her sufficiently that she never resented her isolation. To be alive is so startling, she once wrote, that there is little time for other occupations. She died as she had lived, quietly, but beginning in 1890, when her first poems were published, her reputation grew; now she is considered one of America's foremost poets and an artist well in advance in both thought and technique of her own time and place.

Dostoevsky, Fyodor (1821–81): He was born in Moscow and after completing his education and his two-year stint in the army, burst brilliantly onto the literary scene with his first novel, *Poor Folk* (1846). He was arrested for involvement in a political discussion group deemed seditious by the authorities and sentenced to death. He was reprieved at the last possible moment, when actually facing the firing squad, and spent four years doing hard labor in Siberia and six more in the army before being pardoned in 1859. By the time of his return, his ideas had shifted remarkably: He came to despise much of what was going on in the rest of Europe (an attitude which was only intensified by his travels there) and to see the salvation of humankind and history in Russian Orthodox Christianity. Despite an immense amount of writing (and editing short-lived periodicals), he was almost always deeply in debt, addicted to gambling, and an epileptic. Not until close to the end of his life did he achieve anything like economic stability and critical acclaim. In addition to *Notes from Underground*, the best-known and most critically acclaimed of his many works are *Crime and Punishment* (1866), *The Idiot* (1869), *The Possessed* (1871), and *The Brothers Karamazov* (1880).

Flaubert, Gustave (1821–80): From Rouen, the son of a surgeon. His brother was also a physician, and it has been said that the surgical procedure used in his novels suggests some of the influence medicine had on his work. After a brief attempt to study law, he returned to a small town just outside Rouen, where he spent the rest of his life writing, punctuated by occasional trips to Paris or abroad. He wrote three more novels after *Madame Bovary* (the last one unfinished), and his collection of short stories, *Three Tales* (1877) established his reputation in that genre as well. He was a dedicated craftsman for whom writing was a very deliberate process: He worked on *Madame Bovary* for five years until he was sure that he had every word correctly chosen and placed. Henry James said of him that he was the first writer to treat the novel seriously as an art form, requiring as much concentration and skill as poetry.

Goethe, Johann Wolfgang von (1749–1832): Goethe was a poet, dramatist, critic, novelist, scientist, and statesman who made significant contributions in all of these fields in his own day. He was trained in law, but practiced it in dilatory fashion, preferring a life of arts and letters. He was part of the *Sturm und Drang* movement in Germany, which was the beginning of German Romanticism, and he made his early literary reputation with neo-Shakespearean plays like *Götz von Berlichingen* in 1773. His novel, *The Sorrows of Young Werther* (1774) caused a sensation across Europe and even stimulated a few suicides over lost love in the Werther manner. He was invited to the court of the Duke of Weimar in 1775, where he served for many years as Prime Minister. Over the years, one great work after another came from his pen in every conceivable genre and style. He is considered, for example, both Germany's greatest

Neoclassical and Romantic poet—no small achievement in itself. Toward the end of his life he was lionized by all of Europe and visited by everyone who could get an audience. He began work on *Faust* in the early 1770s and published fragments of it until Part I was published in its entirety in 1808. Part II was finished just before his death and then sealed up and locked away, to be published posthumously.

Higuchi Ichiyō (1872–96): Orphaned when she was 17, she and her mother and sister were left penniless. Her father had wanted to give her a Westernized education, but he was opposed by his wife, who thought that too much education spoiled a girl for marriage, so she received something of a compromise: a few years of grade school and then a finishing school, where she learned classical Japanese literature. In 1893 the family moved to the edge of the pleasure quarter in Edo (Tokyo), where they opened a store selling balloons and candy. She had published a few stories by that time, but her discovery of the stories of Ihara Saikaku in a lending library suggested new directions for her own fiction, since she was now living in the kind of environment that his stories had treated; the result was her classic story, "Child's Play," published just a year before her death of tuberculosis.

Ibsen, Henrik (1828–1906): He was born in southern Norway. Like quite a few other Realist writers, he studied medicine for a time but abandoned it for the theater. He served for eight years as stage manager of a theater in Christiana (now Oslo), and while there began to write plays himself. He exiled himself from Norway in 1864, and in Rome wrote his Norwegian plays, *Brand* (1866) and *Peer Gynt* (1867). He turned to Realist dramas in prose instead of poetry in 1877 with *Pillars of Society*, and then went on to write a series of plays which scandalized Europe and which most theaters refused to produce: *A Doll's House* (1879), *Ghosts* (1881), *An Enemy of the People* (1882), *The Wild Duck* (1884), and *Hedda Gabler* (1890), among others. Toward the end of his life, now recognized as a great writer, Ibsen returned to Norway and wrote a series of haunting symbolic plays which have received ambivalent response from audiences, readers, and critics.

Proust, Marcel (1871–1922): The older son of a doctor who practiced just outside of Paris and had a brilliantly educated mother, with whom Proust was to live until the time of their deaths; Proust was diagnosed with asthma when he was nine. Despite his illness, he graduated and spent a year in the military before he began writing for magazines and attending social events in the fashionable Faubourg Saint-Germain. In about 1905, following the deaths of his parents and a serious turn for the worse in his health, he withdrew from his glittering social life to retreat into a cork-lined room which was kept in semi-darkness, where he spent the last years of his life devoted to writing *Remembrance of Things Past,* emerging only rarely (and then usually to verify a detail of some event that was going into his book). The first volume was published in 1913, and they continued at intervals until his death—and after: The last three volumes were published posthumously.

Pushkin, Alexander (1799–1837): Of aristocratic heritage, he spent his youth in dissipation and poetry, very much as his literary model, Lord Byron, had done. Like Byron, he was always on the edge of trouble because of his liberal political views, which eventually led to his dismissal from his position at the Foreign Office. His early poems earned him instant fame, which he consolidated with his long romantic-satiric poem, *Eugene Onegin*, and a historical tragedy, *Boris Godunov.* He wrote much during his short life and much of his work has been revered by the Russian people ever since. He married a dazzling and much-sought-after beauty in 1831 (by his own count, she was the 113th woman in his life), but the marriage was not a happy one; Pushkin was killed in a duel at the age of 38, fought either over his wife's infidelities or over another man's improper advances toward his wife. His dying words were presumably in French, an indication of the extent to which Western culture dominated Russia during his lifetime—a domination which provided Pushkin with both models and ideas to push against in his own work.

Tagore, Rabindranath (1861–1941): He was the son of an illustrious intellectual family and was born when India was the most important of Britain's colonies. His family connections made part of his education in England possible, and he was thus in a perfect position to understand the ways in which the two cultures could be melded into something both Indian and international. Among his many achievements, he founded a school that became an international university, and became an international lecturer whose topics were the evils of colonialism, the evils of nationalistic war, and the importance of human rights. He supported Gandhi's initiative for Indian independence but warned against the dangers of excessive nationalism in the process. When he returned to India after completing the English part of his education, he became overseer of family estates in the Ganges Valley and rediscovered his native land. His literature thereafter was written in Bengali, the language of the people of northeast India, not English or Sanskrit. He wrote much and was also a musician, writing the words and music to over 2,000 songs, two of which became the national anthems of India and Bangladesh. He was awarded the Nobel Prize for literature in 1913, and he died, venerated by the entire world, in Calcutta in 1941.

Twain, Mark (1835–1910): The pseudonym of Samuel Langhorne Clemens; he grew up in Hannibal, Missouri, on the Mississippi. After a desultory period of schooling, he did a variety of things, including journalism, piloting a steamboat on the Mississippi, and prospecting out west. He began writing humorous regional pieces for newspapers and came to national attention with "The Notorious Jumping Frog of Calaveras County" in 1865, published in newspapers all over America. From then on he was a constant traveler, lecturer, and writer, working from his home base in Hartford, Connecticut. His failed business speculations accumulated serious debts, and a series of family tragedies combined to make him increasingly bitter towards the end of his life. In the judgment of many of his critics, *Huck Finn* is the complicated and extremely interesting transition from his earlier to his later thought. He was born in the year of one appearance of Haley's Comet, and—as he predicted—he died when the comet returned 75 years later.

Bibliography
(Lectures 25–36)

Note: Every work treated in this part of the course is available in multiple editions or translations, many of them excellent. I have listed here the ones from which my text citations were taken. In general, the best strategy is to find an edition that gives you sufficient introductory material to help orient you to the text and sufficient editorial help to understand what you are reading. If you find those things, you have found the recommended text for you.

Essential Reading:

Brontë, Emily. *Wuthering Heights.* New York: Penguin, 1965.

Cao Xueqin. *The Story of the Stone.* David Hawkes, trans. 5 vols. New York: Penguin Books, 1973–1986.

Chekhov, Anton. *Uncle Vanya. Four Great Plays by Chekhov.* Constance Garnett, trans. New York: Bantam, 1968.

Dickinson, Emily. *The Complete Poems of Emily Dickinson.* Thomas H. Johnson, ed. Boston: Little, Brown, 1960.

Dostoevsky, Fyodor. *Notes from Underground.* Michael Katz, trans. New York: W. W. Norton, 1989. See also entry under "Katz" in Supplementary Reading.

Flaubert, Gustave. *Madame Bovary.* Francis Steegmuller, trans. New York: Random House, 1957.

Goethe, Johann Wolfgang von. *Faust. Goethe's Faust Part One and Sections from Part Two.* Walter Kaufmann, trans. New York: Doubleday, 1961.

Higuchi Ichiyō. *In the Shade of Spring Leaves: The Life and Writings of Higuchi Ichiyō, A Woman of Letters in Meiji Japan.* Robert Lyons Danly, trans. New Haven: Yale University Press, 1981.

Ibsen, Henrik. *A Doll's House. Eight Plays by Henrik Ibsen.* Eva Le Gallienne, trans. New York: Modern Library, 1982.

Proust, Marcel. *Remembrance of Things Past.* C. K. Scott Moncrieff and Terence Kilmartin, trans. 3 vols. New York: Random House, 1981.

Pushkin, Alexander. *Eugene Onegin: A Novel in Verse.* Walter Arndt, trans. 2nd ed. Ann Arbor: Ardis, 1992.

Tagore, Rabindranath. *Rabindranath Tagore: Selected Short Stories.* William Radice, trans. London: Penguin, 2005.

———. *A Tagore Reader.* Amiya Chakravarty, trans. New York: Macmillan, 1961.

Twain, Mark. *The Adventures of Huckleberry Finn.* Boston: Houghton Mifflin, 1958.

Supplementary Reading:

Bardhan, Kalpana, trans. and ed. *Of Women, Outcastes, Peasants, and Rebels: A Selection of Bengali Short Stories.* Berkeley: University of California Press, 1990. A selection of stories on the themes indicated by the title of the book. The collection includes Tagore's "Punishment" along with a good analysis of it.

Bayley, John. *Pushkin: A Comparative Commentary.* Cambridge: Cambridge University Press, 1971. A good reading of the poem, touching on most of the points discussed in Lecture Twenty-Eight: the definition of a poetic novel in the context of the 19th century, a good analysis of the verse form, influences on the work and the ways the poem parodies them, and the ways in which Pushkin leans toward Realism.

Bennett, Paula. *Emily Dickinson: Woman Poet.* London: Harvester Wheatsheaf, 1990. A good account of Dickinson's life and poetry, including some fine readings of individual poems, from a feminist perspective.

Briggs, A. D. P. *Alexander Pushkin: A Critical Study.* Totowa, New Jersey: Barnes and Noble, 1983. Briggs is especially good on Pushkin's general philosophy of life and its genial acceptance of things as they are.

Brombert, Victor. *The Novels of Flaubert: A Study of Themes and Techniques.* Princeton: Princeton University Press, 1966. The title indicates the focus of the book. Its chapter on *Madame Bovary* is very helpful.

Brown, Jane K. *Goethe's Faust: The German Tragedy.* Ithaca: Cornell University Press, 1985. A good study of the entire poem, but it is particularly insightful and illuminating about the Faust/Gretchen plot in Part I.

Brustein, Robert. *The Theatre of Revolt: An Approach to Modern Drama.* Boston: Little, Brown, 1964. In what has become something of a classic critical text, Brustein considers not only Ibsen and Chekhov, but also Strindberg, Shaw, Brecht, Pirandello, O'Neill, Artaud, and Genet in the context of the revolution in theater in the late 19th and carrying into the 20th centuries.

Danly, Robert Lyons. *In the Shade of Spring Leaves: The Life and Writings of Higuchi Ichiyō, a Woman of Letters in Meiji Japan.* New York: W. W. Norton, 1992. This book features a biography of Ichiyō as well as parts of her diaries and translations of nine short stories, as well as some useful background and critical information about them.

Fowlie, Wallace. *A Reading of Proust.* 2nd ed. Chicago: University of Chicago Press, 1975. A good introduction to Proust, featuring a clear explication of the most important ideas driving the novel.

Frank, Joseph. *Dostoevsky: The Stir of Liberation, 1860–1865.* Princeton: Princeton University Press, 1986. The brilliantly explicated and argued section of this book on *Notes from Underground* by one of the leading Dostoevsky scholars in the world is excerpted in Katz's work.

Gilman, Richard. *Chekhov's Plays: Opening into Eternity.* New Haven: Yale University Press, 1995. Some very sensitive readings of Chekhov's plays, particularly notable for noticing tiny details and moments that can otherwise go by unnoticed in reading or seeing the play.

Hill, Hamlin and Walter Blair, eds. *The Art of Huckleberry Finn: Text, Sources, Criticism.* 2nd ed. San Francisco: Chandler, 1969. A good collection of materials that is useful in orienting the reader to the book, including some fine critical essays.

Holderness, Graham. *Wuthering Heights. Open Guides to Literature.* Philadelphia: Open University Press, 1985. Like other books in the *Open Guides* series, this one does a pretty thorough reading of the work in a relatively small number of pages, using some modern critical tools and theories to do so.

Hornsby, Richard. *Patterns in Ibsen's Middle Plays.* London: Associated University Presses, 1981. This book is particularly good at relating the structure of Ibsen's plays to that of the well-made play, along the way accounting for some of the meanings Ibsen managed to wring out of the old formula.

Hsia, C. T. *The Classic Chinese Novel: A Critical Introduction.* 1968. Rpt. Ithaca: Cornell University Press, 1996. See also the bibliography for Part II of this course. Hsia is a splendid guide both for the rise and development of the novel in China and individual readings of the great novels from its classical period. He is very illuminating on *The Story of the Stone,* as suggested by the quotations from his book in the lecture.

Katz, Michael R. *Notes from Underground: A Norton Critical Reader.* New York: W. W. Norton, 1989. Like other volumes in the Critical Reader series, this one contains a great deal of useful background material, including passages from the Chernyshevsky novel Dostoevsky was answering and some good critical essays, including Frank's (see entry above).

Keene, Donald. *Dawn to the West.* New York: Holt, Rinehart, Winston, 1984. A splendid survey of modern Japanese literature, including a nice section on Higuchi Ichiyō.

Kilmartin, Terence. *A Reader's Guide to Remembrance of Things Past.* New York: Random House, 1983. This is really a handbook to characters, places, events, and ideas in the novel, and it is keyed to the Moncrieff-Kilmartin translation for easy reference.

Knapp, Bettina Liebowitz. *Emily Dickinson (Literature and Life).* New York: Continuum, 1989. A good account of Dickinson's life and writings, including some fine readings of individual poems from a feminist perspective.

Knoerle, Jeanne. *The Dream of the Red Chamber: A Critical Study.* Bloomington: Indiana University Press, 1972. A very good analysis of the history of the novel in China, its roots in storytelling, and of this novel, whose themes she identifies as the love triangle, the rise and fall of a particular lady within the compound, and the decline of the House of Jia.

Lago, Mary. *Rabindranath Tagore.* Boston: Twayne, 1976. A good introduction to Tagore's life and work.

Miller, J. Hillis. *Fiction and Repetition: Seven English Novels.* Cambridge: Harvard University Press, 1982. As the title suggests, this book places *Wuthering Heights* within the context of English fiction. It is particularly good on questions of narrative technique.

Reed, T. J. *Goethe.* New York: Oxford University Press, 1984. This is a good introduction to the thought and work of Goethe across his entire life and career. Reed is quoted several times on *Faust* in Lecture Twenty-Six.

Smith, Henry Nash. *Mark Twain: The Development of a Writer.* Cambridge: Harvard University Press, 1962. Like almost everything else written by Smith, this book has become something of a critical classic. It focuses on the two voices in Twain—the conventional and the vernacular—and traces their development through Twain's writing.

Thorlby, Anthony. *Gustave Flaubert and the Art of Realism.* New Haven: Yale University Press, 1957. This work is very helpful in placing Flaubert in the context of the Realist Movement and showing the way its precepts are managed by the author of *Madame Bovary.*

Lecture Thirty-Seven
Joyce's *Dubliners*

Scope: In a context of experimentation in all of the arts, we consider James Joyce's *Dubliners* contribution to the modern short story, focusing on Joyce's device of the *epiphany*, or revelation. We examine two stories in detail. "Araby" is a story about an adolescent disillusioned about the romance of the exotic and about love, and it is crafted so that each detail contributes to its overall effect: illustrating Joyce's *symbolic* method by showing how he treats the boy's actions as a metaphoric religious quest, making his epiphany all the more devastating. The second story we consider is "The Dead," in which Gabriel Conroy achieves an epiphany about his own unimportance in the scheme of things and about death. In this story, too, every detail is carefully calculated to contribute to its overall effect. Joyce's methods in *Dubliners*—and in those in the works he was yet to write—had a profound effect on later fiction.

Outline

I. Beginning with Proust in our last lecture, the arts launched into a period of radical experimentation, partly prompted by the massive dislocations of the 20th century and partly by the ongoing quest of artists to find new ways to capture human experience and its significance in art. One of these great experimenters was James Joyce.

    A. Joyce's most accessible experimental work is *Ulysses* (1922), to which an entire Teaching Company course is dedicated.

    B. His most strikingly innovative work is *Finnegans Wake* (1939), which has kept critics and readers busy for the better part of a century.

II. Joyce's collection of short stories, *Dubliners* (1914), connects back to other writers and points ahead to Joyce's later accomplishments.

    A. Joyce was one of the writers who recreated the short story as we discussed it in Lecture Thirty-Four, moving its action and focus from external to internal events.

        1. Joyce called his own version of this internal focus an epiphany.

        2. The word comes from the time in the Christian church year commemorating the visit of the Wise Men—January 6.
        3. Joyce used the term to indicate a sudden revelation or discovery, usually unexpected, that allows the protagonist or reader to see something in a new way.
    B. *Dubliners* contains 15 stories, all set in Dublin, written mostly after Joyce had left Ireland for good in 1903.
        1. Although he set everything he wrote in Dublin, Joyce was always critical of its narrowness, hypocrisy, and subservience to the Catholic Church.
        2. He intended these short stories to be a "chapter in the moral history of Ireland," and in them he finds Dublin "the center of paralysis" that is the result of isolation and excessive conventionality.
        3. The stories are divided into categories: three about childhood, four about adolescence, four about mature life, and three devoted to public life. "The Dead," the last story, is a kind of summary.

III. A partial analysis of two of the stories can illustrate how they work, helping readers to understand better the others in the collection and to see some of the directions Joyce's later work would take.

IV. "Araby" illustrates the devaluation of plot in favor of internal events. It is about a boy with a crush on a friend's sister (known simply as "Mangan's sister") trying to go to a bazaar in another part of town to bring something back for her.
   A. His uncle, with whom he lives, delays him from starting out for the bazaar until nearly nine o'clock at night, and by the time he arrives, the bazaar is closing.
   B. The story ends with an epiphany, as the boy stands looking up into the darkness of the great hall and feeling himself "a creature driven and derided by vanity" while his eyes burn with "anguish and anger."
   C. Joyce's stories seldom feature their plots; every detail of this story is loaded with a double significance for understanding it.
       1. Joyce's evocation and description of the details of the city of Dublin is well-documented, and thousands of literary pilgrims have gone to Dublin to visit the places mentioned in Joyce's works.

2. Joyce also learned from Flaubert, Ibsen, and Chekhov—especially Ibsen, whom he very much admired—how to use every detail in a symbolic way, so that all of the blind alleys, empty houses, dark rooms and passages, and stairways shrouded in shadow become symbolic of Dublin's moral blindness, spiritual emptiness, and emotional repression.
   3. In this story there are also even more explicit symbols: the boy's trip to the bazaar to bring back a gift for Mangan's sister becomes a quest from a medieval romance. The details of the trip, for instance, become obstacles to overcome.
   4. The boy's love for Mangan's sister likewise becomes a religious dedication: He bears his love for her "like a chalice," he utters her name "in strange prayers and praises," the darkening bazaar feels to him like an empty church, and men count money on a silver salver. The combination of these two related sets of symbols suggests a parallel between the boy's quest and that of King Arthur's knights for the Holy Grail.
   5. Two men counting money suggest the money-changers Jesus drove from the Temple in the New Testament story.
   6. The result of plot and the density of symbols and allusions makes the disillusionment of the boy even more crushing—a triumph of commercial and ugly Dublin over a boy's romantic dreams.
V. "The Dead," the last story in the collection, is about Gabriel and Gretta Conroy attending a holiday party thrown by his elderly aunts.
   A. Three events during the course of the party disconcert Gabriel.
      1. A maid snaps at him for what he means as merely a polite question.
      2. His wife teases him in front of his aunts about his concern for galoshes and umbrellas and healthy food.
      3. A colleague teases him about caring more about the continent than he does about Ireland and things Irish.
   B. Gabriel recovers from these events to have a good time at the party, where he is his aunts' favorite nephew and a master of ceremonies who gets to make the speech that goes with the toast.
   C. As he is getting ready to leave, he sees Gretta standing at the top of the steps listening to a tenor sing in the next room. He is struck by her pose, and on the way to their hotel he is overwhelmed by

memories of the intimate moments they have spent together. By the time they reach the hotel, he is eager to make love to her.

D. When pressed, Gretta tells him that the song she was listening to had been sung to her in the rain beneath her window years ago by a young man named Michael Furey, who was already ill and who died soon afterwards. As Gretta says, "I think he died for me."

E. As Gretta goes to sleep, Gabriel has his epiphany, thinking about what a poor part he must have played in Gretta's life next to the memory she carried all these years of Michael Furey.
  1. The scene is like the final one in Ibsen's *A Doll's House*, in which, when Torvald is eager to make love to Nora after she has danced the tarantella, she tells him she is leaving him.
  2. As Gabriel watches the snow fall outside his window, he feels himself drifting towards death, and he feels himself becoming one with both those who have already died and those who, like himself, are drifting towards death.

F. Like all the stories in this collection, every detail matters in this one.
  1. A picture of *Romeo and Juliet* hangs over the piano at his aunts' house, anticipating Michael Furey beneath Gretta's window.
  2. The talk around the table at dinner is about the past.
  3. The song sung by the tenor is "The Lass of Roch Royall," about lovers kept apart by class.
  4. The tapping of snowflakes on the window pane recalls the ghost of Catherine tapping on Lockwood's window in *Wuthering Heights*.
  5. Both Gabriel and Michael's names are taken from angels; in Milton's *Paradise Lost* Michael is given command over Gabriel, which is exactly what Gabriel feels has happened at the story's end.
  6. The party occurs (probably) on January 6—commemorating the visit of the Wise Men.
  7. Snow functions in the story first as a symbol of life and then of death.

G. The story can mean many things.
  1. Gabriel comes to see that death awaits us all, and we are all becoming specters.

2. The story reflects Gabriel's (and perhaps Joyce's) reconciliation with Ireland.
   3. The story is Gabriel's achievement of the kind of detachment Joyce felt that an artist needed.
VI. Joyce's techniques, which make for a very dense prose texture, will become even more marked in his future works and help to make them some of the most stunning works of literature ever written.

Essential Reading:

James Joyce, *Dubliners*.

Supplementary Reading:

John Wyse Jackson and Bernard McGinley, eds. *James Joyce's Dubliners*.

Daniel Schwarz, ed. *The Dead: James Joyce. Case Studies in Contemporary Criticism*.

Questions to Consider:

1. In what ways are Gabriel's three discomfitures on the evening of the party similar in nature, each one simply increasing in intensity? In what ways are they necessary preparations for the epiphany at the story's end? What is their common denominator?
2. In the stories of *Dubliners,* are the epiphanies characteristically understood by the protagonists as well as by the reader? Are there occasions when the epiphany is the reader's but is not entirely grasped or understood by the protagonist? If there are cases like this, what would Joyce's rhetorical point be in structuring the story in this way?

Lecture Thirty-Eight
Kafka's "The Metamorphosis"

Scope: Another stunningly original writer of the period was Franz Kafka, whose innovations in narrative technique can be seen in his "The Metamorphosis," particularly in the way its fantastic premise—a man wakes up to find that he has been transformed into a gigantic insect—is treated in sober realistic fashion. Kafka consistently blocks our attempts to read the story metaphorically or allegorically, yet we cannot resist the effort to try; we look briefly at the story as Expressionist, and as a Marxist, Freudian, or sociopolitical parable. We then consider that this story, like *Notes from Underground*, is prophetic of one aspect of the modern malaise, and we ask about the meaning of the contrast at the story's end between the healthy family that survives and the unhappy lot of the protagonist himself. We conclude by noting some of the writers who have been influenced by Kafka's techniques.

Outline

I. In an era of experimentation in literature, Franz Kafka is particularly innovative in two important ways in "The Metamorphosis."

   A. Instead of telling his story in the standard structure of exposition, complication, climax, and *denouement*, Kafka begins with the climax—in the first sentence. Everything after that is *denouement*, or unraveling.

   B. The first sentence leads the reader into thinking that this is a fantasy, fairy tale, or science fiction, but after that first sentence, the narrator treats Gregor's transformation into an insect in the most literal way possible, forcing the reader to give the story a more or less Realist reading.
      1. In the story, Gregor's family is more annoyed (since he is the family's breadwinner) than surprised or horrified.
      2. For a time they try intermittently to take care of him, but then they get busy and abandon him.
      3. Three times he emerges from his room, each time precipitating a disaster; then he dies, is swept into a dustpan, and the family goes on a picnic.

II. Kafka makes it difficult for readers to give the story an allegorical or metaphoric reading—or to read it as parable—by the prosaic reality of his details.
   A. Experienced readers, encountering in a story a man suddenly metamorphosed into an insect, will immediately try to interpret the story in a metaphoric way and conclude that perhaps modern man has become an insect.
      1. When Gregor gets the hang of using all his legs, he finds it exhilarating to climb across the ceiling, perhaps metaphorically finding pleasure in rising above the drudgery of his old life.
      2. Then the narrator tells us that as Gregor climbs along the ceiling, he leaves behind a slimy trail; his room begins to smell terrible.
   B. In 1977 there had been thousands of articles and books written about Kafka, many of them dealing with "The Metamorphosis," suggesting that even if the narrator discourages us, we feel impelled to try to read the story in some metaphoric or symbolic way.

III. Some of the ways the story has been interpreted may help us in finding our own way of reading it.
   A. The story has been read as part of the movement called *Expressionism*, which tries to describe the way we *experience* the world, not what it looks like in a representational way.
      1. Proust was creating new ways to do that in his work about the same time Kafka was writing this story; Joyce's *Finnegans Wake*—in one of its aspects—does the same.
      2. In the visual arts, Edvard Munch's *The Scream* pictures alienation and terror in a nonrepresentational way.
      3. In an Expressionist way, perhaps Kafka is showing what it feels like to be human in the 20th century.
   B. Marxist critics have read the story as a metaphor for human beings who are alienated and deformed by mechanical work processes. Gregor's metamorphosis—whether deliberate or not—allows him to escape from an inhuman way of life.
      1. These critics see significance in the amount of time spent early in the story showing how terrible Gregor's job is.

      2. Gregor's awful work situation has already, in this reading, turned him into an insect; the metamorphosis merely makes outward what was already true on the inside.
- **C.** Freudian and psychoanalytic critics see the story as primarily about the relationship between father and son.
    1. A few months before he wrote this, Kafka had written "The Judgment," in which a man sentences his son to death, and the son flings himself off the first bridge he comes to; this seems a transparently Oedipal fantasy.
    2. Kafka had read Freud's *The Interpretation of Dreams* (1900), written 12 years before this story, with interest if not always with full endorsement.
    3. In "The Metamorphosis," Gregor has taken over the father's role as breadwinner and head of the family and may very well feel guilty about the usurpation.
    4. In one graphic scene, Gregor's father tries to kill his son, who has come between him and his wife, who, with her clothes half falling off, begs her husband not to kill their son; this is as explicitly Oedipal as it is possible for a story to be.
    5. In this reading, the story is about the guilt of a son who usurps his father's place—guilt which makes him feel like an insect—and it reinforces this reading to notice that as Gregor declines, the father is revived as he reassumes his role as head of the family; at the story's end, he takes his family on a picnic to celebrate Gregor's death.
- **D.** Perhaps the most recurring metaphoric reading focuses on the political, social, and economic circumstances of the modern world and on their implications for modern men and women.
    1. In the modern world, the individual is pitted against vast, impersonal, and relentless systems—government, culture, bureaucracies—which regulate our lives in ways that we never quite understand.
    2. This is a typical Kafka situation: A man has to stand trial, never knowing what he is accused of, who his accusers are, or how he can reach them.
    3. In a parable in *The Trial,* a man goes to the law, before the gate of which sits a gatekeeper who for years keeps him from admission—always just for the time being. As he is dying, the man asks the gatekeeper why in all these years no one has ever tried to pass this gate except himself. The gatekeeper says that

the gate was for this man alone, and now that he is dying, it will be forever sealed up.
   4. In most of Kafka's stories, reality becomes a nightmare in which all institutions that used to be refuges for people fail to recognize them as individuals.
   5. As Dostoevsky's Underground Man has been seen as a foreshadowing of some aspects of the modern city-dweller, so Kafka's Gregor has been seen as representing the plight of anyone with a special need in an increasingly impersonal and regimented world.
  E. An *existential* reading sees Kafka describing a world in which there may well be a God, but one who is merely the vast and impersonal authority behind the inscrutable laws that govern our lives. We recognize their inexorability, but to us they are also incomprehensible, so that the world never makes sense.
   1. The institution in question here is the family, which also seems to operate by inexorable laws that we never quite grasp.
   2. As the story goes on, Gregor moves from a "he" to an "it"; once he is dead, the family goes on an outing, not once thinking of him.
   3. In *Notes from Underground* a man is diminished by the system until he becomes a mouse; here he becomes an insect who dies so that the family can go on with its normal life—whether that normal life is admirable or reprehensible.
IV. In a brilliant article, David Eggenschwiler explicates this story by means of two of Kafka's parables.
  A. In Kafka's reinterpretation of the story of Odysseus and the Sirens from the *Odyssey*, he contends that Odysseus's simplicity in an ironic way defeated the Sirens because they were so astonished by his audacity that they did not sing; Odysseus thought he had heard them singing and had escaped.
   1. In "The Metamorphosis," Gregor's family does not hear the Sirens; Gregor does, so he dies. His family's insight is so much less keen than his that they can escape back into a comfortable middle-class life.
   2. The family *thinks* that it has heard the Sirens and *thinks* that it has defeated them.

- **B.** According to another of Kafka's parables, Gregor escapes into some fabulous yonder and loses his everyday cares. *Interpretation* of parable, however, always reduces it to the dimensions of ordinary life, where it loses its meaning.
    1. Gregor's family acts out an interpretation of the parable, reducing it to the everyday world. They win in ordinary life but lose in parable, while Gregor has won in parable but lost in the everyday world.
    2. This suggests that whenever we try to reduce the story to the level of the everyday, we win in daily life and lose in parable.
- **C.** According to Eggenschwiler, the greatness of "The Metamorphosis" is that it preserves the parable and the mystery of inner life while acknowledging that people like Gregor's family—who never see the mystery—can live life on their own terms and win in everyday life.
    1. The story incorporates both the mysteries of existence as seen by Gregor and the promises of refuge for those whose sight is not so keen, like his family.
    2. How well Kafka did this can be seen by the fact that we are still arguing over the meaning of the story a century after it was written.
    3. For Eggenschwiler, every interpretation of a parable is a reduction by which we can win in life but lose in parable. The story thus can still tease us out of thought.
- **V.** Kafka's techniques have been appropriated by generations of writers; notable among them are Alain Robbe-Grillet, Samuel Beckett, Harold Pinter, Donald Barthelme, Robert Coover, and a special disciple, Gabriel Garcia Marquez, through whom we see that Magic Realism can be traced back to the first sentence of this story.

Essential Reading:

Franz Kafka, "The Metamorphosis."

Supplementary Reading:

Harold Bloom, ed. *Franz Kafka's "The Metamorphosis."*

David Eggenschwiler, "*Die Verwandlung,* Freud and the Chains of Odysseus."

Questions to Consider:

1. How do *you* read this enigmatic and complicated story? What does it mean? What is it about? With whom do you most identify in the story: Gregor or his family? Remembering what we learned in *Don Quixote*—that a text reads us as we read a text—what do you learn about yourself in analyzing where you find your sympathies falling in the story?

2. What is the function of the three boarders who move into the Samsa house for a time? How are they pictured? How do they behave? What do they represent in the larger scheme of the story? Who, or what, in whatever kind of reading you give the story, are they? How does their response to Gregor's presence in the house influence the family's decision about Gregor? That their influence should be so pronounced suggests what about what they represent in the story?

Lecture Thirty-Nine
Pirandello's *Six Characters*

Scope: In this lecture we discuss the rebellion against Realism in drama in the theatricalist movement, led by such figures as Luigi Pirandello, and evident in plays like *Six Characters in Search of an Author*. Pirandello aligns himself with writers like Proust in his examination of the nature of the self. Pirandello challenges the distinction between appearance and reality, and his characters in this play argue that they, as fictional entities, are more "real" than living human beings. All of the play's dialogue centers on his thesis that the "I" or ego that we assume as part of our common sense apprehension of reality may not exist—at least not as we imagine it. We conclude by noting that Pirandello's focus on the diminution of the self and personal responsibility is implied by all of the great "isms" of the turn of the century, which fundamentally change the way we think about ourselves.

Outline

I. Luigi Pirandello is part of a movement in the early 20th century generically called *theatricalism* or *anti-illusionism*.
   A. The purpose of theatricalism in theater was to reject Realism and to substitute for it the dreamlike, the expressive, and the symbolic—anything but the kind of plays that had been made normative by Ibsen, Chekhov, Shaw, and Strindberg.
      1. Theatricalists disapproved of Realism because it had abandoned the defining tools of drama—poetry, interaction between actors and audience, soliloquies, asides, relatively bare stages—as they had been used by the greatest dramatists in Western history: Sophocles, Shakespeare, and Moliere, among others.
      2. They felt that while Realist drama could deal competently with social problems, it could not depict the inner life—the subject of literature as it was being redefined by Proust, Woolf, and Joyce.
      3. One of the most famous of theatricalist plays of this period is Thornton Wilder's *Our Town*, which is anti-illusionist in its use of a bare stage and a stage manager who speaks directly to

members of the audience and reminds them that they are in a theater watching a play. It also features such events as a dead woman returning to spend a day with her family and a scene in a cemetery where the dead speak to each other, both of which express an inner truth that could not have occurred on a Realist stage.

B. Pirandello was also influenced by some of the same people and thought that influenced Proust and T. S. Eliot—including Henri Bergson—and came to some of the same conclusions, including the idea that the self is not fixed and stable but changes across time.

1. Pirandello had already explored these ideas in his short stories and novels, which also treated such themes as appearance and reality.
2. He had come to believe that the "I" which we assume persists through time does not exist—a stunning assertion, since it is the basis for common sense thinking as well as for our legal, moral, and literary systems.

II. All of these ideas are developed in *Six Characters in Search of an Author*.

A. In the play, a rehearsal of a Pirandello play is interrupted by the entrance of six persons who claim to be characters created by a writer who never finished his work; they are looking for a playwright who will finish their story. They act out the two scenes that were written for them, both of them luridly melodramatic.

B. The focus of the play, however, is not on the characters' story but on the interaction between the six characters and the real actors in the theater.

1. The play insists that human beings cannot distinguish between the real and the apparent—the distinction itself is illusory.
2. "Reality" is merely what one happens to believe in at the moment: the appearance to which one commits oneself now.
3. This is a theme we have been exploring since *Don Quixote*, which insisted that what matters is not what is there but how one sees it and interprets it.
4. The Impressionist painters had suggested the same, and the idea that the act of subjective perception had been worked into the novel by such writers as Henry James, Joseph Conrad, and—especially—Marcel Proust.

        5. Pirandello had already written a play titled *Right You Are If You Think You Are,* which suggests that there are as many realities as perceivers.
  C. The distinction between the fictional and the real is violated in the play when six fictional characters enter the plane of reality occupied by the actors and the producer.
    1. The Father—one of the six characters—argues that fictional characters are *more* "real" than living ones, since they are fixed eternally, while a living person is constantly changing and subject to the flux of time.
    2. The idea of art being immortal while humans are transient is not in itself a brand new one; it can be found in Shakespeare's sonnets and in Keats's "Ode on a Grecian Urn," among many other works. Pirandello, however, puts it to different use.
    3. Pirandello, in a preface to the play, says that whenever a reader opens Dante's *Inferno*, Francesca will drift down from the dark wind in her circle of Hell and tell the Pilgrim her story; and it will always be for the first time—just as the Mother in Pirandello's play at one point makes an agonized cry, always for the first time.
  D. In the play each of the six characters sees events and other characters differently from each other.
    1. Each character has a sense of who he or she is and what has happened, but their readings do not match up, which is why it takes so long to get even a provisional draft of their story.
    2. The playwright suggests that any one character is no more correct than another; there are as many versions of the story as there are characters in the play.
    3. Each character is in fact many different characters: each has his or her own sense of who he or she is, but each is also what other characters think he or she is.
  E. There is no guarantee that a character's sense of himself or herself is more accurate than those of other characters. Every self is what it has been at different times and what it has seemed to other characters at different times.
    1. This is illustrated by one of the scenes that was written for the six characters—a scene that occurs in Madame Pace's shop—which each character reads in a different way.

- **2.** The Daughter thinks of the Father as a reprehensible character; he thinks of himself as a decent character who got caught in an aberration which was "out of character" for him.
- **3.** There is no final way to resolve these differences. What *is* a self, apart from what it does from moment to moment? Who is right about the Father? Is there a *real* self that stands outside of things that it does?

III. In exploring these themes, Pirandello is participating in a larger debate that was going on in the first part of the century about the "self" and what it is.

- **A.** Joseph Wood Krutch, in *Modernism in Modern Drama*, argued in 1953 that all three of the great "isms" at the turn of the century—Darwinism, Marxism, and Freudianism—were attacks on the self, the ego that we had always assumed to be in charge of our lives.
    - **1.** Darwinism places evolution in the control of natural selection by the environment to which individual organisms adapt, not in the control of willed choices.
    - **2.** Marxism argues that the means of production determine our beliefs and values, not our own commitments.
    - **3.** Freudianism asserts that most of what we do is the result not of choice or deliberation but impulses of which we are mostly unaware, let alone in control of.
- **B.** In 1875 William Henley's "Invictus" expressed the comforting view that each of us is in total charge of our self. The 20th century was less sure about this, suggesting that the new "isms" make us more *victims* of forces we cannot control than *captains* of our own fate.
    - **1.** The vision is discouraging in that we lose control over our own destinies but comforting in that much of what we do we cannot be held responsible for.
    - **2.** What we get back in place of a continuous ego are states of mind, masks, or personae: the temporary result of forces brought to bear upon us at that moment. The self, then, becomes an anthology of such roles or masks.
    - **3.** Pirandello brings many of these concerns together; it is no accident that his collected plays were titled *Naked Masks*.

IV. Finally, Theatricalists thought that the Realists got it backwards: that life was more like theater than theater was (or should be) like life.

- **A.** As in the theater, in life we put on and take off masks, try out various roles, and make up our lives as we go along.
    1. The process is nicely illustrated in Stephen Sondheim's *Into the Woods*, in the second half of which, with the narrator dead, the characters have to make up their own stories.
    2. This is a situation felt by many people early in the 20th century, when traditional props for identity melted, requiring new conceptions of what had been taken for granted for centuries.
    3. Pirandello sits in the middle of this debate and shift, asking us to think about things that continue to matter to us in the new century.
- **B.** Joseph Wood Krutch predicted (tongue-in-cheek) in 1953 that since Chekhov had gotten rid of plot in drama and now Pirandello had gotten rid of character, there could be no more plays in the modern world. There are, of course, still plays, but our sense of what makes a character, of what makes a self a self, and what that self really is, has changed drastically since the days of William Henley's "Invictus."

Essential Reading:

Luigi Pirandello, *Six Characters in Search of an Author.*

Supplementary Reading:

Robert Brustein, *The Theatre of Revolt.*

Joseph Wood Krutch, *Modernism in Modern Drama.*

Questions to Consider:

1. Pirandello continued to explore his ideas of the relationships between art and life in two other plays which, along with *Six Characters in Search of an Author*, are sometimes called his "Theater Trilogy": *Each in His Own Way* (1924) and *Tonight We Improvise* (1930). In the three plays, Pirandello can argue both ways: Art is superior to life because it is immortal, and art (like death) turns us into stiff statues which can never change. How do you find yourself evaluating the arguments of the Father and the Producer on this question in *Six Characters in Search of an Author?* In your mind, who wins and on what basis?
2. Pirandello wanted this play to not seem like a play but something that happens spontaneously at a rehearsal in a theater. Even the

intermissions are supposed to seem accidental: Once the producer and characters withdraw to his office to work on a script, and once the curtain is dropped by mistake. In how many other ways does Pirandello make this seem more an impromptu than a staged event? How do they express a theatricality's idea of what theater should be, how it should function, and what plays should be about?

Lecture Forty
Brecht's *The Good Woman of Setzuan*

Scope: Bertolt Brecht is part of the same theatricalist movement as Pirandello, but he puts his innovations to social rather than philosophical uses. His epic theater uses *alienation techniques* to prevent emotional identification by the audience with onstage characters and to encourage independent evaluation and thought. This play uses a variety of such techniques to encourage us to consider whether in a capitalist economic system it is possible to be good and successful simultaneously. The play suggests that it is not, and that the gods and religion are irrelevant to the desperate needs of modern humans. Brecht was a Marxist who wanted his plays to advance the Communist revolution, but most readers and critics have seen them as too complex and ambiguous to advocate any particular course of action. His staging techniques have been so widely adopted that now they seem conventional to most theatergoers, not the radical innovations they were at the time.

Outline

I. The plot of Bertolt Brecht's *The Good Woman of Setzuan* involves the gods giving Shen Te money in exchange for her hospitality—money which she uses to buy a tobacco shop, hoping to use the profits for more charity.

    A. Shen Te is so overwhelmed by needy people that she has to invent a ruthless cousin, Shui Ta (herself in disguise), who runs the shop so successfully that he eventually turns it into a sweatshop, employing many people.

        1. Shen Te still hopes to use the profits for good, but there are so many needs that she is forced to bring Shui Ta back more and more often for longer periods of time, until at length Shui Ta is tried for the murder of Shen Te.

        2. At the trial she reveals herself and confesses that all she has done she did to help her neighbors, love her lover, and keep her unborn child from want.

    B. She tells the gods, who are acting as judges at the trial, that they have created an impossible situation in which it is too difficult to be both good and successful. The gods, however, declare themselves satisfied with their experiment and sail off, telling Shen Te to be good. She turns to the audience to ask *them* what can be done.

II. Brecht, like Pirandello, is a theatricalist, using similar techniques to explode Realism in the theater.
  A. Where Pirandello uses his techniques to raise Existential questions, Brecht uses his for *social* purposes.
   1. Brecht had become a Marxist in the 1920s and from then on used his plays to point up contradictions in the capitalist system.
   2. In the process, he effectively reinvented the techniques of modern theater.
  B. Brecht's plays are didactic; beyond that, he wants us to leave the theater wanting to *do* something, to put our new knowledge into action.
   1. Traditional plays using Aristotelian formulae invite emotional identification with characters, so that the audience experiences a *catharsis*, an emotional experience that mimics that of the characters themselves.
   2. The experience of the play is self-contained; an emotionally complete circle that Brecht thought was wasted energy.
   3. Brecht worked with what he called epic theater and its alienation techniques, designed to prevent such identification and to invite thought rather than emotional involvement.
   4. His model was a man in court describing an accident he had witnessed: the man will act out parts of his story and narrate others, *demonstrating* his story rather than fully enacting it.
   5. The point of *epic theater* is to draw us into some emotional identification with stage characters and then to push us back—alienate us—so that we have the emotional leisure to think about what we have seen.
  C. Alienation techniques in *The Good Woman of Setzuan* include direct addresses to the audience by characters, interspersed songs, interludes in which the gods reflect on the action so far, stage action which does not match what the audience is hearing, musicians sitting on stage for the songs, and props which are supposed to look theatrical and nonrealistic.

1. The setting is intended to alienate as well: the city is mythical and suggestive of Berlin or any other large city, but its exotic location allows us to see the familiar with fresh eyes.
2. The ultimate alienation technique is the ending: Brecht knows that we will be unhappy with the way the play concludes, so he has Shen Te come forward to ask us how *we* would rewrite the conclusion to make it a happy one.

III. *The Good Woman of Setzuan* illustrates these Brechtian principles.
  A. It is a parable of the "what if" variety, since in Marxist thought—in which consciousness is determined by the means of production—a woman as good as Shen Te would not be possible in a capitalist system.
   1. Thus, Shen Te invents Shui Ta to do the nasty things she needs to do to survive.
   2. When she is not Shui Ta, she runs the risk of ruining herself because of her natural goodness; her invented cousin must protect her from the consequences of her kind heart.
   3. In the process she becomes a kind of schizophrenic, and we see her better half slowly being corrupted by her alter ego. Whenever Shen Te wins in a material way, she harms herself in a human one.
  B. The point is illustrated in the scenes with her lover, Yang Sun, who wants both Shen Te's goodness and Shui Ta's money simultaneously—which is of course impossible, since they are the same person. He cannot have both at the same time, nor can we, nor can Shen Te herself, which is the point of the play.
  C. When Shen Te becomes pregnant, she more or less permanently disappears in favor of her ruthless cousin, Shui Ta, who is eventually accused of killing her.
   1. It is metaphorically appropriate that he be tried for her murder, since it is only by "killing off" the good woman of Setzuan that the business has been able to grow.
   2. At the trial scene, both Shen Te and Shui Ta admit that Shen Te's focus has changed: She began by assuming her cousin's role only to be able to be charitable, but she has learned that goodness is incompatible with survival.
   3. As always, survival takes precedence over charity—especially when there is her unborn child in the picture.

- **4.** Goodness as a value, the play suggests, cannot survive without fundamental social and economic changes.
- **IV.** The play also insists that solutions for this dilemma have to come from humans themselves, not from the gods or religion.
    - **A.** The gods are not interested in helping people, only in validating their own laws so that they can go back to heaven and the world can go on as it is.
        - **1.** The situation is similar to that in Goethe's *Faust*, where God will be satisfied with his creation if he can find one good person; here the gods will assume that everything is fine if one good person can be found.
        - **2.** The gods represent fixed moral absolutes, which do not allow for any flexibility.
        - **3.** Even good people in Setzuan have compromised in some ways just to stay alive; what makes Shen Te remarkable is that she really *tries* to be good and hopes, as religious people do, that the gods will in some way *help* good people (in one of her songs, Shen Te asks why the gods are not indignant at what happens on Earth).
        - **4.** At the end the gods are satisfied that Shen Te is a good person, which makes goodness possible, and they go back to heaven on a pink cloud.
    - **B.** The gods simply wind up defending the status quo (the rich and powerful), which Brecht feels is what religion does. The gods even become comic figures as the play progresses, suggesting their retreat from relevance.
- **V.** While Brecht recreated stagecraft, his plays were never as successful as Marxist propaganda, as he wished them to be.
    - **A.** He did a series of productions of *Mother Courage and Her Children* in East Berlin where, despite his constant fiddling with the play and its presentation, people kept missing its Marxist point.
    - **B.** Martin Esslin, however, points out in *Brecht: A Choice of Evils* that the entire idea may be based on a non sequitur.
        - **1.** So far as we know, none of the thousands of people who saw Brecht's and Kurt Weil's *The Threepenny Opera* on Broadway ever became Communist.
        - **2.** Beyond that, Brecht wrote plays that are complicated enough that their didactic point invariably gets blunted.

3. In this play, audience hearts always go out to Shen Te, in whom they find a representative of the plight of poor people everywhere.
4. Her last song, which throws the need for a solution into the audience's lap, stresses not any particular solution but the immense *difficulties* in finding one.
5. Perhaps, in a paradoxical way, Brecht's greatness as a dramatist was always at war with his aims as a propagandist.
6. He nonetheless recreated stagecraft and initiated a whole new age for the theater.

Essential Reading:

Bertolt Brecht, *The Good Woman of Setzuan.*

Supplementary Reading:

Bruce Thompson, trans. and ed. *"Der Gute Mensch von Sezuan."*
Alfred D. White, *Bertolt Brecht's Great Plays.*

Questions to Consider:

1. What does it suggest about the function of religion in modern society that all of the rich people to whom the gods appeal for lodging turn them down, and it is only the poor who try to find ways to accommodate them? Wang, the water carrier, is a religious person, but even he has made certain compromises in his faith; what do his presence, his speeches, and his actions contribute to Brecht's point about the uses (and misuses) of religion in a capitalist society?
2. The ordinary people portrayed in this play tend to be greedy, corrupt, opportunistic, hypocritical, and dishonest; why is this so? Is this basic human nature or would these people be different if they lived in a different kind of world? Does the play suggest an answer for this, or is this another one of the ambiguities that make Brecht's plays so interestingly complicated?

Lecture Forty-One
Anna Akhmatova's *Requiem*

Scope: We start with the Yezhov Terror of the late 1930s in Russia as a political context for Anna Akhmatova's *Requiem* and the Imagist revolution in poetry early in the century as an aesthetic context. We also note the increasing alienation of the creative artist from his or her culture since the Romantic period. *Requiem* describes a sick society in which the poet must speak for voiceless victims everywhere. We touch on highlights of the poem cycle, showing how the framing pieces speak with a larger voice for all the oppressed and persecuted women in history, while the inner poems reflect Akhmatova's personal circumstances. The poem's themes include the poet's fight with—and eventual triumph over—madness and her contextualization of her suffering in that of Mary, watching Jesus die on the cross, and Niobe, weeping eternally for her children. The poem commemorates all women who have ever waited outside political prisons and urges us not to forget them.

Outline

I. The political context for the poem is the Yezhov Terror of 1937 and 1938, when there were perhaps 10 million Russians in prisons and prison camps, and millions more had already been executed.

  A. Anna Akhmatova stood outside a prison in Leningrad (formerly St. Petersburg) for 17 months, hoping to see her son (her former and current husband had already been executed).

  B. A woman recognizes her and asks if she can describe this scene; she answers, "Yes, I can." The poem Akhmatova wrote in response was *Requiem*.

II. Prior to all of this, Akhmatova had been a poet well-known for her love poetry, written in the modern style.

  A. The Modernist Movement in Russia was called *Acmeism*, but there were analogous movements throughout the Western world.

   1. Ezra Pound and T. S. Eliot were involved in a movement called *Imagism*, the goal of which was to make poetry more concrete, less musical, and more dependent on images rather than explanation.

       2. The idea was to make poetry richer and to say more with less—which is one of the reasons Emily Dickinson seems so modern, since in some ways she anticipated this movement across Europe.
- **B.** The movements in various countries also point up the increasing alienation of the writer from his or her culture in the 20th century.
  - **1.** Perhaps all literature is subversive in some ways, an expression of irritation or distress like an oyster making a pearl from the irritation of sand.
  - **2.** In earlier literature, writers like Cervantes and Voltaire were reacting against some aspects of their cultures.
  - **3.** From the Romantic period on, writers tended to stand further outside their cultures than they did in the past (e.g., Emma Bovary, the Underground Man, Huck Finn, and Kafka's insect-man).
  - **4.** Proust and Pirandello focused on the isolation of the individual, even within a community or family.
  - **5.** T. S. Eliot suggests in *The Waste Land* a disease pervading all of culture and society, as do many other writers of the period, including Akhmatova.
- **C.** In *Requiem*, Akhmatova is not speaking only as an individual, but first for all the women standing outside all the prisons in Russia in the late 1930s, and then for all women in all times and places, watching as their fathers, husbands, and sons are executed, imprisoned, or disappear. Speaking out for the oppressed is part of the literary tradition everywhere, but it seems especially the case in Russian literature.

III. The poems that make up *Requiem* were written between 1935 and 1961, but they could not be published because for almost 40 years Akhmatova had been forbidden to write or publish poetry.
- **A.** In 1922, Akhmatova was declared an "unsatisfactory poet" whose work did not advance the revolution. She was forbidden to publish and was made an internal émigré; her only published writing for 18 years was a series of essays on Pushkin.
- **B.** Only after Stalin's death in 1953 could she begin to publish these poems, and then she received a series of international awards, including the Etna-Taormina Poetry Prize in 1964 and an honorary doctorate from Oxford in 1965.

- **C.** These poems in fact were not kept during all these years as written manuscripts, but memorized and remembered by Akhmatova and her novelist friend Lydia Chukovskaya, since it would have been too dangerous to have written copies around—or even to speak the poems out loud.
- **IV.** *Requiem* is made up of 10 poems, prefaced by four pieces: three in poetry and one in prose.
  - **A.** The cycle ends with two epilogues. In the second epilogue she asks that if a monument ever be put up for her, it be placed outside this prison as a memorial to the women who waited there with her and for whom she has woven this "mantle"—her poem.
    1. The four prefaces and two epilogues speak with a larger voice for the millions of women who waited outside prisons.
    2. For them, the world has narrowed down to the prison gates, and in a brilliant image, Akhmatova sees all of Leningrad dangling uselessly from its prisons.
  - **B.** The numbered interior poems are the more personal ones.
    1. The first poem describes her husband being arrested; it both describes an emotional breaking point and links the suffering of modern Russian women to that of wives and mothers who in 1698 witnessed the execution of their men under the towers of the Kremlin.
    2. The second and third poems begin the splitting in two of the speaker: one who suffers and one who watches the suffering as she drifts toward an emotional breakdown.
    3. The next three poems contrast her happy youth with the woman who now waits, the 300th person in line, outside the prison; these poems bring her close to madness again as disconnected images float in her mind and the likely death of her son stares down out of the sky like a giant star or the burning eye of a hawk.
    4. The seventh poem, "The Sentence," commemorates the day her son was sentenced to death. Its calm focus on "so much to do" suggests incipient madness once again.
    5. The eighth poem, "To Death," is an invitation to death to come and take her; she will leave the door open to make it easier for him.
    6. In the ninth poem, she once and for all turns away from madness, since to go insane would mean that she would have

to part with all her memories, even of her son; she would rather live in agony for the rest of her life than to part with those.
    7. The tenth poem, "The Crucifixion," places the women in the poem in the context of Mary watching her son die; the recurring religious imagery of the poem is explained at least in part in the awareness that Mary understands, since she too watched her own son die.
  C. In the epilogue there are many cross-references to images and events from earlier in the poem, one of which suggests Niobe, forever weeping for the deaths of her children.
V. *Requiem* is about a specific time and place, but it also remembers all the mothers, wives, and daughters of history who have suffered.
  A. As Elie Wiesel has used his books to speak for the millions who lost their voices in the Holocaust, so Akhmatova does here for the millions of women waiting outside prisons all throughout history and all over the world, who for many reasons cannot speak for themselves.
  B. Her songs are like W. E. B. Du Bois's "sorrow songs," which cannot undo what has been done but can console at least by remembering the pain.

Essential Reading:

Anna Akhmatova, *Requiem*.

Supplementary Reading:

Susan Amert, *In a Shattered Mirror*.

Sam Driver, *Anna Akhmatova*.

Questions to Consider:

1. As you read the cycle, pay particular attention to the religious images and allusions. What is the function of these references? Is the poet suggesting a religious solace in a literal way or must the cycle be read in a metaphoric way, indicating that whatever comfort there is will have to come from someplace other than religion? How do we decide on the basis of the poem itself how we should read and understand the references?

2. The poems are also full of what is sometimes called intertextuality: references and allusions to a lot of other literature, Russian as well as non-Russian. How many other references to other literature can you discover, remembering that some of the references to Russian history and landscape are also references to literary works? How, besides providing a partial cover for the poet, do they function in the poems?

Lecture Forty-Two
Kawabata Yasunari's *Snow Country*

Scope: Kawabata Yasunari's *Snow Country* is a Modernist work, using such techniques as a disciplined point of view and stream of consciousness, learned from contact with Western writers. Kawabata uses these techniques in intriguing ways, since his protagonist, Shimamura, is a detached, remote man, more a spectator than a player, and the novel is about his relationships with two women in a hot springs resort in northern Japan. One woman, Yoko, is for him disembodied, a vision whom he metaphorizes as a star, while the other, Komako, a geisha, is associated with the color red and silk worms. The tension between these relationships is perfectly captured in the novel's final scene, in which a fire, the Milky Way, and an old Japanese folk tale merge to create an ending of nearly perfect ambiguity. We conclude with a series of questions about modern fiction and modern life raised by this novel in the context of Modernism.

Outline

I. In *Snow Country* Kawabata Yasunari uses avant-garde techniques that came to Japan from Western literature.
  A. When Japanese writers first adapted Western techniques for their own works, the most fashionable and up-to-date mode in the West was that of Realism, as we saw in the work of Higuchi Ichiyō.
  B. During the 1930s and 1940s, when this novel was written and published, many of the "isms" mentioned in past lectures made their mark on the novel genre.
    1. Kawabata admitted to being much influenced by James Joyce's *Ulysses* and by the theories of Sigmund Freud.
    2. He belonged to a group of young Japanese writers called *New Sensibilities*, whose aim was to rescue Japanese writing from Realism and Naturalism.
  C. Henry James had established that every story is *somebody's* story, so that first- or third-person limited point of view had become normative for the psychological Realist novel.

1. Kawabata's novel uses a third-person limited point of view, which means that all of our information comes to us through the sensibility of its protagonist, Shimamura.
2. We are inside his head for the entire book, which means that everything we learn has already been colored by his temperament and sensibility.
3. In novels of this sort, we have to get to know our protagonist and his sensibility well enough to make adjustments for his biases and proclivities—a particular issue in this novel because of the nature of Shimamura.

D. Many modern writers—including Proust, Joyce, and Woolf—had argued that our experience of reality is very different from the way it is presented in Realist novels.
1. An accurate account of what goes on in an individual's mind at any given moment would be very different from the logical, rational, prepackaged story that we get in a Realist narrative. What we experience is what Virginia Woolf called "an incessant shower of innumerable atoms" that bombards us all the time.
2. *Stream-of-consciousness* is one technique that writers invented to try to capture more accurately the way reality actually impinges on our consciousness.
3. We see a modest use of stream-of-consciousness in Gabriel Conroy's meditation at the end of Joyce's "The Dead" and its more extensive use in *Ulysses*; Virginia Woolf uses it in *To the Lighthouse* and *Mrs. Dalloway*; and William Faulkner uses it in his novels.
4. Stream-of-consciousness is always a challenging technique for readers, since they must grasp the associative processes by which the mind given them in the novel works and then gather the fragments into some coherent whole or decide that the very incoherence of the fragments is actually an accurate picture of the modern world.

II. The stream-of-consciousness technique is even more challenging in *Snow Country* because of the nature of its protagonist, through whose sensibility all of our information is given to us in this third-person limited account.

A. The action takes place in northwest Japan in the 1930s at a hot-springs retreat for men, noted for the amount of snow it receives in winter. Shimamura visits this place three times in a little less than two years.

- **B.** Shimamura is a detached man: a spectator of life rather than a participant.
    1. He had once become an expert in traditional Japanese dance, but when his expertise was called on by the dance community, he abruptly gave it up.
    2. Now he studies Western ballet, which he never sees and can hence study only in books. As he says, being an expert in Western ballet in Japan is like being in love with someone he has never seen.
- **C.** The novel is about his attraction to two women he meets in snow country.
    1. One is a young woman he sees on the train on his way there, and the other is a geisha he meets at the resort.
    2. He avoids any kind of commitment to either one; he in fact retreats when he feels himself on the verge of a real relationship with the geisha.
    3. It is difficult for us to take Shimamura's measure: His detachment from life keeps him distanced from us as well and leaves us with only a handful of vague impressions and more questions than answers.

III. The two women to whom he is attracted are quite different from each other.

- **A.** The woman on the train—Yoko—stays disembodied for Shimamura as a distant ideal.
    1. The scene in which he sees her on the train is perhaps the most famous in the novel.
    2. He sees her reflection in a window inside the train, but he also sees the landscape moving behind her image in the window, so the effect is like a montage in film.
    3. At one point a light from outside shines directly through her eye in the image in the window, making her eye into a star; throughout, Shimamura will associate her with cold, distance, and stars. She suggests cleanliness and freshness.
    4. It is perhaps possible that he is interested in her *because* of her remoteness and inaccessibility—which would be very much in character for him.

- **B.** The geisha—Komako—is associated with red (not white, as Yoko is), and her physicality is insisted upon.
    1. She and Shimamura become lovers almost immediately: although as a geisha she is not required to have sex with him, she chooses to, seeming to have fallen in love with him.
    2. We can understand his attraction for Yoko—he is a connoisseur who likes his pleasures at a distance—but what appeals to him about Komako?
    3. Perhaps it is her ambiguity: When Shimamura first meets her, she is neither an independent young woman nor a geisha but something in between, which might appeal to him.
    4. Her colors are red and white, but the white is the white of geisha powder, not snow or stars. She, like Shimamura himself, is hard to define, to pin down.
    5. She is deeply associated with silk worms. The progression from larvae to worms to moths moves from red to white too, and Komako lives in an attic previously used for raising silkworms. When she is young, Shimamura associates her with red translucence; when she is a full geisha, he associates her with the white-powdered wings of the moths laying eggs.
    6. A tour that Shimamura takes into the backlands is related to this silkworm lore: Chijimi silk must be spun, woven, finished, and bleached in the glare of sunlit snow by girls between the ages of 12 and 24—the same ambiguous place where Shimamura finds Komako when he first visits snow country.
    7. Eventually, Shimamura realizes that he is becoming too interested in her, and he decides to leave, sometimes vaguely regretting the kind of man he is but knowing that regret would suggest that he had wasted his life up to this point.
- **IV.** The novel's final scene is full of its own ambiguity.
    - **A.** Yoko is killed in a fire that burns down a theater that used to be a silkworm cocoon warehouse; as Komako carries her away, the Milky Way flows into Shimamura, who has thrown back his head.
        1. The scene alludes to the Japanese festival of Tanabata, based on a myth of parted lovers who live on opposite ends of the Milky Way and who can meet only one night a year.
        2. But which two lovers: Shimamura and Komako or Shimamura and Yoko?

- **B.** The references to Tanabata and its legendary heroes, Herd-Boy and Weaver-Girl, are unmistakable, but what do we make of them or of the entire novel?
- **V.** The text is Modernist in a way that was—as we have noted in earlier lectures—invented by Anton Chekhov: open-ended, without any real sense of closure or any tidy conclusions we can draw.
  - **A.** Modern writers are less inclined than were older ones to tell us how to think, what to believe, and how to understand experience in a work of literature.
  - **B.** Here we are inside the mind of a man who has *chosen* not to make commitments, which makes our own judgments even less secure.
  - **C.** Like many Modernist texts, *Snow Country* leaves us with many questions.
    1. Does the fact that this is a *Japanese* work inhibit our understanding of it, since the Nobel Prize Committee awarded Kawabata the prize in 1966 for demonstrating "the essence of the Japanese mind"?
    2. Is this, rather, some part of Modernism generally—we no longer quite know how to evaluate experience or what to make of it or what standards to use to judge it?
    3. Is Shimamura typically Japanese in a way that makes him difficult for us to understand, or is he simply a representative of modern man: aloof, detached, keeping away from commitments and hence unable ever to gather the fragments of experience together into some coherent whole?
    4. These are all central questions of Modernism in literature: Does experience make sense? Are there standards of reference? Who gets to decide whether life has meaning or not? Is it possible to judge other people, and, if we do, on what basis? If we do find a basis, how do we know that it is not simply ethnocentric?

Essential Reading:
Kawabata Yasunari. *Snow Country.*

Supplementary Reading:
Masao Mihoshi. *Accomplices of Silence.*
David Pollack, *Reading Against Culture.*

Questions to Consider:

1. Notice how often mirrors are used in the novel—including the famous moment when Shimamura sees Yoko in a train window. How do mirrors function in the book? Under what circumstances do they appear? Do they help us in any way to understand either Shimamura or the world of the story more completely?

2. Kawabata said that he was far more interested in the character of Komako than he was in Shimamura—that Shimamura is merely a vehicle for us better to understand and see the geisha in the round. How well do you think you understand her at the novel's end? Does she represent—as some have suggested—the physical, as opposed to Yoko's celestial, so that the book is really about the male demand for the female ambiguity between angel and whore, spirit and flesh, or is there more to her than that? What is there about her that so fascinates Shimamura that he eventually has to tear himself away from her?

Lecture Forty-Three
Faulkner—Two Stories and a Novel

Scope: We begin by noticing that the Nobel Prize William Faulkner was awarded in 1950 rescued his works from the realm of the sensational and the regional. His acceptance speech reminded readers that his stories were about traditional values, even if they occurred in unusual circumstances and contexts. We then use two short stories, "Wash" and "A Rose for Emily," to illustrate Faulkner's characteristic combination of human greatness with the bizarre, the grotesque, and even the insane. We account for this unusual combination in the conceptual framework provided by Aldous Huxley's essay, "The Whole Truth." Then we introduce Faulkner's novel, *As I Lay Dying*, in that framework, showing that like all of his works, the comic, tragic, pathetic, sad, funny, grotesque, and the heroic are always so close to each other that they cannot be separated—which is, as Huxley would say, the "whole truth" about human beings.

Outline

I. The Nobel Prize Faulkner received in 1950 began a revival of interest in his work that has by now made him one of the most studied and written about of all American writers.

II. Beginning with his early novel, *Sartoris*, he created a county named Yoknapatawpha and over a lifetime's work told the story of the rise and fall of the Old South and then the history of the post-war South up to about 1940.

  A. Malcolm Cowley had already pointed that out in the Viking Portable Library edition of Faulkner's work in 1946, but it took a while—and the assistance of the Nobel Prize—for most readers to realize how massive the achievement was.

  B. In scale it is somewhat like Balzac's series of novels about life in Paris from about 1815 to 1848, and it allowed Faulkner to produce a body of work that in almost mythical ways shows the history of the South from the days of the indigenous Indians to almost the halfway point of the 20th Century.

III. Faulkner had been dismissed by some earlier critics because his work seemed to them purely regional in interest and overly sensational, featuring a great deal of violence.
  A. In his Nobel Prize acceptance speech, however, he said that his work was about what all good literature is about: love, honor, pride, pity, compassion, and sacrifice.
  B. In Faulkner's world these virtues are always so compounded with the base, the grotesque, and the comic that it is sometimes hard to recognize them.

IV. "Wash," a 1934 short story later revised and incorporated into *Absalom, Absalom!*, illustrates these Faulknerian qualities.
  A. Wash Williams is a no-account white who for years has squatted on the Sutpen plantation.
    1. He admires Sutpen to the point of adoration and finds meaning in his own life through Sutpen's glory.
    2. After the Civil War, in which Sutpen has lost virtually everything, he seduces Wash's granddaughter, Milly, in an effort to have a son and restart his dynasty. Wash knows what is happening but trusts Sutpen to behave honorably.
    3. When the baby—a girl—is born, Wash realizes that Sutpen cares more for his horses than he does for Wash and Milly, and he kills Sutpen with a scythe.
    4. After dark, when the body had been discovered and the inevitable posse comes for Wash, he kills Milly and the baby, douses his old shack with kerosene, lights it on fire, and then runs out, silhouetted in the flames, into a rain of bullets from the posse.
  B. The ending *feels* like—and in some ways resembles—the ending of a Greek tragedy.
    1. The story is about many things, but one of them is Wash's final gesture, which is so compounded with both magnificence and the reprehensible that they cannot be separated.
    2. Aldous Huxley argues in "The Whole Truth" that while tragedy is always a distilled essence with the baseness all eliminated, comedy always tells the whole truth, leaving in all that tragedy distills away.
    3. In that sense, Faulkner's works are always comic, including the warts. It is not that this makes the heroism or courage or endurance we find there any less admirable, it is just that they

are always embedded in the whole character, as they are in Wash.

V. "A Rose for Emily" illustrates the Faulknerian world even more graphically.
  - **A.** This complicated story is about a woman—a descendent of the old aristocracy in Jefferson, the seat of Yoknapatawpha County in 1928—and of the town's assessments of her over the years.
    1. The narrator uses the "we" pronoun, suggesting that he speaks for all of Jefferson.
    2. The story uses the technique of broken chronology to move backwards and forwards in time, the way someone telling a story would do, giving us a sense of the town's perception of Emily Grierson over time.
    3. Among other things, we discover in the story's last paragraph that Emily had years ago poisoned her lover who was about to leave her and kept his body in the upstairs bedroom of her house, where he died; in the story's last paragraph we discover that she still slept in the bed where he lay, now badly decomposed.
    4. Emily is of course mad, but the story's title refers to the town's gift to her of a rose for her refusal to give in, compromise, and adapt herself to the increasingly grubby world around her; as critics have noted, there may be an element of madness in all heroism.
  - **B.** Again, in Huxley's phrase, Faulkner always gives us "the whole truth," the tragic and comic simultaneously mixed together—as are, for the reader, laughter, sorrow, horror, and admiration.

VI. *As I Lay Dying* (1930) illustrates the same point but with some additional technical virtuosity.
  - **A.** The plot concerns a poor family from the country taking the body of their matriarch to Jefferson to bury it.
    1. The family is unlucky, and a series of disasters delays them, so that it takes nine days to get to Jefferson, by which time the body in the wooden coffin has attracted buzzards and offends everyone who comes within nosing distance of it.
    2. On the one hand, the story is that of a heroic journey, through flood and fire, to keep a promise.

  3. We also discover that some of the family members have private motives for wanting to go to Jefferson; once again, at any given moment a gesture can be seen simultaneously in a number of different lights: grotesque, absurd, comic, horrible, or noble.
B. The narrative technique in this novel is particularly striking and innovative.
  1. The story is told in 59 sections by 15 characters, most of them members of the Bundren family, but some are told by other folks who encounter them on their way to Jefferson.
  2. As in Brontë's *Wuthering Heights,* all of the story tellers are *inside* the story, with no omniscient narrator telling us what really happened or how to judge what happened.
  3. Each of the 59 sections uses stream-of-consciousness technique or interior monologue, which foregrounds the normative subjectivity of literature in the 20th century.
  4. Additionally, some of the characters are troubled ones, and their interior monologues illustrate their problems: Vardaman, the youngest son, is totally traumatized by his mother's death; Darl, another son, is so intuitive that he can almost read the minds of other characters but is also unstable enough that the family leaves him in a hospital for the insane when they return from Jefferson.
  5. Nonfamily characters add various perspectives to the family's journey, so that by the time Addie Bundren is actually buried, we get to see the entire series of events in many dimensions.
C. There are, in addition, subplots within the family itself.
  1. Some family members have secrets they wish to keep from the others—secrets which are threatened by Darl's intuitive insights, helping to account for why the family is willing to leave him behind at the story's end—which complicate relations among the family members.
  2. Addie, the corpse, is given a long monologue of her own in which she tells us that one of her children is not her husband's but was fathered by the local preacher, whom she met in the woods when she discovered that her husband could not end her lifelong feelings of isolation. Her monologue in some ways is a key to everything else that happens in the book and to the monologues of the other characters.

VII. The novel also marks a particular moment in modern American history.
- **A.** Faulkner started writing *As I Lay Dying* the day after the stock market crash in 1929.
    1. That event marked the end of the Roaring Twenties, with its stories of individualism and entrepreneurial aggressiveness (as told by F. Scott Fitzgerald, for example), and the beginning of a period of stories about cooperation and communal effort (as told by John Steinbeck in *The Grapes of Wrath,* for example).
    2. *As I Lay Dying* perfectly straddles those two periods: It is about a family on an epic quest, each member driven by personal needs, but each of whom is likewise able to subordinate those needs into larger family purposes; thus, Addie does get buried at last.
- **B.** The book also illustrates the Faulknerian world as one simultaneously comic, tragic, pathetic, sad, funny, grotesque, and heroic. It is another way in which Faulkner always tells "the whole truth."

Essential Reading:

William Faulkner, short stories and *As I Lay Dying.*

Supplementary Reading:

Cleanth Brooks, *The Yoknapatawpha Country.*

James B. Carothers, *William Faulkner's Short Stories.*

Doreen Fowler, and Ann J. Abadie, eds. *Faulkner and the Craft of Fiction.*

Questions to Consider:

1. One interesting exercise is to go through "A Rose for Emily" carefully enough to note its event-chronology, as opposed to its narrative-chronology. When did each event described in the story happen? One of the things this exercise can do is to remind us that Faulkner had a very clear sense of the order of events in Emily Grierson's life; another is to note the artistry that went into the final arrangement of those events in the citizen's narrative.

2. In what ways is Addie Bundren's monologue a key to all that happens in *As I Lay Dying*? What does it explain? How does it help us to untangle family tensions and relationships, and how does it explain some of the events that occur on the journey? If we had Addie's monologue earlier in the novel, some things in the book might be more comprehensible to us as we read it; can you think of some rhetorical reasons why Faulkner might have wished to withhold that information from us until the point at which her monologue occurs?

Lecture Forty-Four
Naguib Mahfouz's *The Cairo Trilogy*

Scope: *The Cairo Trilogy* comes from Mahfouz's Realist phase, patterned on the novels of Flaubert and Tagore. Mahfouz, however, had also mastered Proust, Henri Bergson, and Joyce, whose influences are likewise apparent. The trilogy traces a family's history from 1917 to 1944, showing the erosion of a traditional way of life by Western influences. In the second volume the conflict is focused in the mind of Kamal, whose internal debates we follow in a stream-of-consciousness technique. Kamal's dilemma is symbolized by his infatuation with a half-Westernized young woman who represents the forces in conflict within him. In the third volume, the original family dies, and Kamal is still paralyzed with indecision, but a new generation has opted for political action, and we get a double vision of time—as the destroyer of individuals but also as an evolutionary process in which martyrdom can advance the cause of social justice generations later.

Outline

I. Like William Faulkner, Naguib Mahfouz—while well-known in the Arab world—became a world writer rather than a regional one after he won the Nobel Prize in 1988.

  A. Like Faulkner with his Yoknapatawpha County, Mahfouz's novels give a history of the changes that occur in Cairo from 1917 to 1944.

  B. As Faulkner is now considered one of the greatest American writers, so Mahfouz now ranks as one of the greatest Arab novelists.

II. As in India and Japan, Western influence had a great deal to do with the rise of the Arabic novel.

  A. The Arabs did not really have a novel tradition until the 20th century.
    1. There had been other narrative forms, like the ones in *1001 Nights,* but nothing like the novel as it had developed in the West since *Don Quixote*.

2. Western influence became very marked in Egypt from 1883 on, so Mahfouz and other writers had access to the Western novel, which had gone through many evolutionary stages by that time.
3. The most important literary form in Arabic had always been poetry, so when the novel tradition came to places like Egypt, writers had to master the entire novel tradition in order to begin writing Arabic novels.
4. Mahfouz in his novel career recapitulates the development of the Western novel, beginning in the 1930s with historical romances like those of Walter Scott and moving by about 1945 into Realist novels like those of Flaubert. Starting in about 1959, he began writing more experimental novels using techniques we have seen in Proust, Joyce, and Faulkner—*Mirrors* (1972) in fact is very Faulknerian, using 54 characters to reflect various aspects of Egyptian culture.

B. *The Cairo Trilogy*—composed of *Palace Walk*, *Palace of Desire*, and *Sugar Street*—is from Mahfouz's Realist phase.
1. The three novels feature essentially chronological plots, clearly defined characters, and enough references to Cairo and Egyptian history to give the stories a sense of authenticity.
2. Their subject is a middle-class family traced across three generations from 1917 to 1944; their point of view is third-person omniscient—all features of the Realist novel.
3. By the time Mahfouz wrote these, he had also read Joyce, Bergson, and Proust (among others), so there are some elements in the books that can be considered Modernist.
4. Beginning in the second novel, he uses the stream-of-consciousness technique we have seen in Joyce, Kawabata, and Faulkner.
5. Bergson and Proust allow him to see time as duration rather than as measurable units; time is—as in Proust—one of the real protagonists of Mahfouz's novels.
6. The books have a lot to do with memory, as in Proust, one of the writers Mahfouz most admired.

III. The history of the period in Egypt from 1917 to 1944 features largely in the three novels.

- **A.** In 1917, when *Palace Walk* begins, Egypt is still a part of the Ottoman Empire but has been occupied by England since 1883 and was made a British Protectorate in 1914.
  1. Anti-British feeling is therefore strong in Cairo, and many Egyptians hope that the Germans will win World War I—especially since one of their allies is the Ottoman Empire.
  2. When the Allies win in 1918, the English maintain control, and a movement for Egyptian independence breaks out. The demonstrations of 1919 produce many martyrs, including one member of the family at the center of the trilogy.
- **B.** The struggle does not end, however, since the King, the English, and various Egyptian leaders still make shifting alliances for control of the country. When the third novel ends in 1944, two grandsons of the original family are in prison detention camps as political prisoners.

IV. The novels use this political history as a background against which the life of a family is told across three generations.
- **A.** The first novel, *Palace Walk*, establishes a way of life that in Cairo in 1917 was very traditional.
  1. The father, Ahmad Abd al-Jawad, is a merchant who is an absolute autocrat in his family.
  2. He is also a "bundle of contradictions": Outside the house he is a witty and cheerful friend, and at night he is a libertine, drinking and spending time with mistresses drawn from the world of professional singers.
  3. Modern readers have some trouble with this character, but it is clear that he is representative of a long cultural tradition. At any rate, his children adore him, and his sequestered wife considers herself a blessed woman to have a man like him.
  4. Every afternoon the family meets for coffee to talk about the day's events, and we notice how more and more discussion time is taken up with political talk as the novel progresses.
  5. Close to the end of the first novel, the favorite son of the family, Fahmi, is killed in a demonstration. Despite the family's efforts to reestablish their routines, life is never quite the same.
- **B.** The second novel, *Palace of Desire*, charts the slow decline of the parents but focuses on the next generation, especially on Kamal.

1. Social changes in Cairo are evident in the marriages of the two daughters of the family who live on terms of relative equality with their husbands—very unlike the way their mother lived and they were brought up.
2. The oldest son tries to maintain his father's patriarchal control, which leads to two quick divorces; he achieves a stable marriage only later, marrying one of his father's past mistresses, who is shrewd enough to allow him some liberty while still maintaining control of the marriage.
3. The focus of the second novel is the youngest son, Kamal, whose encounters with Western thought have undermined the traditional beliefs and values with which he was raised.
4. In a great symbolic scene, his father reprimands him harshly for having published an article on Charles Darwin, who contradicts the Quran's version of creation.
5. Kamal's dilemma—caught between the old and the new—is captured in his infatuation for a young woman named Aida, who was raised in Paris and is hence more Western than Egyptian, more Catholic than Islamic.
6. The narrator allows the reader to see the more negative sides of Aida, but insofar as she is an embodiment of the Western forces pulling Kamal away from his family and childhood, she is an ambiguous symbol.
7. Kamal never quite recovers from his polarized self; by the end of the third novel, he is still single, living in the old family house with one semi-demented sister and still unable to make up his mind or commit to anything. He still hopes that one day truth will reveal itself to him.
8. Much of what we learn about Kamal we learn from his internal monologues, a technique Mahfouz learned from Western writers.

C. The third novel, *Sugar Street*, follows the fortunes of the family up to 1944.
1. Ahmad Abd al-Jawad dies on the night of an air raid. He has to be carried to his bed by Kamal, one sure sign of the reversal that inevitably happens to father and son.
2. Mahfouz, like Flaubert and Ibsen, also uses realistic details as symbols: Kamal's seduction from traditional beliefs is symbolized by a half-Westernized woman, and the great traditionalist father dies in an air raid—the airplane being in

its time the most advanced product of Western science and technology.
    3. Kamal's mother dies in a coma, unable even to speak to the family she has produced and raised.
    4. Kamal realizes when she dies that he has lost the person who loved him most, but he also realizes that he had given up her belief system years ago and is still caught between two worlds—a skeptic even of his own skepticism—and is a representative of the dilemma of modern human beings.

V. In many ways, time is the ultimate protagonist of the trilogy.
  A. By the end of *Sugar Street*, the family has declined: There have been a series of deaths, the certainties of the grandparents' generation have all been eroded, and two grandchildren are in prison awaiting trial as political subversives.
    1. As in *Gilgamesh*, time has taken the once vital and nearly godlike Ahmad Abd al-Jawad and turned him into a pitiful old man who needs to be carried to his deathbed by his son; it has also sent his wife, whose love and care balanced her husband's autocratic control, into a coma in which she cannot even say goodbye to those she loves the most.
    2. Individual human beings succumb to time's power, and the trilogy records the process in precise detail.
    3. There is also a collective time, an evolutionary time, in which individuals serve as building blocks for mankind, which is eternal and can therefore transcend the ravages of time on the individual.
    4. In that collective time, Fahmi wills the time he has not used in his life to the next generation. At the end of the trilogy, two of his nephews (had he lived to be their uncle) are in prison for carrying on the revolution for which he gave his life.
    5. At the end of the trilogy, Kamal, still paralyzed with doubt, visits his nephews in prison and is inspired by one of them, who tells him that as human beings we all have obligations to the "perpetual revolution"; he promises that he will find some beliefs by which to live, wherever they lead him.
  B. This collective time is the other side of time in the novels.
    1. It destroys individuals, but it also has moved Egypt from political freedom to an awareness of the need for social justice.

2. Every political revolution is not an end in itself but a step forward in collective and evolutionary time.
3. In this way, Mahfouz's trilogy is both the story of individuals destroyed by time *and* the story of generations moving forward in time towards some ideal, making this one of the greatest—if slightly belated—achievements of the Realist Movement.

Essential Reading:

Naguib Mahfouz, *The Cairo Trilogy: Palace Walk, Palace of Desire, Sugar Street.*

Supplementary Reading:

Roger M. A. Allen, *The Arabic Novel: An Historical and Critical Introduction.*

Rasheed El-Enany, ed. *Naguib Mahfouz: The Pursuit of Meaning.*

Questions to Consider:

1. Both *The Story of the Stone* and *The Cairo Trilogy* deal with the decline and fall of a family. While there are differences—of class, culture, and time period—is there a generic similarity in the way the two authors treat their subjects? How, for example, is time treated in each? Is there a villain, or at least an understandable cause, for the decline of the two families? Is there a character like Kamal in the earlier Chinese novel? What kinds of commentary are made on their respective cultures in the two works?
2. Is there a center of consciousness or a single sensibility that more or less pervades this three-volume work? If so, whose? What is the effect of making that character, rather than another, the center of our attention as we read?

Lecture Forty-Five
Achebe's *Things Fall Apart*

Scope: Chinua Achebe's novel, in the Realist tradition, is a reaction against Western novelistic depictions of Africans. The first two-thirds of *Things Fall Apart* describe the life of the Igbo people before the coming of the British, and they deal with conflicts between the people and one of their most impressive representatives: Okonkwo, a flawed character who cannot deal with the gentle side of his nature because he fears resembling his father, a notorious failure. The last third deals with the coming of the missionaries and the inroads they make into the village—including converting Okonkwo's son, Nwoye. The fall of Igbo culture to the British is explained metaphorically in Yeats's poem, "The Second Coming," from which the novel's title is taken. The novel's climax occurs when the village is required to deal with Okonkwo and the missionaries simultaneously—a juxtaposition that leads to tragedy for both him and his people.

Outline

I. Realism in literature has almost always implied a social agenda.
   A. Flaubert, Ibsen, and (to a lesser extent) Chekhov criticized the middle classes, Dostoevsky attacked Utilitarian Utopianism and Romantic sentimentality, and Mahfouz implicitly endorsed the need to work for social justice.
   B. Achebe has a social agenda as well, based on his shock at discovering how Africans were depicted in novels about Africa by white authors—as savages with the undeveloped minds of children.
      1. His first novel, *Things Fall Apart*, was written to refute this notion and to show what colonialism feels like from the *inside*.
      2. He demonstrates that Africans had a rich and complex culture before the coming of Westerners, one which—along with their dignity—was mostly lost in the colonial period.
      3. His hope was to restore some of that dignity by reminding his people of their own pre-colonial culture; it is part of the complexity of the situation that the book should be written in

English, with its title taken from a poem by William Butler Yeats.

II. The first-two thirds of the novel give a picture of life among the Igbo people before the coming of the missionaries, and its focus is on one of the most powerful and important men in the village: Okonkwo.
  A. Okonkwo is a man driven to achieve at everything.
    1. Because his father was a failure, Okonkwo lives his life proving that he is not his father.
    2. He worries about his son, Nwoye, who seems to take after his grandfather too much.
    3. In a raid he captures another boy, Ikemefuna, who comes to live with Okonkwo and who turns out to be a nearly perfect son, even stimulating Nwoye into behavior that pleases his father.
    4. The village oracle decrees that Ikemefuna must be killed; the village elders caution Okonkwo that since the boy calls him "father," he should not take part in the ritual killing. Okonkwo, not wishing to appear weak, kills the boy with his own hands, and Nwoye is devastated.
    5. Okonkwo is banished to his mother's village for seven years for a (different) crime against the earth goddess; while he is there, missionaries make inroads into his home village.
    6. There is trouble when he returns, and when he tries to rouse his village into action against the English, killing one of their messengers, the village fails to respond, and Okonkwo hangs himself.
  B. Okonkwo is a warrior, wrestler, grower of yams, and a man of wealth who at an early age already has two barns, three wives, and two titles. In rejecting his father's weakness, Okonkwo also rejects gentleness, affection, and emotion—qualities which seem feminine to him.
    1. In feeling this way Okonkwo shows that despite being "one of the greatest men of his time," he is not entirely in harmony with his people, for whom feminine values play an important part.
    2. Women are not men's equals in the village, but its most important deity is Ani, the earth goddess, and the oracle in the village is an important and honored person.

©2007 The Teaching Company.

3. Ani is the ultimate judge of morality and conduct, and all three of Okonkwo's punishable crimes are committed against her.
4. When Okonkwo is exiled to his mother's village, an elder explains to him why the Igbo people say that "mother is supreme."
5. This and other details of the novel suggest that there is a balance between masculine and feminine values—a balance which is threatened by Okonkwo because of his obsessive need not to be his father.

C. Nwoye, Okonkwo's son, is a throwback to his grandfather, a gentle boy without his father's hardness.
1. His masculine side is brought out by Ikemefuna when he lives with the family, and Ikemefuna himself comes very close to embodying a perfect balance of masculine and feminine virtues.
2. When Ikemefuna is killed, something inside Nwoye snaps, and so he is ripe for conversion by the Christian missionaries when they arrive—as are all others who do not quite fit into the Igbo culture.

III. In most ways, Okonkwo is a perfect representative of his people: He gets his values of hard work and the drive to excel from them, but he overdoes them and pushes them too far.

A. While he is gone, his people have enough flexibility to allow the missionaries to build their church and to live side-by-side with them, even while they are losing some of their members to the new faith.
1. When Okonkwo returns, he sees violence as the only possible response; when his people fail to join him after he has killed the messenger, he kills himself.
2. He dies representing what he sees as the values of his society—values which he thinks have been betrayed.
3. What he does not see is the flexibility built into his culture, a flexibility illustrated in many of its proverbs.

B. Okonkwo is in many ways like the figures in Greek tragedy: someone who is neither entirely right nor entirely wrong and whose weaknesses are the reverse of his strengths.
1. Okonkwo is not inherently a cruel man, as we see when he decides that he must kill Ikemefuna with his own hands, and

on the night the priestess carries his daughter through the nine villages.
   2. It is simply that because of the weakness of his father, he cannot express the gentler sides of his nature and of his culture.
   3. His tragedy is also that of his people, who cannot manage to deal with Okonkwo and the missionaries at once, as they could have had they not coincided so disastrously.
IV. The title of the novel comes from Yeats's "The Second Coming," and the poem's vision of history is used to explain the confrontation between Igbo and British cultures.
   A. According to Yeats's poem, every civilization is a construct which excludes as it defines and hence pushes what is unacceptable outside its parameters. Over time, the excluded values gather strength until they overwhelm the civilization itself, replacing its values with their reverse.
   B. The first two thirds of the book portray the Igbo culture which, among its many values, asserts that the community is always more important than the individual.
      1. This culture's values are courage, self-reliance, strength, and success, and while other virtues can be tolerated, they are not honored. They are, in Yeats's terms, the values which the definition of Igbo culture excludes.
      2. When the Christians arrive, they give expression to the values excluded by Igbo culture: kindness, gentleness, and above all personal relationships, and they inevitably appeal to the outcasts of the community.
      3. These values beat on the walls of Igbo civilization, and when some village members become Christian, the community is for the first time divided against itself.
      4. The second missionary to arrive, Mr. Smith, is far less tolerant than the first and less flexible than the Igbo people; when Okonkwo returns home, spoiling for a fight, the disaster is precipitated.
   C. The ending of the novel illustrates Yeats's thesis.
      1. The forces that loose anarchy into the Igbo village come from the Evil Forest, the place where excluded values have been gathering strength.

2. The missionaries emphasize personal relations versus the communal ones of the culture, and those are the values that break down the walls of the Igbo construct and bring about "the second coming."
3. When one of the elders lashes out at the English commissioner at the novel's end, he laments not just the death of Okonkwo, one of their best, but of an entire culture.

V. There is an irony in the book's ending—an irony of which Achebe is himself very much aware.
   A. Achebe himself is a post-colonial writer writing in English, which makes him a descendent not so much of Okonkwo as of Nwoye, since Nwoye is the one who takes the first step that will allow an Igbo writer to record his people's history in English.
   B. Nwoye's movement away from tribal values is the first step in the journey of the Western-educated Nigerians of Achebe's generation, making Achebe the inheritor of Nwoye's revolt. He can celebrate the Igbo culture, but he does so through tools gained by its destruction.

Essential Reading:

Chinua Achebe, *Things Fall Apart*.

Supplementary Reading:

C. L. Innes and Bernth Lindfors, eds. *Critical Perspectives on Chinua Achebe*.

G. D. Killam, *The Novels of Chinua Achebe*.

Questions to Consider:

1. Why are the masculine virtues so important in traditional Igbo society? Why is it said that "yams are a man's crop"? Why is the man taking care of a child who opens the gate allowing a cow into the yam field given a stiff fine by the elders? Why is calling someone an *agbala* an insult?

2. Can you identify the stages of Nwoye's realization that his people's ideals are not his own? What might have become of him had the missionaries not shown up when they did? To what extent is his father responsible for Nwoye's unhappiness and sense of alienation? To what extent do you share Nwoye's emerging values as opposed to those of his people?

Lecture Forty-Six
Beckett's Plays

Scope: In this lecture we take up our first Postmodernist writer, Samuel Beckett. We define that movement in part as the assumption that we live in an absurd world which gives us no meanings or definitions of ourselves which we can use as guides for living. We illustrate this assumption with other Postmodernist writers: Jean-Paul Sartre, Albert Camus, John Barth, Kurt Vonnegut, and Salman Rushdie. Then we look at three Beckett plays, *Waiting for Godot, Endgame,* and *Happy Days,* showing that the stage picture perhaps counts for more than the words in Beckett's plays, even though both contribute to the theme of absurdity. The solipsism of a Beckett play is emphasized by its frequent allusions to games and the theater itself. We conclude with a radio drama by Beckett, *All That Fall*, which portrays an extinguished world falling toward nothing, a perfect illustration of an absurd world.

Outline

I. In this and the next two lectures we move from Modernism to *Postmodernism*.
  - **A.** We have been defining Modernism in two ways.
    1. The first definition involves the technical experiments used by most of the fiction writers and dramatists we have looked at since Marcel Proust.
    2. The second definition has to do with subject matter: secular instead of religious, urban rather than rural, and radically subjective.
    3. Universals have pretty much been abandoned, and some of the most basic assumptions of the past—including a belief in an ego or self that persists through time—have been questioned.
    4. In some ways the intellectual shifts of the early 20th century required writers to create new literary forms to record a human experience which seems very different from what it was in the past.
  - **B.** In Postmodernism, subject, themes, and assumptions move another step beyond those of Modernism.

1. Modernists were reacting against the literature that came before them and refuting concepts that no longer seemed to work.
2. Postmodernists *assume* this breakdown of most of the foundations of thought and literature of the past and then move forward.
3. Most Postmodernists would agree with the French Existentialists, Sartre and Camus, who argued that we live in an absurd universe—or at least in one whose meanings are inaccessible to us.
4. In the past, humans could define themselves in religious, natural, or scientific contexts, each of which implies rules for conduct.
5. For the Existentialists, on the other hand, there are no external definitions: Each of us creates human nature with every action that we take.

C. These themes are nicely illustrated in John Barth's *The Floating Opera.*
1. The book is about Todd Andrews, who investigates the meaning of his own life in term-paper fashion.
2. He comes up with five conclusions: Nothing has any intrinsic value; the reasons for which people attribute value to things are always ultimately irrational; there is, therefore, no ultimate "reason" for valuing anything; living is action and there is no final reason for action; and there is no final reason for living.
3. He tries, and fails, to commit suicide, after which he amends his fifth principle: "There's no final reason for living (or for suicide)."
4. This is the world of Camus's "The Myth of Sisyphus," in which he argues that the only philosophical question is whether life is worth living or not.

D. Kurt Vonnegut's works make many of the same points.
1. They portray a world in which existence precedes essence, and they assume no identifiable meaning or purpose for existence.
2. Things just happen, often cruelly and pointlessly, and efforts to change them are generally futile.

E. Salman Rushdie's "The Prophet's Hair" makes some of the same points.

1. Its point is that there is no going back to the certainties of the past; we have to move on from where we are without trying to recapture the foundations of our ancestors.
2. The story's amazing combination of genres is also Postmodernist—a point we will come back to in the next two lectures.

II. Samuel Beckett's plays work from the same set of assumptions.
   A. The Nobel Prize Committee in 1969 said that Beckett had recognized the central dilemma of the century: the contradiction between the human effort to discover meaning and the awareness that there is no meaning that we have not created ourselves.
      1. His characters try to create or find meaning, wait for explanations that never arrive, and fill up their time to keep terror at a distance.
      2. Beckett himself wrote in 1949 that the condition of art is that there is nothing to express, no desire to express anything, no way to express it if there were something to express, and still an obligation to express something.
   B. Beckett reinvented drama one more time in the 20th century.
      1. It is in some ways the future drama that Joseph Wood Krutch predicted in Lecture Thirty-Nine: a drama without plot or characters in the way we usually understand them.
      2. What Beckett dramatizes is uncertainty, incoherence, and nonmeaning.
      3. In *Waiting for Godot*, Didi and Gogo fill up time with arguments, reconciliations, eating, and doing vaudeville routines while waiting for someone who will probably never show up.
      4. In *Endgame*, four characters wait in an enclosed room while outside there is only death; three are going blind, one is deaf, one is half-crippled, and one has only stumps for limbs. We are at the end of some road here.
      5. The metaphor in the title is from chess, a game of attrition. By the end of the play, the board is nearly bare: endgame.
      6. As a game of chess is self-contained—referring only to itself and not to something outside it—the title reinforces the idea that drama, too, is a game, a "play" which is self-contained and reflexive.

7. *Happy Days* shows a couple: the wife (buried up to her waist in sand in Act I and up to her neck in Act 2) who fills up her time with ritual acts like combing her hair or brushing her teeth while keeping up a steady stream of chatter to Willie, her inattentive husband.
8. Her talk seems designed to ward off the hopelessness of her situation, in which there is not even night and day—only a bell to signal time for sleep and time to wake.

C. As in absurdist drama, the stage pictures are perhaps more important than the words spoken by the characters.
1. What these characters do is repetitive, and all of them seem dimly aware that they are in a play which repeats itself night after night. Frequently they use the language of theater; in *Endgame*, Hamm even says that he is making an "aside" and is warming up for his final "soliloquy."
2. Winnie breaks her mirror, and she says that she does this every time, but when the bell rings there is always a new unbroken one—perhaps put there by a stage hand.
3. One of the points made would seem to be that as chess is only a game, so is a play. In an absurd world a game or play is what we do to pass the time, to keep from thinking. The windows out of which one can see nothing and Hamm's blindness in *Endgame* perhaps suggest solipsistic isolation.
4. When Hamm asks whether his father—who lives in the dustbin—is still alive, he is told, "He's crying." To live is to weep, and to wait for the end of the game and the play.

D. *All That Fall* is a radio drama which may be a perfect vehicle for Beckett: words surrounded by silence.
1. The story is about a woman going to meet her husband at a train station; the train is delayed because—as it turns out—a young child fell from the train and was run over.
2. Precisely what happens (and the extent to which Mr. Rooney may be responsible for the fall) is never quite clear.
3. The play is full of references to death and full of the sadness of decline and fall. It is also full of humor and charm, but it probably expresses Beckett's outrage at the universe, in which we are alone, and in which *our* voices sound in a vast emptiness. As Mrs. Rooney says, "We are alone. There is no one to ask."

Essential Reading:

Samuel Beckett plays.

Supplementary Reading:

Beryl S. Fletcher and John Fletcher, *A Student's Guide to the Plays of Samuel Beckett.*

Andrew K. Kennedy, *Samuel Beckett.*

Questions to Consider:

1. Beneath the sometimes nearly incomprehensible dialogue of characters in Beckett's plays, we can still sense real relationships: friend and friend, husband and wife, father and son. How would you characterize these relationships as they appear in the dramas? Do these relationships provide comfort and help for the characters or do they exacerbate already painful situations? What is the value of relationship in Beckett drama?

2. What do you think really happened on the train in *All That Fall*? Is Mr. Rooney in any way responsible for the death or was it pure accident? Is there any way to tell? What difference does in make in understanding what the play is about to decide one way or another?

Lecture Forty-Seven
Borges's *Labyrinths*

Scope: We continue our exploration of Postmodernism in the short stories of one of its avatars—Jorge Luis Borges. The absurd universe is perfectly illustrated in his "The Library of Babel," which suggests that the universe, or reality, is so vast as to be incomprehensible to us. Then we explore Borges's awareness of the untranslatable gap between reality and the human constructions of logic and language—a gap which encourages him to write stories using language or logic, rather than reality, as his guide. We go on to an analysis of "Tlön, Uqbar, Orbis Tertius," which shows the superiority of a world constructed purely from human logic to the actual one in which we live. The lecture concludes with references to other stories in the collection, *Labyrinths,* treats some salutary reasons why Postmodernists write the way they do, and ends with a reminder of how influential Borges has been in Postmodernism.

Outline

I. If the universe is absurd, as most Postmodernists believe, then what is there to write stories about—besides pointing out its absurdity? Jorge Luis Borges provides one answer to this question.

II. That the universe is absurd is asserted in one of Borges's most famous stories, "The Library of Babel."

    A. The story pictures the universe as a library made up of a presumably infinite number of identical hexagonal galleries; its exact center is any one of its hexagons and its circumference is inaccessible.

        1. Identical books (35 per shelf, each book being 410 pages long, each page containing 40 lines of 80 letters and spaces) line the identical shelves.

        2. A comma, 22 letters, a period, and a space make up the 25 characters used in the books, all used in apparently random but unrepeated ways on the pages of the books.

        3. Occasionally there is a comprehensible line—"O time thy pyramids" is one such—but for every line of sense there are

"leagues of senseless cacophonies, verbal jumbles, and incoherences" that cannot correspond to any known language.
4. The books would thus register every possible combination of the 25 symbols—a number that would be vast but not infinite, and they would express everything that could be expressed in all possible languages, meaning that all solutions to all problems and questions, including the origin of the library itself, would be in books somewhere—books which the librarians take to calling the Vindications.
5. When this idea was first introduced, librarians from every hexagon traveled through others, looking for the Vindications, forgetting that the chances of finding even one could be computed at zero.
6. The narrator assumes that the library is infinite and cyclical, so that, traveling in any direction and after many centuries, one would find the same volumes repeated in the same disorder, which—thus repeated—would be an order: *the* Order.
7. The order implies a God or an architect, since a library like this could not simply happen. There is an order here, but it is on a scale so vast that it is entirely incomprehensible to us—which experientially is the same as if there were no order at all.

B. The important implication is that if reality is incomprehensible to us, then all the structures by which we live are "fictions," contingent, made up by us.
1. In "The Analytical Language of John Wilkins," Borges makes up a Chinese encyclopedia which contains an absurd classification of animals, totally bizarre and arbitrary.
2. His point is that all human classifications are arbitrary, and that it is impossible to give linguistic form to reality because language and reality operate by different logics. There is no classification of the universe that is not arbitrary and conjectural because we do not know what the universe is.
3. Logic and language work by their own rules—rules which we have invented—and reality works by its rules; there is no necessary connection between them.
4. He frequently refers to Zeno's Paradox, in which it can be logically demonstrated that Achilles cannot ever catch up with a turtle; of course, if the race were to take place, Achilles *would* catch up.

5. From this discrepancy we can decide that our sense perceptions are more reliable than our logic or vice versa (the latter being the one that started Plato toward his philosophical system).
6. Borges uses the discrepancy to show the independence of the two systems of reality and logic, and he suggests that reality is apprehensible to us either via our senses or our logic; the gap between the two cannot be bridged.
7. He uses infinite regress in the same way. Infinite regress is logically possible, but it cannot be done in reality; two of his examples of infinite regress come from works we have looked at in this course: *Don Quixote* and *1001 Nights*.

C. Borges prefers to structure his stories by the order of logic rather than that of reality, since the latter can only reproduce the universe's incomprehensibility, while the order of logic and language can produce astonishingly beautiful structures.
1. In his story "Funes the Memorious," he gives us a character with a perfect memory, which means that he cannot abstract or cut and paste, so that he an absolute victim of the "disordered chance of realistic representation." It takes him exactly the same amount of time to tell about an experience as it took for him to have the experience—which, for Borges, is what realistic fiction does.
2. Borges's favorite authors included writers like Rudyard Kipling and Robert Louis Stevenson, who are usually denigrated for their implausibility and for the unrealistic tidiness of their stories. That is precisely what Borges admired about them—that they make no attempt to be realistic.
3. He also, along with virtually all Postmodernists, admired the *1001 Nights* and the stories and novels of Kafka for the same reason: because they are perfect, beautiful, and give us a formal perfection and meaning that incomprehensible reality never can.

III. All of this is illustrated in another famous story, "Tlön, Uqbar, Orbis Tertius."
A. The story is about the gradual discovery of a society which over the past three centuries has created first an imaginary land and then an imaginary planet.

1. One of its founding members was Bishop Berkeley, the Idealist philosopher, so it turns out to be a most intriguing and interesting kind of place.
2. It is, of course, also logically consistent and coherent because it was made by humans using the rules of human logic and language.
3. When word of this imaginary planet gets out into the world, the world begins to adapt itself to Tlön; even objects unique to this created world begin to show up in ours.
4. The reason for this is clear: Tlön is made up, but it is orderly, rational, and understandable vis-à-vis our own reality, whose order and rules and meaning we never grasp.
5. As Oscar Wilde said half a century earlier, reality is merely process looking for form. Art *is* form, and when someone creates something of formal perfection, we try to adapt reality to it; thus, the world is becoming Tlön.

B. In one way or another, that is what most Postmodernists assert.
1. Art and literature can construct for us fictions by which we can live—so long as we remember that they are fictions which have no more necessary connection to reality than a chess game.
2. Postmodernists can still promote things they believe in, as do John Barth, Gabriel Garcia Marquez, and Kurt Vonnegut; even as they are writing their novels and stories, however, they keep reminding us that these are *fictions,* not accurate pictures of reality.
3. Borges himself largely avoids political and social agendas in his stories, of which there are many brilliant ones in *Labyrinths.*
4. There are important implications for us in Borges's stories, even though he does not reach for them. Fascist ideology in Nazi Germany was certainly an imaginary world, hobbled together out of the most disparate sources. Once the creators of the ideology had invented it, however, they came to believe that it was true and were willing to die and kill for it, which for a Postmodernist is the ultimate madness.
5. As in Dr. Seuss's story of *Yertle the Turtle*, every idea and structure by which we live is made up by us, all the way down to what we think is bedrock. If these structures and theories help us to live more happily and better, they are useful, but we

must never forget that we made them up, that they are contingent, and that they are not a reflection of the real world.

IV. Borges has by now influenced several generations of Postmodernist writers, as the tribute from Umberto Eco in *The Name of the Rose* suggests.

Essential Reading:
Jorge Luis Borges, *Labyrinths*.

Supplementary Reading:
Jaime Alazraki, ed. *Critical Essays on Jorge Luis Borges.*

Beatriz Sarlo, *Jorge Luis Borges.*

Questions to Consider:
1. "The Garden of the Forking Paths," like many stories in *Labyrinths*, is about the relationship between art and life. What relationship is indicated in that (and other) stories?
2. Borges, like many Postmodernists, is fond of detective stories. Why, given his ideas about reality and human logic and language discussed in the lecture, would he find detective and mystery stories so attractive?

Lecture Forty-Eight
Rushdie's *Haroun and the Sea of Stories*

Scope: In this lecture we deal with Salman Rushdie's *Haroun and the Sea of Stories*, a children's book about the importance of stories in our lives. After a brief account of the book, we identify it as Postmodernist via its *intertextuality*—i.e., its construction of itself out of other literature and its narration of the process of its own composition. We illustrate this intertextuality by noting some of the many multicultural allusions that permeate the book. We conclude by considering its theme: that stories are one of the most important tools in history for helping humans stay free—whether that freedom is conceived in imaginative or political terms; and we use that idea as a way of reviewing the stories and storytellers of our entire course, concluding with William Faulkner, that stories are one of the ways in which humans can not only "endure," but may even "prevail."

Outline

I. *Haroun and the Sea of Stories* was written while Rushdie was in hiding, protected by the British Secret Service during the time that Iranian authorities had called for his death at the hands of faithful Muslims for writing *The Satanic Verses* in 1988.

    A. It was dedicated to Rushdie's son, both to fulfill a promise to the boy and to explain something of the family's circumstances.

    B. It also deals with the relationship between authority and a creative artist, censorship, and the question Haroun asks in the book, "What's the use of stories that aren't even true?"

    C. For us, it can help in our ongoing definition of Postmodernism and provide the basis for a generalization or two about literature.

II. The story tells of a boy, Haroun, who travels to the Sea of Stories to try to restore his father's gift for storytelling (his father is a professional storyteller) after a series of family crises has rendered him mute in front of audiences.

    A. The problem turns out to be even more serious when he discovers that the Sea of Stories—the source of all stories in the world—is being deliberately polluted by the dictatorial Khattam-Shud, who is

the enemy of all books and whose name in Hindustani means "completely finished" or "over and done with."
- **B.** After a series of complicated and exciting adventures, all ends happily for Haroun's family, and the Sea of Stories is cleansed.
- **C.** The book is in some ways an allegory of Rushdie's own circumstances when it was written, but the allegory can be interpreted in a number of ways, and for us it probably limits the power of the book to see it too simply as an allegory.

III. *Haroun and the Sea of Stories* is a Postmodernist book, as we have been defining the term in the past two lectures.
- **A.** Its most notable Postmodernist component is its intertextuality, meaning that it is made up of other literature and it is also about literature.
    1. We have seen this tendency ever since Proust's *Remembrance of Things Past,* which was a book about how the book came to be written.
    2. We have seen it in Borges's "The Library of Babel," in which the universe is conceived as a library, in "Tlön, Uqbar, Orbis Tertius," in which the imaginary planet of Tlön invades ours via sets of encyclopedias, and in "Pierre Menard and the *Quixote,*" in which an author recreates *Don Quixote* word-for-word for modern readers.
    3. We have seen this kind of reflexivity in Beckett's plays, whose allusions to games and the theater keep reminding us that they are self-contained and reflexive.
    4. If we think of Realist literature as being about the external world and Modernist literature as being about the subjective inner world, then we can think of Postmodernist literature as being about literature—about itself.
- **B.** *Haroun and the Sea of Stories* is richly intertextual.
    1. Most notably, it is full of references to the *1001 Nights*: The names of the two central characters; the many allusions to the stories of Sinbad the Sailor; and the fact that Rashid, Haroun's father is—like Shahrazad—a storyteller, all recall that great collection of stories for us.
    2. And the "Sea of Stories" part of the title, as well as its crucial importance to the entire story, recalls the famous collection of stories from India, in translation called *Ocean of the Rivers of Story* (see Lecture Twelve).

3. Western literature is part of the book's intertextuality as well, and (among others) we get references to Grimm Brothers' fairy tales, Lewis Carroll's *Alice in Wonderland* and *Through the Looking Glass*, *The Wizard of Oz,* Indian movies, punning references to Gogol and Kafka, and perhaps even to a Beatles' song, "I Am the Walrus."
  4. The book also notices the way all of these diverse cultural traditions flow together to produce something new. In the Sea of Stories, different-colored streams flow together to alter one another; Haroun at one point thinks of storytelling as a kind of juggling, keeping a lot of different tales from different places in the air and not dropping any of them.

IV. Two important themes of the book have to do with enemies of stories and storytelling.
  A. Khattam-Shud's hatred of stories is the more obvious, and he uses the most tyrannical means to suppress both the stories themselves and even speech and language.
    1. When he finally meets the dread figure, Haroun asks him why he hates stories, and he says that they make it more difficult for him to control the world.
    2. Inside every story is a place where people can be free, and they can imagine and live in alternate worlds, which makes the job of tyrants nearly impossible.
    3. At the novel's end, Rashid tells the story of what has happened in the novel so far to help drive the tyrannical Snooty Butto out of town, suggesting that stories can have political as well as imaginative liberating powers.
  B. But Khattam-Shud is not the only enemy of stories in the book. There is also Mr. Sengupta, the man who hates stories and has run off with Haroun's mother, thus precipitating the family crisis.
    1. Mr. Sengupta is the one who asks the book's basic question: "What's the use of stories that aren't even true?" Haroun, who hears the question, asks it of his father as well.
    2. Significantly, when Haroun first sees Khattam-Shud, he is reminded of Mr. Sengupta, suggesting that tyrants and people who want to suppress the imagination in favor of *fact* are allies in the campaign against stories and storytelling.

V. Throughout history stories and storytelling have served a variety of functions.

- **A.** In most of the earliest literature, Sin-liqe-uninni, Homer, Virgil, and the scop of *Beowulf* created heroes that embodied the favored features of their cultures, serving in some measure as official spokespersons for those cultures.
- **B.** Later, writers like Chaucer, the creators of *1001 Nights*, and Cervantes created space between the author, the storyteller, and the tale, allowing the reader room for interpretation.
- **C.** Realists like Flaubert, Ibsen, Tagore, and Mahfouz learned to take themselves out of their stories, which purported to be unmediated pictures of reality.
- **D.** In the 20th century, in an age of eroding certainties, authors came to see that every story is *somebody's* story and thus placed the storyteller inside the work itself, forcing the reader to make up his or her own mind about the teller and the tale; that gave us the works of Brontë, Twain, Proust, Yasunari, and Faulkner.
- **E.** Finally, at the end of history (so far), authors see their work as self-contained art, detached from a reality that we cannot understand and on which therefore we cannot base our values.
- **F.** We do not know what the future holds, but it seems certain that whatever it is, there will always be storytellers inventing new forms and uses for stories.
    1. As Rushdie reminds us, inside every story is a world not subject to the control of tyrants or hard-headed practical people, both of whom try to control us by suppressing our imaginations.
    2. Inside those worlds there is room for alternate ways of thinking, as there was for Emily Dickinson in her poems, which took her far beyond the confined and respectable life she lived in Amherst.
    3. As *Haroun and the Sea of Stories* reminds us, we never know where such imaginative freedom will take us: The people of the Valley of K. did, after all, free themselves from Snooty Butto after they had heard a story.

VI. There are other values in stories as well.
- **A.** Gabriel Garcia Marquez said that the stories his grandmother told him could not change the external world, but they did make him feel better.

B. William Faulkner, in his Nobel Prize acceptance speech, said that literature could help humans not only to endure, but to prevail.
   1. Faulkner did not exactly say it this way, but part of the reason it helps us prevail is by keeping our inner worlds free from the Khattam-Shuds and Mr. Senguptas of the world, who are always interested in manipulating us into accepting their vision of the world.
   2. Perhaps one of the most powerful sentences in all of human history is, "Tell me a story."

Essential Reading:

Salman Rushdie, *Haroun and the Sea of Stories.*

Supplementary Reading:

Catherine Cundy, *Salman Rushdie.*

Sabrina Hassumani, *Salman Rushdie: A Postmodern Reading of His Major Works.*

Questions to Consider:

1. There is a great deal of attention paid in *Haroun and the Sea of Stories* to the values of societies in which open discussion is allowed, particularly in the depiction of the cultures of the Chupwalas and the Guppees. What are the advantages and disadvantages of free speech and the right to criticize one's leaders in the book?

2. Sinbad the Sailor stories receive a lot of allusive attention in the book. Since you have already encountered those stories in *1001 Nights,* do you see any connections between the values of those stories and the values of Rushdie's book? Are there ways in which knowing the Sinbad stories helps to illuminate what is happening in *Haroun and the Sea of Stories*?

Timeline
(Lectures 37–48)

1902	Joseph Conrad's *Heart of Darkness*.
1914	James Joyce's *Dubliners*.
1914–18	World War I.
1915	Einstein's General Theory of Relativity.
1915	Franz Kafka's "The Metamorphosis."
1918	Bolshevik Revolution in Russia.
1921	Luigi Pirandello's *Six Characters in Search of an Author*.
1922	T. S. Eliot's *The Waste Land*.
1929	The Stock Market Crash; beginning of the Great Depression.
1930	William Faulkner's *As I Lay Dying*.
1934	Stalin begins purges of the Communist Party.
1935–47	Kawabata Yasunari's *Snow Country*.
1938–40	Bertolt Brecht's *The Good Woman of Setzuan*.
1939–45	World War II.
1941	Jorge Luis Borges's *The Garden of Forking Paths*.
1945	Atomic bombs dropped on Hiroshima and Nagasaki.
1947	Independence for India.
1953	Samuel Beckett's *Waiting for Godot*.
1956–57	Naguib Mahfouz's *The Cairo Trilogy*.
1957	Samuel Beckett's *Endgame*.

1958	Chinua Achebe's *Things Fall Apart*.
1963	Anna Akhmatova's *Requiem*.
1967	Gabriel Garcia Marquez's *One Hundred Years of Solitude*.
1969	First man walks on the moon.
1988	Salman Rushdie's *The Satanic Verses*.
1989	The Berlin Wall torn down.
1990	Salman Rushdie's *Haroun and the Sea of Stories*.

Glossary
(Lectures 37–48)

alienation techniques: Associated with epic theater, alienation techniques are dramatic and theatrical devices intended to prevent too close an emotional identification on the part of the audience with events and characters on stage. They can include, among others, direct addresses to the audience, songs, stage sets and props which look deliberately stagy, placards, and slides shown on the walls of the set. The basic idea is to remind audiences that they are watching a play, not a slice of real life.

catharsis: Aristotle said that a *catharsis*, or purgation, of the emotions of pity and fear on the part of the audience occurs in tragedy. While there is serious disagreement as to his precise meaning, for our purposes a *catharsis* is the emotional engagement and release that is the result of sympathetic identification with characters on stage.

denouement: The unraveling of a plot in drama or fiction; the tying up of loose ends after the story's climax.

epic theater: Most closely associated with Bertolt Brecht, epic theater uses a combination of dramatic action and narrative both to draw audiences into emotional engagement with events and characters on stage and to allow sufficient emotional distance for intellectual consideration. In order to prevent too close an emotional identification, epic theater uses alienation techniques.

epiphany: The Christian festival celebrating the visit of the Magi to the infant Jesus. It literally means a showing-forth, suggesting Christ's manifestation to the Gentiles. Its date in the Christian calendar is January 6. The term was adapted by James Joyce to indicate a moment in which something is seen as though for the first time or becomes immediately clear; each of the stories in his *Dubliners* is organized around such moments, or epiphanies.

Existentialism: A philosophical formulation that asserts that existence precedes essence: that is, we exist but without having any external reference point by which to define who we are, the meaning of our own existence, or the meaning of the universe. Rather, we create whatever meaning there is ever going to be with our decisions and actions. Although they did not invent it, Existentialism in the 20th century is most closely associated with Jean-Paul Sartre and Albert Camus. As a fully developed system of thought it is much more complex than this, and there are few true Existentialists around anymore, but this much of it is an assumption shared by many—not all—Postmodernist writers, including the three in our course.

Expressionism: A movement in the arts whose purpose was to depict inner experience by abandoning representation of the external world and using objects as signs or symbols of inner states. It reached its height in all the arts in the first decades of the 20th century. In literature, Franz Kafka probably came closest to embodying its ideals and goals in fiction, as August Strindberg did in drama.

intertextuality: The technique of making literature out of other literature. In a way, this has always happened in literature—as Virgil made his *Aeneid* out of Homer's *Iliad* and *Odyssey*—but it is a more explicit and important technique for Postmodernists, for whom literature (and all art) is reflexive and self-contained. In a way, they would argue, literature is always intertextual, since it cannot be about anything other than itself—or at least that it operates by its own laws, not those of reality.

Modernism: The term is used to designate writing which makes a deliberate break with traditional forms of expression. It particularly denotes early 20th-century writers who were trying in various ways to reject all aspects of Victorianism, moral as well as literary. Its techniques include an extreme subjectivity, a sense that the external world is as it is perceived by the individual, and such devices as interior monologue, broken chronology, stream-of-consciousness, and the Magic Realism of writers like Kafka. It also involves a rejection of many traditional values and assumptions, based on the work of such thinkers as Darwin, Marx, and Freud, and is enhanced by the sense that traditional values had been proven inadequate by World War I and the Great Depression. Virtually all of the writers in this course from Proust onward are in one way or another Modernists, as their experimentation with narrative and expression illustrates. The movement blends into Postmodernism, which continues some aspects of Modernism but sends them off in new directions.

Postmodernism: A complex and many-faceted movement growing out of Modernism. It was first used in architecture to describe an eclectic (and sometimes) playful use of allusions to past styles in contemporary buildings. In literature it can mean many things. For our purposes in this course, three of its elements have been developed in the last three lectures: (1) its general (not universal) assumption that the universe is absurd, or at least that its meanings are incomprehensible to us; (2) its assertion that literature (like language and all art) is reflexive and about itself, not about reality—which we cannot know anyway; and (3) its tendency to make literature out of other literature and to foreground the processes of its own creation.

stream-of-consciousness: A phrase invented by William James to describe the mixture of sensations, thoughts, memories, associations, and reflections that occupy our consciousness at any given moment. As a literary technique it involves efforts to capture this flow in words and images, thus coming closer than traditional narrative to the way reality actually impinges on the individual consciousness.

symbol: Something which is both itself and suggests or means something else, as a flag is a piece of colored cloth but which stands for a state or nation. In literature a symbol functions on a literal level as part of a setting or as an object but also suggests other, larger meanings. Some symbols are more or less conventional, like the sea, and others are created for particular uses by a writer. Snow in Joyce's "The Dead" functions in both of these ways.

theatricalism: Sometimes also called anti-illusionism, this is a generic term which includes a variety of individual movements: e.g., Expressionism, Futurism, Dadaism, and Surrealism. All have in common an aversion to Realist drama with its meticulously recreated sets, its naturalistic prose dialogue and characters, and its avoidance of contact between actors and audience. Theatricalists wanted the stage to be expressive, symbolic, and dream-like in order to be able better to show on stage the *inner* life of individuals. They also wanted to restore to the stage some of its essential tools—tools that had been used by the greatest dramatists in history—such as poetry, asides, soliloquies, and music. They wanted nonrepresentational stage sets that could be used as, for example, projections of inner life, dreams, and other nonrational aspects of our lives. Thornton Wilder's *Our Town* is a theatricalist work in many of these ways, as are the plays of Pirandello and—for very different reasons—Brecht.

Biographical Notes
(Lectures 37–48)

Achebe, Chinua (b. 1930): Achebe was born in Nigeria to missionary teachers and was therefore raised a Christian. He attended University College in Ibadhan and received his B.A. in 1953. He worked for the Nigerian Broadcasting Service until 1967, when civil war broke out following Nigerian independence from Britain in 1960, in which he supported the Igbo people's efforts to create a separate state, Biafra. He taught at the University of Massachusetts-Amherst in the early 70s and late 80s and at the University of Connecticut-Storrs, as well as at the University of Nigeria-Nsukki. He has traveled widely, lecturing and bringing the needs and dreams of his people to a world audience, and he has been throughout his life active in Nigerian politics, primarily as a commentator. His first novel, *Things Fall Apart* (1958), was designed to undo the false impressions of Africans generated in English books he had been required to read as part of his education. He has since written more novels and nonfictional books about Nigeria, he has garnered a room full of awards and prizes for his writing, and he is sometimes thought of as the father of the African novel in English, a title which has involved him in some controversy with Africans who believe that literature should be written in tribal languages. He continues his work as author, patron of young writers, and ambassador of Nigeria to the world.

Akhmatova, Anna (1889–1966): Born in Odessa as Anya Gorenko, she grew up in pleasant circumstances just outside of St. Petersburg, which she loved nearly as much as she loved Pushkin, who had also lived nearby. She changed her name to Anna Akhmatova when she started publishing poetry to avoid bringing what her father thought would be disgrace on the family for harboring a poet. She married and spent three months with her husband in Paris, where she met Modigliani and learned about the ground-breaking work of Braque, Picasso, and Stravinisky, all of whom were working in Paris at the time. She had published several volumes of (mostly) love poetry before she was declared counterrevolutionary by Stalinist censors and silenced in the 1920s. Divorced by then and remarried, her former husband was executed for his part in an anti-Bolshevik conspiracy. Silenced for 40 years, she wrote literary criticism, especially on the works of Pushkin. In 1935 her third husband and only son were arrested in the first stages of the Yezhov Terror following the assassination of the Secretary of the Communist Party. They were released but re-arrested: Her husband died in a prison camp in Siberia, and her son was not released until 1956. During these years she wrote both *Requiem* and what many consider her greatest work, *Poem Without a Hero*. After Stalin's death in 1953 she was allowed to publish again, but *Requiem* was not published in Russia in her lifetime because of censorship. It did appear in other languages and countries, however, and by the end of her life she was receiving recognition and awards as one of the greatest Russian poets of the century.

Beckett, Samuel (1906–89): Beckett was born in Dublin, and he received his B.A. from Trinity College in 1927. While teaching English in Paris he met James Joyce, and he spent some time as Joyce's secretary (he also translated part of *Finnegans Wake* into French). He returned to Dublin to take an M.A. degree in 1932 and stayed on to teach French for a year. After traveling about, he settled in Paris, and he was living there when he published his first novel, *Murphy* (1938). After World War II he preferred to write in French, later translating his own works into English. In addition to his plays, he wrote novels which have received high critical praise, including *Watt* (1953) and a trilogy: *Molloy* (1951), *Malone Dies* (1951), and *The Unnameable* (1953). He achieved worldwide recognition for *Waiting for Godot* (which opened in Paris in 1953 and New York in 1955), and was awarded the Nobel Prize in 1969.

Borges, Jorge Luis (1899–1986): Borges was born in Buenos Aires into an educated and literate family. Since his grandmother was English, he grew up speaking both Spanish and English, and he read voraciously in his father's library, which included books in both languages. By the age of nine, he published a translation into Spanish of Wilde's "The Happy Prince" in a local newspaper. Later he added Latin, French, and German to his list of languages. He began his adult writing career primarily as a poet and essayist. His first collection of short stories was published in 1941. He worked at a library in Buenos Aires but was stripped of his position because of his opposition to Juan Perón. After Perón's fall in 1955, he became Director of the National Library, a post he continued to hold even after he became almost totally blind. He continued to publish until 1970, after which he spent time lecturing at universities across the world. In 1961 he shared the International Publishers' Prize with Samuel Beckett.

Brecht, Bertolt (1898–1956): He was born in Bavaria, and he studied science and medicine at Munich University. While still in school he started writing theater reviews for a local newspaper and writing plays. He served as an orderly in a hospital during World War I. After the war, in Berlin he wrote a series of plays before he became a Marxist in the 1920s. From that point on, his plays were largely didactic, intended to satirize capitalism and to advance the socialist revolution. When the Nazis came to power, his German citizenship was revoked, and he traveled, first to Denmark, then Sweden and Finland before arriving in the United States, where he worked in the film industry. Most of his greatest plays were written during these years, including *The Life of Galileo* (1938–39), *Mother Courage and Her Children* (1939), *The Good Woman of Setzuan* (1938–40), and *The Caucasian Chalk Circle* (1944–45). After the war he and his wife, actress Helene Weigel, directed the famous Berliner Ensemble in East Berlin, where he had a chance to perfect his ideas of epic theater as a director. He died in East Berlin in 1956.

Faulkner, William (1897–1962): Faulkner was born in New Albany, Mississippi, but grew up primarily in Oxford, where the family moved when he was five. He was descended from what had once been an important Mississippi family. He left high school after two years but continued to read widely on his own. During World War I he trained as a fighter pilot in Canada, but the war ended before he got into action. Back in Oxford, he enrolled briefly at the University of Mississippi. He went to New York, returned to Oxford to serve as postmaster at the university, and wrote poetry. In 1925 he went to New Orleans, where he met Sherwood Anderson, who encouraged him to write fiction and helped him get his first novel, *Soldier's Pay* (1926) published. After a year in Europe, he returned to Oxford and began to write about Yoknapatawpha County: his first novel set in his mythical place was *Sartoris* (1929). Then came his best-known novels: *The Sound and the Fury* (1929), *As I Lay Dying* (1930), *Light in August* (1932), *Absalom, Absalom!* (1936), and *Go Down, Moses* (1942), among many others. He was also writing short stories during this time, selling about 30 of them to journals between 1930 and 1932. After the Nobel Prize, which he received in 1950, he also won a Pulitzer Prize and a National Book Award. He lived in Oxford for the rest of his life, where he died in 1962.

Joyce, James (1882–1941): Joyce was born in Dublin and received a solid Jesuit education, despite his large family's headlong descent into poverty. Early in his life he left Ireland to become an international figure, living in Trieste, Zürich, and Paris, where he taught languages and wrote his books. He did not, however, leave Ireland in those books, which are set in his home country—mostly in Dublin. He became friends with such other notable writers as Ezra Pound, T. S. Eliot, Ernest Hemingway, and Samuel Beckett, and acquired over the years a series of patrons—most importantly Harriet

Shaw Weaver, a British editor—who eventually allowed him to devote his time to his literary work. In addition to *Dubliners* (1914), his other best-known works are *A Portrait of the Artist as a Young Man* (1916), *Ulysses* (1922), and *Finnegans Wake* (1939). He fled Paris after it had been occupied by the Germans in World War II, and he died in Zurich a few weeks later.

Kafka, Franz (1883–1924): Born in Prague, Czechoslovakia, he was pressured by his father to become a businessman and earned a law degree from the German University in Prague. He took a job at the Workers' Accident Insurance Institute, where he had a chance to see bureaucracy in action from the inside. He lived most of his life at home, writing in his spare time while doing a creditable job at his semi-governmental occupation. He became aware that he had tuberculosis in 1917, and he died of the disease in Vienna in 1924. Aside from a few short stories and novellas, he published little during his lifetime. His three great novels, *The Trial* (1925), *The Castle* (1926), and *Amerika* (1927) were published posthumously from his manuscripts by his friend and first biographer, Max Brod. "The Metamorphosis" was published in 1915.

Kawabata Yasunari (1899–1972): Born in Osaka, he was orphaned early by nearly all of his family, both immediate and extended, and spent much of his adolescence in dormitories. By the time he graduated from Tokyo Imperial University in 1924, he had already published short stories, and he continued to write throughout his life, leaving behind a large body of work. He was proficient in Western literature, and as a young man he and several of his colleagues formed a club dedicated to freeing Japanese literature from Realism and Naturalism. He also worked as a journalist and wrote many reviews of other writers, many of whom he had helped to discover and promote. He was awarded the Nobel Prize in 1968, only the second Asian to win it. His works are characterized by roaming and loneliness, which gives a certain melancholy tone to all of them. Of his many novels, *Snow Country* is his best-known and most- translated; it became an instant classic almost from the moment that it was published.

Mahfouz, Naguib (1911–2006): He was born in Cairo, attended government schools, and graduated from Cairo University in 1934 with a degree in philosophy. He began writing while in college and published his first volume of short stories in 1938. Even after he had become a famous and popular writer, he had to support himself and his family with a variety of jobs in government and on newspapers. He later adapted novels for films and for a time was the director of the Cinema Organization, a nationalized institution. After his *Cairo Trilogy* made him famous (1956–57), he continued to write, but his novels and short stories also continued to evolve, both in content and form, and he became a more controversial figure in Egypt and in the Arab world generally thereafter. When he attacked the Ministry of Culture's plan to censor books prior to publication as "terrorism," he was stabbed and lost the use of his writing hand. He continued to argue and write for internationalism and freedom until his death in 2006. He was awarded the Nobel Prize in 1988.

Pirandello, Luigi (1867–1936): Born in Sicily, the son of a sulfur merchant, he earned a doctorate in romance philology in 1891. He started his career as a poet and short story writer, but when the sulfur mines went under in 1904 (his wife was the daughter of a sulfur merchant as well), both families went bankrupt, and Pirandello then had to depend for a living on a job as a teacher he had formerly used as a kind of hobby. His wife also became insane and lived most of the rest of her life at home (she was not institutionalized until much later) until her death in 1918. For the rest of his life, Pirandello continued to write, turning more towards drama about 1916. He became director of his own Art Theatre in Rome in 1925 and took his plays to great cities all over the world. He was awarded the Nobel Prize in 1934, and at his death in 1936 he left behind a prodigious amount of literature in many genres—an amazing amount of it is very good.

Rushdie, Salman (b. 1947): Rushdie was born in Bombay but educated primarily in England, including Cambridge University. He came to international attention with his second novel, *Midnight's Children* (1981), when he was awarded the Booker of Bookers award as the best novel to have won the Booker Prize in its 25 years of existence. His acknowledged models are Jorge Luis Borges and Gabriel Garcia Marquez, and he generally writes in the mode sometimes called Magic Realism. In 1988 his *The Satanic Verses* was condemned by Iranian authorities as blasphemous, and a *fatwa*, calling for his death, was pronounced. He spent the next 10 years in hiding, protected by the British Secret Service, and even since the fatwa was lifted, he has lived in constant danger. It was during his 10 years in hiding that he wrote *Haroun and the Sea of Stories*.

Bibliography
(Lectures 37–48)

Note: Every work treated in this part of the course is available in multiple translations and editions, many of them excellent. I have listed here the ones from which my text citations were taken. In general, the best strategy is to find an edition or translation that gives you sufficient introductory material to help orient you to the text and sufficient editorial help to understand what you are reading. If you find those things, you have found the recommended text for you.

Essential Reading:

Achebe, Chinua. *Things Fall Apart.* London: Heinemann, 1958.

Akhmatova, Anna. *Requiem. The Complete Poems of Anna Akhmatova.* Judith Hemschemeyer, trans. 2nd ed. Boston: Zephyr Press, 1992.

Beckett, Samuel. *The Complete Dramatic Works of Samuel Beckett.* London: Faber, 1986.

Borges, Jorge Luis. *Labyrinths: Selected Stories and Other Writings.* Donald A. Yates and James E. Irby, eds. Various trans. New York: New Directions, 1962.

Brecht, Bertolt. *The Good Woman of Setzuan. Parables for the Theatre: Two Plays by Bertolt Brecht.* Eric Bentley, trans. Minneapolis: University of Minnesota Press, 1965.

Faulkner, William. *As I Lay Dying.* New York: Random House, 1957.

———. *Collected Stories of William Faulkner.* New York: Random House, 1977.

Joyce, James. *Dubliners.* New York: Viking, 1964.

Kafka, Franz. *"The Metamorphosis," "In the Penal Colony," and Other Stories.* Joachim Neugroschel, trans. New York: Simon and Schuster, 1995.

Kawabata Yasunari. *Snow Country.* Edward G. Seidensticker, trans. New York: Berkley, 1960.

Mahfouz, Naguib. *The Cairo Trilogy: Palace Walk, Palace of Desire, Sugar Street.* William Maynard Hutchins, Olive E. Kenny, Lorne M. Kenny, Angele Botros Samaan, trans. New York: Doubleday, 1990-1992.

Pirandello, Luigi. *Six Characters in Search of an Author.* John Linstrum, trans. London: Eyre Methuen, 1979.

Rushdie, Salman. *Haroun and the Sea of Stories.* New York: Granta Books, 1990.

Supplementary Reading:

Alazraki, Jaime, ed. *Critical Essays on Jorge Luis Borges.* Boston: G. K. Hall, 1987. This is a collection of essays by various hands on many aspects of Borges's thought and writing, including some good readings of individual stories.

Allen, Roger M. A. *The Arabic Novel: An Historical and Critical Introduction.* 2nd ed. Syracuse, New York: Syracuse University Press, 1995. This is a standard reference work which places Mahfouz in the context of the development of the Arabic novel.

Amert, Susan. *In a Shattered Mirror: The Later Poetry of Anna Akhmatova.* Stanford: Stanford University Press, 1992. A detailed close reading of Akhmatova's later poetry, including *Requiem.* Amert is particularly adept at discovering references and allusions—some of them quite veiled—to other literature; these allusions carry part of the meaning of the poems.

Bloom, Harold, ed. *Franz Kafka's "The Metamorphosis."* New York: Chelsea House, 1988. This is part of Bloom's *Modern Critical Interpretations* series, and like the rest of the volumes in the series, it features a collection of good and interesting modern essays as well as a stimulating introduction by Bloom.

Brooks, Cleanth. *William Faulkner: The Yoknapatawpha Country.* New Haven: Yale University Press, 1963. In a classic Faulkner critical text, Brooks sees the achievement rooted in a specific region—roots which allow the author to see the problems of the modern world through a particular lens. A helpful index of characters and genealogical tables is also included.

Brustein, Robert. *The Theatre of Revolt.* Boston: Little, Brown, 1964. In what has become a critical classic, Brustein treats Pirandello, Ibsen, Strindberg, Chekhov, Shaw, Brecht, O'Neill, Artaud, and Genet in what he defines as the "theatre of revolt" which remade modern drama.

Carothers, James B. *William Faulkner's Short Stories.* Ann Arbor: UMI Research Press, 1985. An examination of the short stories in relation to Faulkner's novels.

Cundy, Catherine. *Salman Rushdie.* New York: Manchester University Press, 1996. A good overall view of Rushdie, his career, and his works.

Driver, Sam. *Anna Akhmatova*. New York: Twayne, 1972. A good general introduction to Akhmatova's life and works, including detailed commentary on *Requiem*.

Eggenschwiler, David. "*Die Verwandlung*, Freud, and the Chains of Odysseus." *Modern Language Quarterly* 39, no. 4 (December 1978); rpt. in Bloom above, pp. 71–93. A brilliant essay on Kafka's enigmatic story, which is less about what it means than about the *way* it means. Many of the insights in Lecture Thirty-Eight were borrowed from this essay.

El-Enany, Rasheed, ed. *Naguib Mahfouz: The Pursuit of Meaning*. New York: Routledge, 1993. This is an essential work for understanding Mahfouz. It includes analysis of many of his works, a biography, and sends the reader off in new directions with an excellent bibliography.

Fletcher, Beryl S. and John Fletcher. *A Student's Guide to the Plays of Samuel Beckett*. 2nd ed. Boston: Faber and Faber, 1985. These are good introductions to the plays, featuring contextual information as well as annotations and commentary.

Fowler, Doreen and Ann J. Abadie, eds. *Faulkner and the Craft of Fiction: Faulkner and Yoknapatawpha County*. Jackson: University of Mississippi Press, 1989. A collection of papers delivered at a Faulkner conference; the emphasis is on themes, narrative strategies, and structures in a number of different Faulkner works.

Hart, Clive, ed. *James Joyce's Dubliners: Critical Essays*. New York: Viking, 1969. A collection of essays by various hands from various perspectives on different aspects of the stories.

Hassumani, Sabrina. *Salman Rushdie: A Postmodern Reading of His Major Works*. Madison, New Jersey: Fairleigh Dickinson University Press, 2002. As its title suggests, this book considers Rushdie as a Postmodernist writer.

Innes, C. L. and Bernth Lindfors, eds. *Critical Perspectives on Chinua Achebe*. Washington, D. C.: Three Continents Press, 1978. This is a collection of essays on various aspects of Achebe's work, including the one by Gareth Griffiths referred to in Lecture Forty-Five and a very good one by A. G. Stock on the ways in which Achebe uses the Yeats poem of the title in *Things Fall Apart*.

Jackson, John Wyse and Bernard McGinley, eds. *James Joyce's Dubliners: An Illustrated Edition with Annotations*. New York: St. Martin's Press, 1995. Each story is generously documented with notes and photographs which give a detailed sense of the Dublin in which it is set and suggest the ways in which many of the items function symbolically. Each story is followed by a short interpretive essay.

Kennedy, Andrew K. *Samuel Beckett.* New York: Cambridge University Press, 1989. This book features both a broad look at Beckett's career as well as chapters on each major play and novel.

Killam, G. D. *The Novels of Chinua Achebe.* New York: Africana Publishing, 1969. This book gives a good reading of *Things Fall Apart*, showing how Achebe manages to locate the historical crises of colonialism within the individual consciousness.

Krutch, Joseph Wood. *Modernism in Modern Drama: A Definition and an Estimate.* New York: Russell and Russell, 1953. Included in this book—another critical classic—is a splendid section on the ideas of Pirandello. This book was cited liberally in Lecture Thirty-Nine.

Masao Mihoshi. *Accomplices of Silence: The Modern Japanese Novel.* Berkeley: University of California Press, 1974. A good account of the context for *Snow Country* as well as a convincing account of its growth over a 14-year period. According to this thesis, Kawabata's great gift is in placing human actions and life on a larger canvas.

Pollack, David. *Reading Against Culture: Ideology and Narrative in the Japanese Novel.* New York: Cornell University Press, 1992. Pollack gives a good reading of *Snow Country* and in addition provides useful information about Tanabata, silkworms, and weaving as central metaphors and images in the book.

Sarlo, Beatriz. *Jorge Luis Borges: A Writer on the Edge.* New York: Verso, 1993. This is a comprehensive examination of the career of Borges, with particular attention paid to his early work. It includes good analyses of many of the stories in *Labyrinths*.

Schwarz, Daniel, ed. *"The Dead": James Joyce. Case Studies in Contemporary Criticism.* New York: St. Martin's Press, 1994. This book provides the text of "The Dead" and then gives five essays by different critics from five different contemporary critical perspectives: psychoanalytic, reader-response, new historicist, feminist, and deconstructive. Each interpretive essay is prefaced by an essay on how that kind of criticism works.

Thompson, Bruce, ed. *"Der Gute Mensch von Sezuan."* London: Methuen, 1986. The text of the play is in German, but the introduction—which is excellent—is in English and provides a useful and readable orientation to the play itself.

Permissions Acknowledgments

Anna Akhmatova, excerpts from "Requiem" from *The Complete Poems of Anna Akhmatova*, translated by Judith Hemschemeyer, edited and introduced by Roberta Reeder. Translation copyright © 1983, 1984, 1986, 1989, 1992, 1997 by Judith Hemschemeyer. Used by permission of Zephyr Press, www.zephyrpress.org

"Classic of Poetry XXVI: Boat of Cypress" and "Written Crossing the River to Qing-he," translated by Stephen Owen, from *An Anthology of Chinese Literature: Beginnings to 1911*, edited and translated by Stephen Owen. Copyright © 1996 by Stephen Owen and The Council for Cultural Planning and Development of the Executive Yuan of the Republic of China. Used by permission of W. W. Norton & Company, Inc.

Jorge Luis Borges, excerpts from "The Library of Babel" and "Everything and Nothing," translated by James E. Irby, from *Selected Stories & Other Writings*. Copyright © 1962, 1964, 2007 by New Directions Publishing Corp.

Li Po, "Drinking Alone Beneath the Moon, Two Selections" and "Sitting Alone in Ching-t'ing Mountain," translated by Irving Yucheng Lo, in *Sunflower Splendor: Three Thousand Years of Chinese Poetry*, edited by Wu-chi Liu and Irving Yucheng Lo (Bloomington: Indiana University Press, 1975).

Poems from *Kokin Wakashu: The First Imperial Anthology of Japanese Poetry*, translated by Helen Craig McCullough. Copyright © 1985 by the Board of Trustees of the Leland Stanford Jr. University. Used by permission of Stanford University Press, www.sup.org.

Poetry is used by permission of the publishers and the Trustees of Amherst College from *The Poems of Emily Dickinson*, Thomas H. Johnson, ed., Cambridge, Mass: The Belknap Press of Harvard University Press, Copyright © 1951, 1955, 1979, 1983 by the President and Fellows of Harvard College and from *The Poems of Emily Dickinson: Reading Edition*, Ralph W. Franklin, ed., Cambridge, Mass: The Belknap Press of Harvard University Press. Copyright © 1998, 1999 by The President and Fellows of Harvard College. All rights reserved.

Tu Fu, Poem "11465," in *The Great Age of Chinese Poetry: The High T'ang*, edited by Stephen Owen (New Haven and London: Yale University Press, 1981). Copyright © 1981 Yale University Press. Used by permission of Yale University Press.

White, Alfred D. *Bertolt Brecht's Great Plays*. New York: Barnes and Noble, 1978. This is a work on a number of Brecht plays, and its essay on *The Good Woman of Setzuan* is lucid and interesting.